THE OFFICIAL BLENDER GAMEKIT
Interactive 3-D for Artists

D1604206

THE OFFICIAL BLENDER GAMEKIT

Interactive 3-D for Artists

Edited by Ton Roosendaal and Carsten Wartmann

NO STARCH PRESS

San Francisco

Publisher: William Pollock
Managing Editor: Karol Jurado
Compositor: Wedobooks
Proofreader: Stephanie Provines

Authors: Michael Kauppi, Carsten Wartmann
Tutorials, game demos, CD-ROM content: Joeri Kassenaar, Freid Lachnowicz, Reevan McKay, Willem-Paul van Overbruggen, Randall Rickert, Carsten Wartmann
Editor: Carsten Wartmann
Cover Design: Samo Korosec, froodee design www.froodee.com

Distributed to the book trade in the United States by Publishers Group West, 1700 Fourth Street, Berkeley, CA 94710; phone: 800-788-3123; fax: 510-658-1834.

Distributed to the book trade in Canada by Jacqueline Gross & Associates, Inc., One Atlantic Avenue, Suite 105, Toronto, Ontario M6K 3E7 Canada; phone: 416-531-6737; fax 416-531-4259.

For information on translations or book distributors outside the United States, please contact No Starch Press, Inc. directly:

No Starch Press, Inc.
555 De Haro Street, Suite 250, San Francisco, CA 94107
phone: 415-863-9900; fax: 415-863-9950; info@nostarch.com; http://www.nostarch.com

Library of Congress Cataloguing-in-Publication Data

Roosendaal, Ton.
        The official Blender GameKit: interactive 3-D for artists / Ton
Roosendaal and Carsten Wartmann.
        p. cm.
        ISBN 1-59327-002-X (pbk.)
1. Computer animation. 2. Three-dimensional display systems. 3. Computer graphics. 4. Blender
(Computer file) I. Wartmann, Carsten. II. Title.
        TR897.7.R65 2003
        006.6'96--dc21
                                                        2003006895

Special thanks to the NaN Technologies crew:

Management:
Gil Agnew, Jan-Paul Buijs, Maarten Derks, Loran Kuijpers, Ton Roosendaal, Jan Wilmink

Software Engineers:
Frank van Beek, Laurence Bourn, Njin-Zu Chen, Daniel Dunbar, Maarten Gribnau, Hans Lambermont, Martin Strubel, Janco Verduin, Raymond de Vries

Content Developers:
Joeri Kassenaar, Reevan McKay, WP van Overbruggen, Randall Rickert, Carsten Wartmann

Website, Support and Community:
Bart Veldhuizen, Willem Zwarthoed

Marketing:
Elisa Karumo, Sian Lloyd-Scriven

System Administrators:
Thomas Ryan, Marco Walraven

Administration and Backoffice:
Maartje Koopman, Annamieke de Moor, Brigitte van Pelt

BRIEF CONTENTS

CONTENTS IN DETAIL

QUICKSTART

1
QUICKSTART

PART ONE:
INTRODUCTION

2
WHAT IS THIS BOOK ABOUT?

3
INTRODUCTION TO 3-D AND THE GAME ENGINE

4
BLENDER BASICS

PART TWO:
PLAYING WITH 3-D GAME TECHNOLOGY

5
MODELING AN ENVIRONMENT
57

6
APPENDING AN OBJECT FROM ANOTHER SCENE
63

7
START YOUR (GAME) ENGINES
67

8
INTERACTIVITY

9
CAMERA CONTROL
77

10
REAL-TIME LIGHT
79

11
OBJECT ANIMATION
81

12
REFINING THE SCENE
85

13
ADDING SOUND TO OUR SCENE
89

14
LAST WORDS
91

PART THREE:
BEGINNER TUTORIALS

15
TUBE CLEANER: A SIMPLE SHOOTING GAME

16
LOW POLY MODELING

PART FOUR:
INTERMEDIATE TUTORIALS

17
SUPER-G

18
POWER BOATS

19
BALLERCOASTER

20
SQUISH THE BUNNY —
CREATING WEAPON EFFECTS
FOR A FIRST-PERSON SHOOTER

PART FIVE:
ADVANCED TUTORIALS

21
FLYING BUDDHA MEMORY GAME

22
GAME CHARACTER ANIMATION USING ARMATURES

23
BLENDERBALL

PART SIX:
REFERENCE

24
BLENDER WINDOWS AND BUTTONS

25
REAL-TIME MATERIALS

26
BLENDER'S GAME ENGINE

27
GAME LOGICBRICKS

28
PYTHON

29
INSTALLATION AND SUPPORT

GLOSSARY 320

INDEX 325

QUICKSTART

1

QUICKSTART

Have you ever wanted to personalize a computer game? While many game level editors allow you to do so, Blender goes a step further: allowing you to create a completely new game.

In this quickstart chapter, I will show you how to map a face onto a game character. (The game character used here was made by Reevan McKay. You can read more about this in Chapter 22, which will also demonstrate many other elements of character animation.)

NOTE *I have attempted in this quickstart to keep the discussion as self-contained as possible. Although it will be helpful if you already know something about graphics, if you follow the instructions here step-by-step all should go well.*

Figure 1-1 shows an image of a real-time 3-D animation created using the method that will be briefly described in this chapter. (The scene is on the CD and called Tutorials/Quickstart/CalliGoingMad1.blend.)

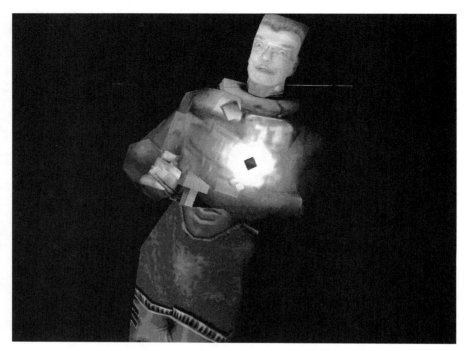

Figure 1-1: Calli going mad . . .

NOTE   *If you have not installed Blender yet, please do so. The installation process is described in Section 29.1. Further hints about graphics hardware are given in Section 29.2.*

1.1. Simple Face Mapping

This section will show how to put a new face onto a ready-made character. There are some drawbacks to this method but it will get you started quickly.

To begin, start Blender by double-clicking its icon. It will open a screen as shown in Figure 1-2.

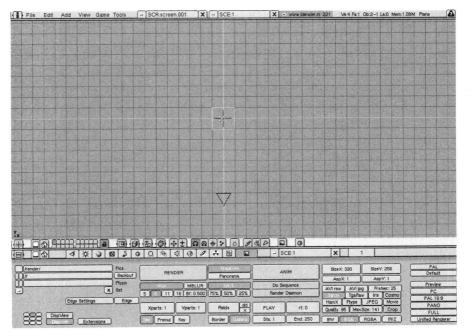

Figure 1-2: The Blender opening screen

Locate the File menu on the top left of the screen and choose Open by clicking it with the left mouse button (or LMB). A big FileWindow appears, which is used for all Blender loading and saving operations.

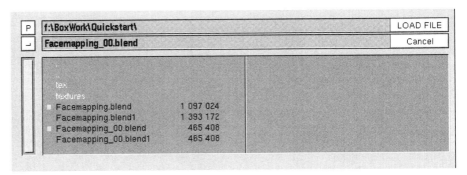

Figure 1-3: Blender FileWindow

The button labeled with a "P" at the upper left corner of the FileWindow puts you one directory up in your path. The MenuButton ☑ below it brings you back to the last directories you have visited, as well as your mapped drives in Windows. Click and hold it with the LMB to change to your CD-ROM.

Now enter the directory Tutorials/Quickstart/ and click with the LMB on Facemapping_00.blend. Confirm your selection by clicking LOAD FILE at the top right of the FileWindow. Blender will load the file needed for the tutorial.

NOTE *Please have a look at Section 4.1 for a explanation on how we will call interface elements and keyboard shortcuts (i.e. PKEY) in the tutorials.*

To have a quick look what this file is about, press CTRL-RIGHTARROW. The window layout changes to a bigger view of the character. Now press PKEY and the game engine will start. Using the controls from Table 1-1 walk around to have a closer look at the character.

Table 1-1: Quickstart Controls

Controls/Keys	Quickstart Controls
WKEY	Move forward
DKEY	Move left
AKEY	Move right
SKEY	Move backward
CTRL	Shoot
Spacebar	Duck

Stop the game engine by pressing ESC when you have seen enough. Press CTRL-LEFTARROW to return to the window layout that we will now use to map a different face.

Move your mouse cursor over the left window with the 3-D view of the head and press FKEY. This will start the so-called FaceSelectMode, which is used to manage and change textures on objects.

All polygons that belong to the face are now outlined and you can see them also in the right view showing the 2-D texture image of the face. This procedure is called *mapping* and will make the 2-D image appear where we want it on the 3-D object.

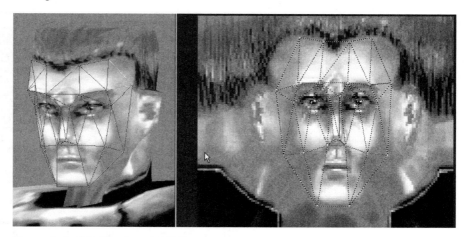

Figure 1-4: 3-D head and 2-D face map

Locate the Load button in the right ImageWindow and click it with the LMB. A FileWindow (in this case an ImageFileWindow) will open and lets you browse through your hard disks and the CD-ROM again. Go to the directory Tutorials/Quickstart/textures/. The ImageFileWindow displays little thumbnail images to ease the choice of images (see Figure 1-5).

TIP *You can also choose a picture of you or another person. But if you are a beginner, I would suggest using the supplied image for your first attempt. Blender can read and write Targa (.tga) and JPEG (.jpg), which are both common file formats.*

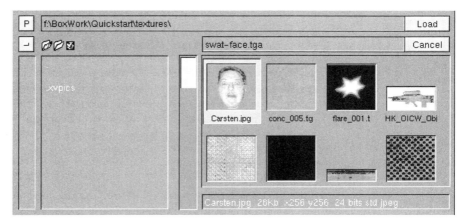

Figure 1-5: ImageFileWindow

Click the image Carsten.jpg (yes, it's me, your tutorial writer), and click the Load button at the top right of the ImageFileWindow to load it. The image will immediately appear in the 3-D view to the left.

TIP *Depending on your screen resolution you may need to zoom the right ImageWindow out a bit. Use the PAD- and PAD+ keys for zooming.*

The dimensions of my ugly face don't fit the previous mapping, so it'll look a bit distorted. Also, the color may not match exactly, making it look like a cheap mask.

Now move your mouse over the ImageWindow on the right and press AKEY; this selects (yellow color) all the control points here, called *vertices* in Blender. Now press GKEY and move your mouse, and all vertices will follow and you can watch the effect on the 3DView. Try to position the vertices in the middle of the face, using the nose as a reference. Confirm the new position with the LMB. If you want to cancel the move, press the right mouse button (or RMB) or ESC.

TIP *To have a better look at the head in the 3DView, you can rotate the head around using the middle mouse button, or MMB (if you are using a two-button mouse, hold ALT and use the LMB) and moving the mouse.*

To refine the placement of the texture on the head, you may now need to move the vertices more. Move your mouse over the ImageWindow on the right and press AKEY to deselect all vertices (they will turn purple). Now press BKEY.

This will start the BorderSelect, and a crosshair will appear. Press and hold the LMB to draw a rectangle around vertices you want to select and release the mouse button. Now you can move these vertices by pressing GKEY and using the mouse. Press LMB to confirm the move. Control the effect by watching the head on the 3DView.

TIP   *Don't give up too soon! Mapping a face needs practice, so take a break and play with the games on the CD, and try again later.*

If you want to look at your creation, switch to the full-screen scene by pressing CTRL-RIGHTARROW and start the game engine with PKEY.

1.2. Using 2-D Tools to Map the Face

Here's a brief overview of how to use a 2-D paint program to montage a face into a face map. If you don't already know how to work with layers in your application, see the documentation for your image-editing program. I use the free GPL software GIMP (http://www.gimp.org/) as my paint program, but any image-manipulation program that supports layers will do.

To begin:

1.   Load the image swat-face.tga (.tga files are Targa images) and the face you want to use in your paint program.
2.   Place the new face in a layer below the swat-face.tga and make the upper layer slightly transparent so that you can see the new face through it as shown below.

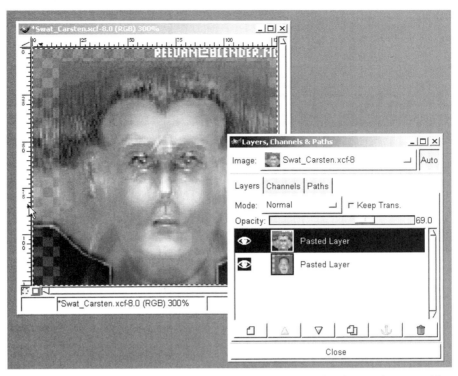

3. Scale and move the layer containing the new face so that it matches up with the swat-face.tga layer. (Use the eyes, nose, and mouth as guides to help you match them up.) Try to match the colors of the layers using the color tools of your 2-D program, too.

4. Make the upper layer non-transparent again.

5. Now use the eraser from your 2-D paint program to delete parts of the upper layer; the new face should appear at these points. Use a brush with soft edges so that the transition between the two layers is soft.

6. Collapse the layer to one and save the image as a Targa (.tga) or JPEG (.jpg) image. You may want to touch up the collapsed image, too, by blurring or smearing areas of transition to improve the look of your montage as shown on the next page.

7. Now load the scene Facemapping_00.blend from the CD. Press FKEY with your mouse over the 3DView on the left to enter FaceSelectMode.

8. Move your mouse to the right over the ImageWindow and click the Replace button to replace the current texture in the entire file with the texture you made.

9. Find the map with your face on your hard drive, select it with the LMB and press Load in the ImageFileWindow. The new texture should now appear on the head.

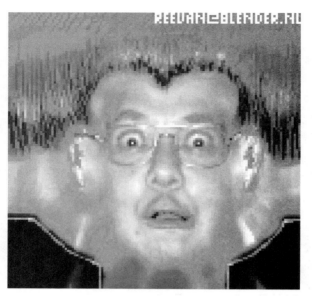

10. Finally, switch to the full-screen view again (CTRL-RIGHTARROW) and test the scene by starting the game engine with PKEY.

PART ONE
INTRODUCTION

2

WHAT IS THIS BOOK ABOUT?

Blender offers you a new and unique way to explore interactive 3-D graphics. As you'll soon see, this book will guide you through many aspects of making your own games and interactive 3-D graphics with Blender. While you can have fun with the ready-made games on the CD instantly, changing them or creating your own game is also great fun.

Blender is a fully integrated 3-D creation suite with all the tools you need to make linear animation and nonlinear (interactive) 3-D graphics. Because Blender provides all of these features in one application, the artist using Blender can follow a very smooth workflow, from design, to modeling and animation, and on to publishing 3-D content.

In contrast, if you were not using such an integrated suite as Blender, and you wanted to make a demo trailer of a game, you would need to use several separate tools including a modeler, a renderer, a video-editing application, and the game engine itself to produce your video. Blender makes it easy by combining all these tools to make it easier for you to produce interactive and linear 3-D content.

With Blender we give you the tools you need to make your creative ideas come true. With this book, we show you how to achieve your dreams using Blender.

Contents

This book contains:

- Sample game scenes for you to play with
- Sample games and tutorial scenes that you can change and personalize
- Coverage of Blender basics for making interactive 3-D graphics
- Coverage of 3-D game technology basics
- Advanced tips and tricks from professional Blender artists
- References for the Blender game engine

How to Use This Book

Before beginning with this book you should install Blender on your computer. Blender is usually simple to install, but if you encounter any difficulty installing or running Blender, please read Section 29.1. Once Blender is installed, you can explore the games on the CD bundled with this book.

Chapter 1 and Part II of this book introduce you to Blender. You'll have some fun with 3-D game technology, and you will learn how to use Blender by following the many practical examples. If you are not already familiar with Blender, you should then read Blender Basics in Chapter 4.

Once you've got the basics down you are ready to start with the tutorials. The tutorials are divided into beginner, intermediate, and advanced levels. If you run into problems please see the index and the glossary to find further information on what is available in this book. Also, be sure to join the huge and lively Blender Community (see Section 29.4), or ask our support if you run into trouble.

Once you complete the tutorials, the reference section in Part IV will be a great resource to help you in creating your own interactive 3-D scenes. We also provide further documentation to help you get the most out of Blender (details are in Section 29.5).

I hope you enjoy reading this book. My thanks go to the tutorial writers who have helped to produce the wonderful content of this book, the developers of Blender, and all other people who have made this book possible.

Carsten Wartmann, February 2002

3

INTRODUCTION TO 3-D AND THE GAME ENGINE

by Michael Kauppi

3.1. Purpose of This Chapter

This chapter is aimed at those who have little or no experience in 3-D or with game engines. It will introduce you to the world of three-dimensional (3-D) computer graphics, first by introducing the general concepts behind 3-D and then by showing how those concepts are used in computer graphics. Next, it will introduce you to game engines and Blender's game engine in particular, as well as three characteristics often found in good games.

3.2. General Introduction to 3-D

3.2.1. 2-D overview

We'll begin our journey into 3-D with an overview of 2-D. If you're like most people reading this book you should already know the concepts behind 2-D or at least be able to grasp them fairly quickly.

XY axes

You can think of 2-D as being a flat world. For example, imagine putting a blank piece of paper down on a table and looking down at that paper. If that paper represented the 2-D world, how would you describe where things are located on it? You'd need some kind of reference point from which to measure distances in order to determine position.

This determination of position is generally done by drawing two lines, called axes: one horizontal and the other vertical (see Figure 3-1). The horizontal line is called the *X-axis*, and the vertical line is called the *Y-axis*. Where the axes cross is your reference point, usually called the *origin*.

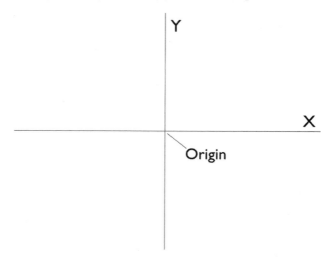

Figure 3-1: X- and Y-axes

Along these axes, imagine a series of regularly spaced hash marks, like the lines on a ruler. To describe where something is, you count the distance along the X- and Y-axes. Distances to the left and below the origin on the X- and Y-axes, respectively, are negative, while distances to the right and above the origin on the X- and Y-axes, respectively, are positive (see Figure 3-2).

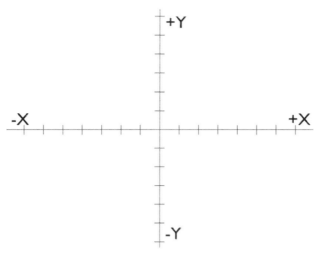

Figure 3-2: Positive and negative axes

For example, to describe where the dot in Figure 3-2 is located, you would count four units along the X-axis (known as the X coordinate) and five units along the Y-axis (known as the Y coordinate).

Now, with a default origin and XY coordinates, we can begin to describe 2-D geometry.

Points

The dot shown in Figure 3-3 is the simplest object that can be described in 2-D, and is known as a *point*. To describe a point you need only an X and a Y coordinate, as shown in the figure.

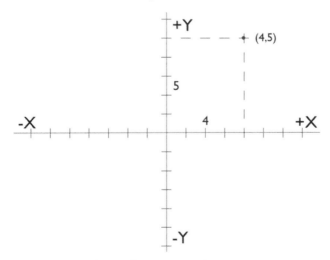

Figure 3-3: Defining the position of a point in 2-D space

Lines

The next simplest object we can describe in 2-D space is the line. To describe a line, you need only describe two points, as shown in Figure 3-4.

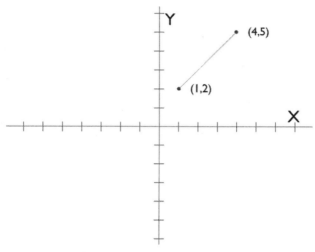

Figure 3-4: A line in 2-D

Polygons

By connecting three or more lines, you can begin to describe shapes, known as *polygons*. The simplest polygon is the three-sided triangle; next is the four-sided quadrangle or quadrilateral (usually shortened to *quads*), and so on, to infinity. For our purposes, we'll only work with triangles and quads.

With this knowledge, it's now time to expand from 2-D to 3-D space.

3.2.2. 3-D, the third dimension

As the name implies, *3-D* has an extra dimension to it (compared with 2-D space) but the concepts we covered in the 2-D discussion above still apply.

Z-axis

As with 2-D, we need a reference point from which to describe the location of things in 3-D. This is done by drawing a third axis that is perpendicular to both the X and Y axes and that passes through the origin. This new axis is usually called the *Z-axis*, and values above and below the origin are positive and negative, respectively (see Figure 3-5). By using this new axis we can describe objects as they exist in the real world.

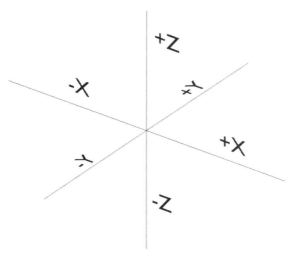

Figure 3-5: Introduction of the Z-axis

Points

To describe a point in 3-D, we now need three coordinates: the X, Y, and Z coordinates, as shown in Figure 3-6.

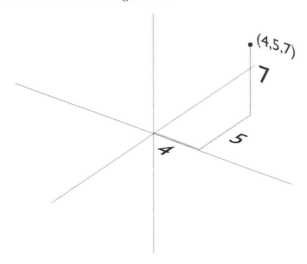

Figure 3-6: Defining a point in 3-D

Lines

As in 2-D, we can describe a line by defining two points, but now our line does not have to lie flat; it can be at any angle imaginable (Figure 3-7).

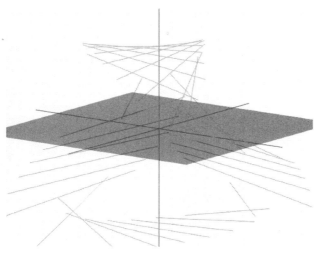

Figure 3-7: Lines are not confined to 2-D

Polygons

By connecting lines, we can form polygons just like in 2-D. Our polygons, just like our lines, are no longer confined to the flat 2-D world, as shown in Figure 3-8. Because of this, our flat 2-D shapes can now have volume.

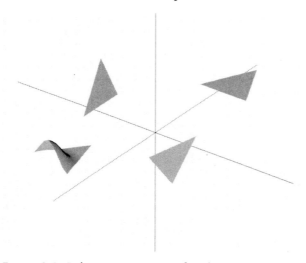

Figure 3-8: Polygons are not confined to 2-D

For example, a square becomes a cube, a circle becomes a sphere, and a triangle becomes a cone, as you can see in Figure 3-9.

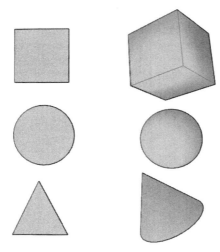

Figure 3-9: Some 2-D shapes and their 3-D counterparts

Now with the basics of 3-D covered, let's see how these concepts relate to 3-D computer graphics.

3.2.3. 3-D computer graphics

By now, you should have a basic understanding of the general concepts of 3-D. If not, go back and reread the previous sections. Having these concepts in mind will be very important as you proceed through this guide.

Next, we'll show you how the concepts of 3-D are used in 3-D computer graphics, also known as *computer graphic images (CGI)*.

Terminology

A slightly different set of terms is used for CGI. Table 3-1 shows how those terms relate to what you have learned so far.

Table 3-1: CGI Terminology

3-D Term	Related CGI Term
Point	Vertex
Line	Edge
Polygon	Polygon

Armed with our new terminology, we can now discuss CGI polygons.

Triangles, quads

While theoretically, a polygon can have an infinite number of edges, the more edges there are, the more time it takes a computer to calculate that shape. This is why triangles and quads are the most common polygons found in CGI; they allow the creation of just about any shape and do not put too much stress on the computer to calculate. But how do you form shapes with triangles and quads?

Mesh

As discussed previously, our polygons are no longer confined to the flat 2-D world. We can arrange our polygons at any angle we choose, even "bending" them if necessary. By combining a series of polygons at various angles and sizes, we can create any 3-D shape we want.

For example, six squares can be combined to form a cube, and four triangles and a square can form a pyramid, as shown in Figure 3-10.

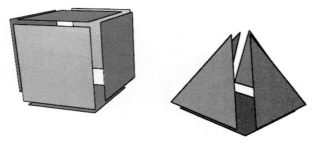

Figure 3-10: Combining polygons to more complex shapes

By increasing the number of polygons and manipulating their locations, angles, and sizes we can form complex objects like those shown in Figure 3-11.

As you can see, the more complex an object, the more it takes on a meshlike appearance. In fact, the object in Figure 3-11 is being viewed in *wire mesh* mode. You'll often hear the term *mesh* used to describe any combination of CGI polygons.

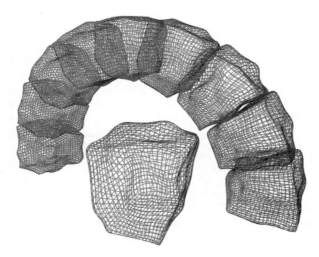

Figure 3-11: Arch made of quad-based blocks

Primitives

As demonstrated above, we can create shapes by combining polygons, but to form basic shapes by hand (such as spheres, cones, and cylinders) would be very tedious. Thus, 3-D applications like Blender have preprogrammed shapes called *primitives* that you can quickly add to a 3-D scene. Blender's mesh primitives include planes, cubes, spheres, cones, cylinders, and tubes. There are other primitives as well (not all of them mesh-based), and you will learn about them as you develop your Blender skills.

Faces

Polygons can be *faced* or *unfaced*. You can think of an unfaced polygon as being made of just wire, while a faced polygon has a "skin" stretched over that wire as shown in Figure 3-12.

Figure 3-12: Unfaced (left) and faced polygon (right)

When you tell Blender to draw your 3-D scene, called *rendering*, the faced polygons will appear solid, while the unfaced polygons will appear as holes as shown in Figure 3-13.

Figure 3-13: Unfaced polygons appear as holes in objects

Materials

Look at some objects around you, and you will see that they have many characteristics. Some are shiny; some are matte. Some are opaque; some are transparent. Some appear hard, while others appear soft. To re-create these characteristics in the 3-D world, we apply a *material* to an object, which tells Blender how to render the object's color, how shiny the object should appear, its perceived "hardness," and other properties, like the spheres shown in Figure 3-14.

Figure 3-14: Sphere objects with different materials

Textures

Take a look at the things around you again. Besides their material properties, they also have *texture*. Texture affects not only how something feels (whether it is smooth or rough), but also how it looks (its colors and patterns). Because we can't touch what we make in the 3-D CGI world, we will focus on how things look.

Image maps

A common method for applying textures is through the use of *image maps*, which are 2-D images which we "wrap" around an object. For example, Figure 3-15 shows a map of the earth wrapped around a sphere.

Image maps allow us to represent minute detail on our models (objects) that would be difficult to model directly and that would greatly increase the number of polygons if we did model them. By using image maps we keep the number of polygons low on our models, thus letting Blender render our scenes faster, which is especially important for real-time rendering in the game engine.

Figure 3-15: Map of the earth (back) wrapped around a sphere

UV mapping

One common challenge with image maps is that of accurately wrapping the maps around an object, especially a complex one. Many times the texture will not be aligned as we wish or it may "stretch," as shown in Figure 3-16. A popular way to overcome this problem is to use *UV mapping*.

Figure 3-16: Poorly mapped earth texture

UV vs. XY coordinates

What are UV coordinates? As mentioned in the 3-D overview, you can describe a point (vertex) by giving its X, Y, and Z coordinates. If you want to map a 2-D image onto a 3-D object, the XYZ coordinates have to be transformed into two dimensions, usually called the *UV coordinates*.

Instead of calculating UV coordinates automatically, you can define them yourself in Blender. This means that, for each vertex, not only a an XYZ coordinate is stored, but also the two values for U and V.

How does UV mapping work? Take a look at the head object in Figure 3-17. Each corner of the faces is a vertex, and each vertex has an XYZ and UV coordinate as explained earlier. Using Blender's UV editor, we unwrap the mesh, much like we do when we take a globe and lay it flat to make a map of the world, and lay that mesh on top of our 2-D image texture.

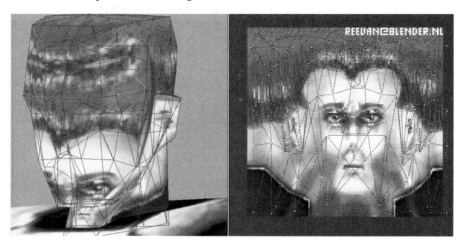

Figure 3-17: Poorly positioned head texture

Then, by moving the unwrapped mesh's UV coordinates, we can tell Blender exactly where the texture should go when Blender wraps the texture around our 3-D object, as shown in Figure 3-18.

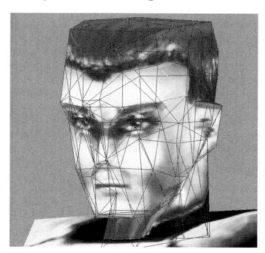

Figure 3-18: Final placement of texture

NOTE   *The reason it is called a UV editor and not a UVW editor is that we make our adjustments in 2-D (UV), and Blender automatically takes care of the W coordinate when it wraps the texture around our model. Not having to worry about the third dimension makes our job easier in this case.*

Viewing 3-D space

To do anything in 3-D, we need to be able to see what we are doing. We do so using *views*.

This section will discuss the various views available in Blender (*standard, interactive,* and *camera* views), and the two view modes available; it will not cover the steps you need to follow to use the views. (Those will be explained in Section 4.10.) We will also look at the use of lights, which, though not actually views, are necessary if you want to see anything when you render your 3-D scene. Lighting is also an important tool we can use to alter the mood of our scenes.

Standard

There are six preprogrammed standard views in Blender, each looking along a particular axis as shown in Figure 3-19. These views are generally used when modeling objects because they help to provide a sense of orientation. They are also useful if you get disoriented using the interactive view.

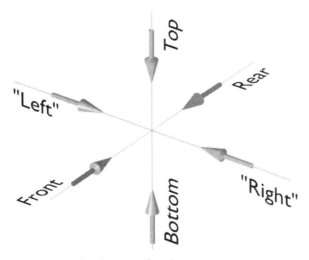

Figure 3-19: Blender's six fixed views

Interactive (free)

While the standard views are very useful for modeling, sometimes they don't help us visualize how an object will look in 3-D, as you can see in the example shown in Figure 3-20. This is when Blender's interactive view becomes useful.

Figure 3-20: Guess the true shape of this object!

Blender's interactive view allows you to rotate your entire 3-D scene in any direction interactively (in real time) to let you view things from any angle, as shown in Figure 3-21. This helps you visualize how your scenes and models will look.

Figure 3-21: Object from Figure 3-20 in a perspective view

Cameras

The standard and interactive views are generally not used when it is time to render your scenes (stills, animations, or real-time rendering in the game engine). Instead, you use a camera view for rendering.

You might think of this like a movie set: You are the director and you can walk around and look at your set from any direction (standard and interactive views) to make sure everything is just as you want it, but when it is time to shoot the scene you need a camera. This is what your audience will see, and the same holds true for camera views, as shown in Figure 3-22.

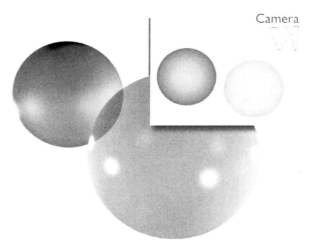

Figure 3-22: Image from Figure 3-14 showing how the camera was positioned in the scene

View modes

Here are two viewing modes for all the views in Blender: *orthogonal* and *perspective*. Orthogonal mode views everything without perspective, whereas perspective mode, as the name implies, uses perspective (Figure 3-23). Orthogonal mode is useful when creating your models because it lacks the "distortion" associated with perspective mode, which helps your accuracy. Perspective mode, like the interactive view, can help give you a sense of what your model will look like, but without the need to rotate the entire 3-D scene. (Rotating the entire scene can be slow if the scene is very complicated.)

Figure 3-23: Orthogonal and perspective modes

Lights

When you are ready to render your scene or play your game, you will need at least two things: a camera and lights. If you try to render without a camera you will get an error message, but if you try to render without a light all you will get is a black image.

This is one of the most common mistakes for new Blender users, so if you try to render something and all you get is a black square, be sure to check whether you've put in a lamp. For the interactive 3-D graphics, there can be scenes without light, but they usually look flat.

There is more to lights than helping you to see. As in real life, lights can help set the atmosphere or mood of a scene. For example, using a low blue light helps to create a "cool/cold" atmosphere, while a bright orange light might create a "warm" one (Figure 3-24). Lights can be used to simulate ambient light, muzzle flashes, or any other effect where you would expect to see light.

Figure 3-24: Same scene rendered with different lights

Because you will be creating games with objects that move and change, we must cover:

Transformations

As touched on earlier, we describe the locations of objects in our 3-D worlds by using an origin and a XYZ coordinate system of measurement. The coordinates calculated from this default origin are known as *global coordinates*. In addition, an object's center serves as its own origin, and so the object can have its own XYZ axes as shown in Figure 3-25. This is called a *local origin* and a *local coordinate system with local coordinates*.

But why is this important?

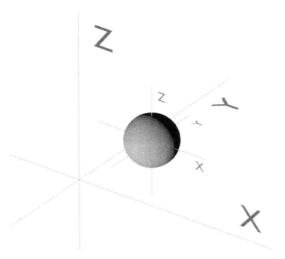

Figure 3-25: Local axis of an object

A game where nothing moves or changes will not get much of a following. The objects in your games need to move, and this is one place where the concept of transformations becomes important. The three most common transformations are *translation, rotation,* and *scaling,* as listed in Table 3-2.

Table 3-2: Transformations

Transformation	Description
Translation	When an object moves from point A to point B
Rotation	When an object spins around a particular point or axis
Scaling	When an object increases or decreases in size

When you make your games, remember that transformations are relative and can affect game play. When an object translates from point A to B in the global coordinate system, from that object's point of view, its local coordinate system doesn't necessarily move. For example, a character standing in a moving train seems to be stationary from their point of view. The train's speed may be 65 mph, but the character feels like they are standing still. Their local origin (their center) doesn't move, as far as they are concerned.

However, if we look at the same character from the point of view of someone standing still outside the train, the character is now moving. From this second character's local point of view, they are standing still and the first character is moving, but neither are rotating. Or are they?

If we look from the point of view of another character, hovering in space, not only are both of the other characters on the earth, rotating as the earth rotates on its axis, but also as the earth rotates around the sun.

So, how does this affect game play? Imagine everyone is trying to hit a stationary target on the train. The first character has the easiest job, a stationary target; the second character has to hit a moving target; and the third character has to hit a target that is moving and experiencing two forms of rotation. This shifting of points of view is called *coordinate transformation*, and as you can see, it can have an important impact on game play.

In most 3-D software packages you can work with these coordinate systems using so-called hierarchies. You can define one object as being the "parent" of another object, which then becomes a child. Now all transformations of the parent are also applied to its children. That way you only have to define motion for a parent to have all its children moving in the same way. In the solar system example, we humans all are in fact "children" of the earth, which in turn is a "child" of the sun.

One last point: Transformation is not restricted to just shapes. Materials, textures, and even lights can be moved, rotated, and scaled. In fact, anything that exists in your 3-D world is actually an object and so is subject to transformations.

NOTE *As your 3-D skills develop, you will learn how to use global, local, and relative transformations to affect game play and to create interesting effects.*

Now that you have received a basic introduction to 3-D CGI, it's time to talk about game engines and aspects of good games.

3.3. Game Engines and Aspects of a Good Game

3.3.1. What is a game engine?

A *game engine* is software that simulates a part of reality. Through a game engine, you interact with a 3-D world in real time, controlling objects that can interact with other objects in that world. If you have ever played a video game on a computer, on a console, or in a game arcade, you have used a game engine of some kind.

The game engine is the heart of a game and consists of several parts. One part displays the 3-D world and its objects on your screen, drawing and redrawing your scenes as things change. Another part deals with decision making (known as *game logic*), for example, deciding when events like doors opening should occur. Another part simulates physics, such as gravity, inertia, momentum, and so on. Yet another part detects when objects collide with each other, while another actually moves objects. The game engine tries to simulate all these things as quickly as possible to provide a smooth fluid simulation.

For example, in a computer baseball game, the game engine will have the pitcher throw you a pitch (moving an object). As the ball travels the game engine will calculate all the physics that act on the ball, such as gravity, air resistance, and so on. Then you swing the bat (or more accurately, you tell the game engine to swing the batter's bat) and hopefully hit the ball (i.e., collision detection between the ball and bat).

This is a very simplified example. The game engines you have used are much more complicated and can take a team of programmers and a great deal of time to create. (At least, that was the case until Blender's game engine was released.)

3.3.2. Blender's game engine—Click-and-drag game creation

Blender is the first game engine that can create complete games without the need to program. Through its click-and-drag graphical user interface (GUI), even those with no programming experience can enjoy the challenge of creating fun and exciting games.

After you create your 3-D world and 3-D objects, you only need to use a series of pull-down menus, simple key strokes, and mouse clicks to add behavioral properties to that world and those objects and bring them to life. For professionals, this allows for the rapid prototyping of games, and for non-professionals, it's the first chance to produce their own games without having to spend years learning to program or the need for large programming teams. (Of course, for those who can program, Blender uses the Python scripting language to allow programmers to extend Blender's game engine even further.)

This relative ease of use, though, hides the Blender game engine's true innovation. . . .

3.3.3. "True" and "fake" 3-D game engines

Blender is a "true" 3-D game engine. Until recently, game logic wasn't done on an object level. This meant that a "higher intelligence" (HI) in the game had to control all the objects, moving them when appropriate or keeping track of their condition (e.g., alive or dead). With the advent of "true" 3-D game engines, each object in a game is its own entity and reports such information back to the game engine.

For example, if you are playing a game where you walk through a maze that has hidden doors, in the past the HI would have had to decide when you were close enough to a hidden door and then open it. With Blender's game engine, the door itself can have a sensor function and will determine when another object is close enough, then the door will open itself.

Another example would be a shooting game. The gun has logic attached that detects when you pull the trigger; the gun then creates a new bullet object with a certain starting speed. The bullet, which is now its own entity, shoots out of the gun and flies through the air all the while being affected by air resistance and gravity. The bullet itself has sensors and logic as well, and detects whether it hits a wall or an adversary. On collision, the logic in the bullet and the logic in the collided object define what will happen.

In the past, when you pulled the trigger, the game engine would calculate whether a bullet fired at that time would hit the target or not. There was no actual bullet object. If the game engine determined that a hit had occurred, it then told the object that had been hit how to react.

The advantage of Blender's "real" 3-D game engine is that it does a better job of simulating reality because it allows for the randomness that occurs in the real world. It also distributes the decision load so that a single HI isn't required to decide everything.

While Blender provides you with the technology to create good games, it doesn't create them automatically. To create good games, you need to understand three important aspects of games.

3.3.4. Good games

If you analyze successful games, you will find that they have three aspects in varying degrees. This is known as the "toy, immersive, goal" theory of game creation.

Toy

The *toy* aspect of a game refers to the immediate fun of just playing it. You don't need to think too much; you can just grab the mouse or the game controller and start playing, much like you did with your toys when you were a child. You didn't need to read a manual on how to play with your toy cars or spend time figuring out complicated strategy.

In short, games with a high degree of toy are very intuitive. Think of your favorite arcade game at your local game arcade. Most likely you only needed one joystick and two or three buttons, or a simple gun with a trigger. This doesn't mean that such games don't require skill, just that you can gain immediate enjoyment from playing them.

Immersive

The *immersive* aspect of a game is the degree to which the game makes you forget you are playing a game, sometimes called the "suspension of disbelief." Flight simulators or racing simulators are good examples.

Realism is an important factor in the immersive aspect of a game, which is why simulators have reached such an advanced level of realism. The MechWarrior series and WarBirds are two excellent examples of immersive games that have very realistic environments, animations, and sounds. They are fairly low on the toy aspect and take some time to learn to play, with almost every key on the keyboard used for some function.

The old one-button joysticks have been replaced with HOTAS (Hands on Throttle and Stick) systems consisting of a joystick with seven to ten buttons for one hand, a throttle device with an equal number of buttons or dials for the other, and even pedals for your feet. These systems combine with the game to create an incredibly immersive environment. These games also often have a high degree of goal.

Goal

The *goal* aspect of a game is the degree to which a game gives you a goal to achieve. This often involves a lot of strategy and planning. Age of Empires and SimCity are two games that are very goal oriented.

Goal-oriented games are often very low on the toy aspect. SimCity, for example, comes with a thick manual explaining all the intricate details of "growing" a successful city. This is not always the case, though: Quake is a goal-oriented game that also has a good deal of toy and immersive aspects to it.

Balance

When you create your games, you will have to strike a balance between the toy, immersive, and goal aspects of your games. If you can create a game that has a high degree of each aspect, you'll most likely have a hit on your hands.

3.4. Conclusion

This chapter has introduced you to the basic concepts of 3-D, including vertices, polygons, materials, textures, origins, coordinate systems, and transformations. You have also been introduced to what makes a game work, both on a technological level with the discussion of game engines and on a conceptual level with the discussion of what makes good games good.

The rest of this book will show you how to use Blender to put these concepts to work when creating games. Once you have finished this guide, you'll have all the tools you'll need to make games; the rest will fall to your own creativity. Good luck, and we look forward to seeing you announce your games on Blender's discussion boards (see Section 29.4).

4

BLENDER BASICS

The Blender user interface can be a little confusing for beginners because it differs from other 3-D software packages. But persevere! Once you familiarize yourself with the basic principles behind the user interface, you'll start to realize just how fast you can work in your scenes and models. Blender optimizes the day-to-day work of an animation studio, where every minute costs money.

NOTE   *Installing Blender is simple: just unpack it and place it in a directory of your choosing (or let the installer do it). The installation is described in detail in Section 29.1.*

When you first start Blender, you'll see a screen like the one shown in Figure 4-1. The big Window is a 3DWindow where your scene and objects are displayed and where you will manipulate them. The smaller window, located below the 3DWindow, is the ButtonsWindow where you can edit the various settings of the scene and selected objects.

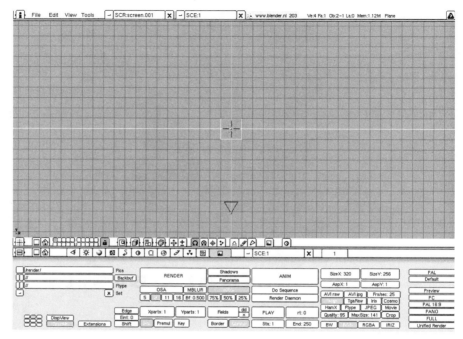

Figure 4-1: The first start

4.1. Keys and Interface Conventions

During its development, which followed the latest 3-D graphics developments, an almost new language also developed around Blender. Nowadays, the entire Blender community speaks that language, which Ton Roosendaal — the father of Blender — often calls *Blender Turbo language*. This language makes it easy to communicate with other Blender users worldwide.

In this book, we refer to key presses as AKEY, BKEY, 1KEY, 2KEY, and so on. (Note that numbers that are to be entered using the numeric keypad on the keyboard will be listed as PAD1, PAD2, and so forth.) This will allow you to see what is done in a tutorial at a glance, once you know the shortcuts. Key combinations appear as (for example) SHIFT-D or CTRL-ALT-A.

Also, we refer to the mouse buttons as LMB, MMB, and RMB for left, middle, and right mouse button.

4.2. The Mouse

Blender is designed to be used with two hands: one hand on the keyboard and the other using the mouse. This prompts me to mention the Golden Rule of Blender:

Keep one hand on your keyboard and one hand on your mouse!

The mouse is particularly important because by using it you can control more than one axis at time. We recommend that you use Blender with a three-button mouse. If you have a two-button mouse you can substitute for the MMB by holding ALT and using the LMB.

The mouse usually has the same functionality in all of Blenders's sections and windows.

Left Mouse Button (LMB)

With the LMB you can activate buttons and set the 3D-Cursor. You will often click and drag the LMB to change values in sliders.

Middle Mouse Button (MMB)

The MMB is used predominantly to navigate within windows. In the 3DWindow it rotates the view; when used with SHIFT it drags the view, and with CTRL it zooms. While manipulating an object, the MMB is also used to restrict a movement to a single axis.

NOTE   *On systems with only two mouse buttons, you can substitute the MMB with the ALT key and the LMB.*

Right Mouse Button (RMB)

The RMB selects or activates objects for further manipulation. Objects change color when they are selected. Holding SHIFT while selecting with the RMB adds the clicked object to a selection. The object last selected is the active object, and it will be used for the next action. If you SHIFT-RMB an already selected object, it becomes the active object. Click again to deselect it.

4.3. Loading and Saving

In the Header of the InfoWindow, normally located on the top of the screen, you should see the FileMenu, as shown in Figure 4-2. This menu offers you standard operations for working with files and changing views.

Figure 4-2: FileMenu

Pressing the spacebar brings up the Toolbox (Figure 4-3), a large pop-up menu with the most commonly used Blender operations. The FILE entry gives you access to file operations. Every command shows its associated hotkey.

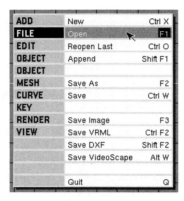

Figure 4-3: Blender's main menu, the Toolbox

NOTE *Use the Toolbox to learn the hotkeys in Blender!*

The most common file operations in Blender are the loading and saving of scenes, and the quickest way to do so is with hotkeys: F1 offers you a FileWindow to load a scene and F2 a FileWindow to save a scene.

FileWindow

However you decide to initiate a file operation, you will always get its appropriate FileWindow.

The main part of a FileWindow is the listing of directories and files as shown in Figure 4-4. File types known by Blender are shown with a yellow square. LMB-click a directory to enter it. Click with the LMB to select a file and put its name into the file name input (TubeCleaner_11.blend, in this example). Press ENTER or click LOAD FILE to load the file shown, or press ESC or click Cancel to cancel the operation. MMB-click a file to quickly load it, or enter the path and file name by hand in the two inputs at the top of the FileWindow to load a file. Use the RMB to select more than one file. The selected files are highlighted in blue.

P	/mero2/home/cw/work/texte/NaN/BoxWork/TubeCleaner/Tutorial/	LOAD FILE
↵	**TubeCleaner_11.blend**	Cancel

```
                                        4 096
                                        4 096
        textures                        4 096
    TubeCleaner_11.blend          1 625 120
    TubeCleaner_12.blend            151 052
    TubeCleaner_10.blend            150 332
    TubeCleaner_09.blend            149 832
    TubeCleaner_08.blend            149 536
    TubeCleaner_07.blend            149 020
    TubeCleaner_06.blend            148 272
    TubeCleaner_03.blend            147 440
    TubeCleaner_02.blend            146 940
    TubeCleaner_04.blend            147 524
    TubeCleaner_05.blend            147 852
    TubeCleaner_01.blend            146 284
    TubeCleaner_00.blend            145 172
        test
    TubeCleaner_final.blend       3 735 132
```

Figure 4-4: Blender FileWindow

NOTE *The PAD+ and PAD- keys increase and decrease the last number in a file name, respectively. This is handy for saving different versions of a file as you work.*

The button labeled with a "P" at the upper left corner of the FileWindow puts you one directory up in your path. The MenuButton below it shows the last directories you visited, as well as your hard disk drives in Windows.

Now let's look at the FileWindow Header, shown in Figure 4-5. Here, the button labeled A/Z sorts alphabetically; the clock button sorts by the file date, and the next button sorts by file size. To the right of these buttons you'll see a description of what the FileWindow will do, LOAD FILE in this case.

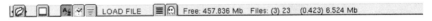

Figure 4-5: FileWindow Header with valuable information

The next button to the right selects between long (size, permissions, and date) and short file names. The little ghost hides all files beginning with a dot, then to its right you have information about the free space remaining on the disk, and the size of the selected files in megabytes.

Version control and backup files

Blender follows a simple, straightforward method to provide an undo. When you enlarge the InfoWindow by pulling down the edge, you can see the controls for backups and version control as shown in Figure 4-6.

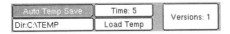

Figure 4-6: Version control and backup settings in the InfoWindow

With the Auto Temp Save button activated, Blender will automatically write a backup after the number of minutes specified in the Time field to the directory entered in the Dir field. Clicking Load Temp will load the last written temporary file.

When you write a file, Blender keeps the old file as *.blend1 for backup. "Versions:" controls how many version files are written.

NOTE   *Besides these possibilities for disaster recovery, Blender writes a file, quit.blend, containing your last scene into the temporary directory Dir when you quit the program.*

4.4. Windows

All Blender screens consist of Windows that represent data, contain buttons, or request information from the user. You can arrange Blender's Windows in many ways to suit your working environment.

Header

Every Window has a Header containing buttons specific to that window or presenting information to the user. For example, here's the Header for the 3DWindow.

The leftmost button shows the window type; clicking it pops up a menu to change the window type. The next button switches between a full screen and a tiled screen window. The button featuring a house graphic fills the window to the maximum extent with the information it is displaying.

Figure 4-7: HeaderMenu

A RMB-click on the header pops up a menu asking you to place the Header at the top, the bottom, or nowhere for that window. Click and hold the MMB on the header, and then drag the mouse to move the header horizontally in case it doesn't fit the width of the window.

Edges

Whenever you place the mouse cursor over the edge of a Blender window the cursor changes shape and the following mouse keys are activated:

LMB

Drag the window edge horizontally or vertically while holding down the LMB. The window edge always moves in increments of four pixels, making it relatively easy to move two window edges so that they are precisely adjacent to each other, thus making it easy to join them.

MMB or RMB

Clicking an edge with MMB or RMB pops up a menu prompting you to Split Area or Join Areas. Split Area lets you choose the exact position for the border; it always works on the window from which you entered the edge. Join Areas joins Windows with a shared edge, if possible, which means that joining works only if Blender doesn't have to close more than one Window for joining. You can cancel the operation with ESC.

4.5. Blender Button Types

Buttons offer the quickest access to DataBlocks. In fact, the buttons visualize a single DataBlock and are grouped as such. Always use an LMB click to call up buttons, as described below:

Button

`Clear` This button, which is usually displayed in salmon color, activates a process such as New or Delete.

TogButton

`Shadeless` This button, which displays a given option or setting, can be set to either off or on.

Tog3Button

`Emit` This button can be set to off, positive, or negative. When set to negative mode the text is yellow.

RowButton

`Glob` `Orco` `Stick` `Win` `Nor` `Refl` This button is part of a line of buttons. Only one button in the line can be active at once.

NumButton

`sizeX 1.00` This button, which displays a numerical value, can be used in these ways:

- Hold the button while moving the mouse. Move to the right and up to assign a higher value to a variable or to the left and down to assign a lower value. Hold CTRL while doing this to change values in steps, or hold SHIFT to achieve finer control.
- Hold the button and click SHIFT-LMB to change the button to a TextBut. A cursor appears, indicating that you can now enter a new value. Enter the desired value and press ENTER to assign it to the button. Press ESC to cancel without changing the value.
- Click the lefthand side of the button to decrease the value assigned to the button slightly, or click the righthand side of the button to increase it.

NumSlider

`R 0.800` Use the slider to change values. The lefthand side of the button functions as a TextBut.

TextButton

`ME:Plane` This button remains active (and blocks the rest of the interface) until you again press LMB, ENTER, or ESC. While this button is active, the following hotkeys are available:

- ESC: Restores the previous text.
- SHIFT-BACKSPACE: Deletes the entire text.
- SHIFT-LEFTARROW: Moves the cursor back to the beginning of the text.
- SHIFT-RIGHTARROW: Moves the cursor to the end of the text.

MenuButton

This button calls up a PupMenu. Hold the LMB while moving the cursor to select an option. If you move the mouse outside of the PopUpMenu, the old value is restored.

IconButton

Button type "But" activates processes.

IconToggle

Button type "TogBut" toggles between two modes.

IconRow

As button type "RowBut," only one button in the row of buttons can be active at once.

IconMenu

⊟ Click with the LMB to see the the available options.

4.6. Windowtypes

🖉 DataSelect, *SHIFT-F4*

For browsing the data structure of the scene and selecting objects from it.

⊞ 3DWindow, *SHIFT-F5*

Opens the main window while working in the 3-D space. It visualizes the scene from orthogonal, perspective, and camera views.

🔟 IpoWindow, *SHIFT-F6*

Opens the IpoWindow, for creating and manipulating IpoCurves, Blender's animation curve system.

⊟ ButtonWindow, *SHIFT-F7*

The ButtonWindow contains all the buttons needed to manipulate every aspect of Blender. A brief overview follows this section; for a more detailed explanation see the Reference section at the end of this book.

▦ SequenceEditor, *SHIFT-F8*

The SequenceEditor; used for post-processing and combining animations and scenes.

🎛 OopsWindow, *SHIFT-F9*

The OopsWindow (Object-Oriented Programming System) shows a schematic overview of the current scene's structure.

🖼 ImageWindow, *SHIFT-F10*

The ImageWindow shows and assign images to objects. It is especially important when working with UV texturing.

ℹ️ InfoWindow

The InfoWindow header shows useful information and contains the menus and the scene and screen MenuButtons. The InfoWindow itself contains the options that let you set your personal preferences.

▣ TextWindow, SHIFT-F11

Opens a simple text editor, mostly used for writing Python scripts, but also useful for inserting comments about your scenes.

⊘ ImageSelectWindow

Lets you browse and select images on your disk and includes thumbnails for previewing them.

◁ SoundWindow, SHIFT-F12

Use the SoundWindow to visualize and load sounds.

ButtonsWindow

The ButtonsWindow shown below contains the buttons needed for manipulating objects and changing the general aspects of a scene.

The ButtonsHeader contains icons to switch between the different types of ButtonsWindows, as follows.

◁ ViewButtons

ViewButtons has the 3DWindow settings for a Window. It only has buttons when it is selected from a 3DWindow, at which point it will offer settings for the grid or background images. Every 3DWindow can have its own settings.

※ LampButtons, F4

The LampButtons only display when a lamp is selected, allowing you to change all of the parameters of a lamp, like its color, energy, type (e.g., Lamp, Spot, Sun, Hemi), quality of shadows, and so on.

◉ MaterialButtons, F5

These appear when you select an object with a material assigned. This clutch of buttons allows you to control every aspect of the look of the surface.

▣ TextureButtons, F6

These buttons let you assign textures to materials, including mathematically generated textures, as well as the more commonly used image textures.

∫ AnimationButtons, F7

Use the AnimationButtons to control various animation parameters. The section of the buttons at the right is used for assigning special animation effects to objects, such as particle systems and wave effects.

⊕ RealTimeButtons, F8

These buttons are part of Blender's real-time section. (This book covers only linear animation.)

⊡ EditButtons, F9

The EditButtons offer several ways for you to manipulate objects. The buttons shown in this window depend on the type of object that is selected.

⊕ WorldButtons

Configure global world parameters, like the color of the sky and the horizon, mist settings, and ambient light settings.

⬠ Face/PaintButtons

Use these buttons for coloring objects at the vertex level and for setting texture parameters for the UV-Editor.

⬥ RadiosityButtons

Blender's radiosity renderer, which is not covered in this book.

▦ ScriptButtons

Assigns Python scripts to world, material, and objects (BlenderCreator).

▭ DisplayButtons, F10

The DisplayButtons allow you to control the quality and output format of rendered pictures and animations.

4.7. Screens

Screens are Blender's fundamental framework. You can have as many screens as you like, each one with a different arrangement of windows, thus allowing you to create a personalized workspace for every task you perform. You can browse your screens with Screen browse, as shown in Figure 4-8. The screen layout is saved with the scene, allowing you to have scene-dependent workspaces. For example, you might have a screen for 3-D work, another for working with Ipos, and a complete file manager to arrange your files and textures.

→ SCR:screen.001   X

Figure 4-8: Screen browse

4.8. Scenes

Scenes allow you to organize your work and to render multiple scenes in the Blender game engine — to display an instruments panel overlay, for example. You might also switch scenes from the game engine and thus changing levels of a game. Browse your Scenes with Scene browse, as shown in Figure 4-9.

Figure 4-9: Scene browse

When adding a new scene you have these options:

Empty: Create a completely empty scene.

Link Objects: All Objects are linked to the new scene. The Objects layer and selection flags can be configured differently for each Scene.

Link ObData: Duplicates Objects only. ObData linked to the Objects, such as Mesh and Curve, are not duplicated.

Full Copy: Everything is duplicated.

4.9. Setting Up Your Personal Environment

The options listed above allow you to create your own environments. To make your personal environment the default when Blender starts, or after you reset Blender with CTRL-X, use CTRL-U to save it to your home directory.

4.10. Navigating in 3-D

Blender is a 3-D program, so we need to be able to navigate in 3-D space — a challenge because our screens are only 2-D. We use the 3DWindows as "windows" to the 3-D world created inside Blender; ways to navigate in 3-D space from within 2-D screens.

4.10.1. Using the keyboard to change your view

To change your view, place your mouse pointer over the big window on the standard Blender screen. This is a 3DWindow used for showing and manipulating your 3-D worlds.

NOTE   *Remember that the window with the mouse pointer located over it (no click needed) is the active window! This means that only this window will respond to your key presses.*

Pressing PAD1 (the number "1" key on the numeric pad) gives you a view from the front of the scene. In the default Blender scene, installed when you first start Blender, you are looking at the edge of a plane with the camera positioned in front of it. Hold down the CTRL key (on some systems SHIFT is also possible) to get the opposite view, which in this case is the view from the back (CTRL-PAD1).

PAD7 returns you to the view from the top. Now use the PAD+ and PAD- to zoom in and out. PAD3 gives you a side view of the scene.

PAD0 switches to a camera view of the scene. In the standard scene, you see only the edge of the plane because it is at the same height as the camera.

PAD/ only shows selected objects; all other objects are hidden. PAD. zooms to the furthest extent of the selected objects.

Use PAD7 to switch back to a top view or load the standard scene with CTRL-X. Now, press PAD4 four times, and then PAD2 four times. You should be looking from the left, above the scene and down onto it.

Use the cross of keys on the number pad (PAD8, PAD6, PAD2, and PAD4) to rotate the actual view. If you use these keys together with SHIFT, you can drag the view.

Press PAD5 to switch between a perspective and orthogonal view.

NOTE *Use CTRL-X followed by ENTER to get a fresh Blender scene. But remember, this action will discard all changes you have made!*

Try experimenting with these keys to get a feel for how they work and what they do. If you get lost, use CTRL-X followed by ENTER to return to the default scene.

4.10.2. Using the mouse to change your view

The MMB is the main button to use for navigating with the mouse in the 3DWindow. Press and hold the MMB in a 3DWindow; then drag the mouse to rotate the view with the movement of your mouse. Try using a perspective view (PAD5) while experimenting for a very realistic impression of 3-D.

NOTE *When used with the SHIFT key, the above procedure translates the view. With CTRL, it zooms the view.*

The 3DHeader is shown below. The following overview should give you a good idea of how to use the buttons on the 3DHeader to look around in 3-D scenes.

The leftmost icon switches the window to different window types (3DWindow, FileWindow, and on). The icon to its right toggles between a full-screen representation of the window and its default representation. The icon with a house on it zooms the window so that all objects become visible.

The LayerButtons (including the icon with the lock on it) will be discussed later in this book.

 The LocalView icon switches the modes for the local view and is the mouse alternative to the PAD/ key. With the following icon you can switch between orthogonal, perspective, and camera views (keys PAD5 and PAD0).

This button toggles between the top, front, and side views. SHIFT selects the opposite view, just as it does when you use the keypad.

 The DrawMode button switches between different methods of drawing objects. You can choose from a bounding box, a wireframe, a faced, a gouraud-shaded, and a textured view.

The ViewMoveZoom icons translate and zoom the view with a LMB click on the icon and a drag of the mouse.

4.11. Selecting Objects

To select an object, click it with the right mouse button (RMB). Clicking an object also deselects all other objects. To extend the selection to more than one object, hold down SHIFT while clicking the RMB; selected objects show as purple in the wireframe view. The last object selected is colored a lighter purple and it is the active object. Operations that only apply to one object, or need one object as reference, always work with the active object.

Objects can also selected with a border by pressing BKEY (Border Select), then drawing a rectangle around the objects. Draw the rectangle with the LMB to select objects; draw with the RMB to deselect them.

Selecting and activating

Blender distinguishes between selected and active objects. The active and selected object is displayed in a lighter color than other selected objects, and the name of the active object is displayed in the InfoHeader. Only one object can be active at any time (or example to allow visualization of data in buttons), and multiple objects can be selected at once. Almost all key commands affect selected objects.

A single RMB-click is sufficient to select and activate an object. All other objects (in the visible layers) are then deselected in order to eliminate the risk of key commands unintentionally changing those objects, and all relevant buttons are also drawn anew.

Selections can be extended or shrunk using SHIFT+RMB, in which case the last object selected (or deselected) then becomes the active object. Use Border Select (BKEY) to more rapidly select a number of objects at one time, but remember that none of the objects selected using this option will become active.

4.12. Copying and Linking

Blender uses an object-oriented structure to store and manipulate objects and data, which allows an object to have its own data (in the case of the Blender Game Engine Polygon-Meshes) or share a Mesh with other objects. This system offers several advantages, including:

- Reducing the size of the scene in memory, on disk, or when publishing on the Web.
- Changes to the ObData inherit to all objects at the same time. Imagine how important this becomes when you decide to change a house object you have used 100 times in your scene, or when changing the Material properties of one wall.
- You can design the logic and game play with simple placeholder objects, then swap them against the finished objects with a click of the mouse.
- The shape of objects (the MeshData) can be changed during the game's runtime without affecting the object or its position.

Copy

Copying a selected object duplicates it. Copying is fastest with the key command SHIFT-D or with the Duplicate entry in the EditMenu.

Linked Copy

To create a linked copy of an object use ALT-D. Unlike copying with SHIFT-D, the mesh forming the object is not duplicated, but rather linked to the new objects.

User Button

Another common way to create and change links and Blender interface elements is with the UserButton, as shown below. To use this MenuButton to change links, LMB-click it and choose a link from the menu that appears. If there are more possibilities than the menu can show, a DataBrowseWindow is opened instead.

If an object has more than one user, the UserButton will be blue, and a number indicates the number of users (in the above image three). Selecting this number will make a copy of the Data and makes the object single-user.

Linking

To link data from the active to the selected objects use CTRL-L. A menu (shown below) will ask what data you want to link. You can choose to link the objects between scenes or link Ipos, MeshData, or Materials.

You can see the object structure created by copying or linking actions in the OopsWindow, SHIFT-F9, as shown in Figure 4-10. This figure shows that the object linked was copied two times with ALT-D. You can see that all three objects (Blender automatically generates unique names by appending numbers) are linked to the same MeshData "Plane_linked." The object "Copied" was copied with SHIFT-D, resulting in two objects with their own MeshData.

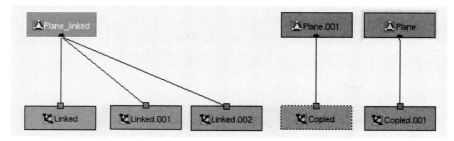

Figure 4-10: Object visualization in the OopsWindow

4.13. Manipulating Objects

Most actions in Blender involve moving, rotating, or changing the size of items, and Blender offers a wide range of options for doing so. The options are summarized here. (See the 3DWindow section for a full list.)

Grab mode

GKEY. Move the mouse to translate the selected items, then press the LMB, ENTER, or the spacebar to assign it to its new location. Press ESC or the RMB to cancel. Translation is always corrected for the view in the 3DWindow.

Use the MMB to limit translation to the X-, Y-, or Z-axis. Blender determines which axis to use, based on the already initiated movement.

RMB and hold-move allows you to select an Object and immediately start Grab mode.

Rotate mode

RKEY. Move the mouse around the rotation center, then press the LMB, ENTER, or the spacebar to assign the rotation. Press ESC to cancel. Rotation is always perpendicular to the view of the 3DWindow.

The center of rotation is determined by use of the buttons in the 3DWindowHeader. Starting from the left, the leftmost button rotates around the center of the bounding box of all selected objects. The next button to the right uses the median points (shown as yellow/purple dots) of the selected objects to find the rotation center. The button with the 3D-Cursor on it rotates around the 3D-Cursor and the last button rotates around the individual centers of the objects.

Scale mode

SKEY. Move the mouse from the rotation center outward, then press the LMB, ENTER, or the spacebar to assign the scaling. Use the MiddleMouse toggle to limit scaling to the X-, Y-, or Z-axis; Blender determines the appropriate axis based on the direction of the movement.

The center of scaling is determined by the center buttons in the 3DHeader (see the explanation in the preceding Rotate mode section).

While in scaling mode, you can mirror the object by pressing XKEY or YKEY to mirror at the X- or Y-axis.

NumberMenu

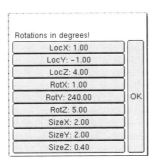

To input exact values, you can call up the NumberMenu with NKEY. SHIFT-LMB-click to change the buttons to an input field and then enter the number.

EditMode

When you add a new object with the Toolbox, you are in EditMode. In EditMode, you can change the shape of an Object (e.g., a mesh, a curve, or text) by manipulating the individual points (the vertices) that form the object.
Selecting with the RMB and the Border Select BKEY also selects vertices. To select more vertices you can use Circle Select by pressing BKEY-BKEY. "Painting" with the LMB selects vertices, painting with the MMB deselects.

When you enter EditMode, Blender makes a copy of the indicated data. The hotkey UKEY serves as an undo function, restoring the copied data.

NOTE   *As a reminder that you are in EditMode, the cursor shape changes to a cross.*

PART TWO
PLAYING WITH
3-D GAME TECHNOLOGY

In this part of the book, we'll use the "Pumpkin-Run" example file that you'll find on the CD to explain and illustrate most of the core techniques for making a 3-D game. While we can't make you a professional game designer in a few pages, or even with a complete book, you'll learn the basics in this section and have fun at the same time. You will learn:

- How to load and save Blender scenes
- Manipulate objects and navigate in a scene
- Basic texture mapping
- How to play interactive 3-D in Blender's integrated 3-D engine
- How to add interactivity to control game elements
- How to control the camera and lights
- Object animation
- How to add and use sound

Although there seems like a lot to learn, and there is, don't despair: Game play is the most important thing. Even technically simple games (like Tetris) can be entertaining for long periods of time. So concentrate on making your game fun for others, or just enjoy creating stuff yourself!

Advanced Topics Covered in Later Chapters

- Character animation is the art of bringing computer models to life. This complex topic demands many different capabilities from the game designer. It requires texturing, modeling, animation, a good knowledge of natural motions, and so on.

- Special effects like bullets and explosions.

- Overlay interfaces and multiple scenes.

- Python scripting to simplify complex game logic. Python is a modern and efficient scripting language which is integrated into Blender. Complex things can often be simplified with a few lines of Python.

5

MODELING AN ENVIRONMENT

When you start Blender, it opens with the default scene, as shown in Figure 5-1. The big window shown in the figure is the 3DWindow, our window to the world of 3-D inside Blender scenes. The pink square is a simple plane drawn in wireframe. In this figure, we are looking onto the scene from above, a so-called TopView. The triangle represents a Blender camera. Let's navigate the scene a bit, a quick review of what you learned in Section 4.10. These actions should give you a basic idea of how navigating in Blender's 3-D space through a 2-D window works.

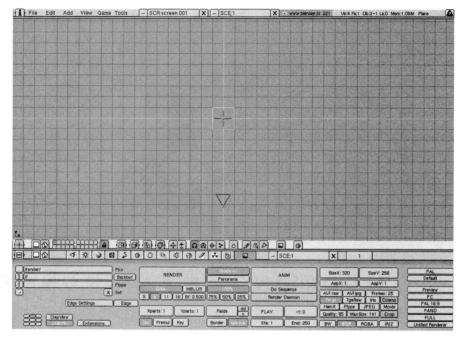

Figure 5-1: Blender, just after starting it

1. Move your mouse cursor over the camera and press your right mouse button (RMB) to select the camera.

NOTE *Blender uses the RMB for selecting objects!*

2. Now we will change the view of the scene. Move the mouse cursor into the big 3DWindow and press and hold the middle mouse button (MMB) and move the mouse to rotate the view.

NOTE *Remember: Blender is designed to work best with a three-button mouse. However, if you have only a two-button mouse you can substitute for the middle mouse button by holding ALT and the left mouse button (ALT-LMB).*

3. Return to the TopView of the scene by pressing PAD7.
4. Select the plane again by mousing over it and pressing the RMB. The plane will be drawn in pink when your selection has been successful. Now let's change the scale of the plane.
5. Move the mouse over the selected plane, press SKEY, and move the mouse again. You should see that the plane changes its size according to how your mouse moves.

6. Now hold CTRL while moving the mouse. The scale will only change in increments of 0.1. Scale the plane until the size is 10.0 for all axes by checking the scaling information in the bar below the 3DWindow (see Figure 5-2), and then press the LMB to finish the scaling operation.

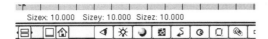

Figure 5-2: Scaling info in the 3DWindow Header

NOTE   *If you can't scale to 10.0 or want to stop the scaling action, press the RMB or ESC. ESC will abort every Blender procedure without making any changes to your object.*

7. Now let's customize the Blender screen and the window layout. Move your mouse slowly over the lower edge of the 3DWindow (see Figure 5-3) until it changes to a double arrow. Now press the MMB or RMB; a menu will appear:

Figure 5-3: Splitting a window

8. Select Split Area and then move the line that appears to the middle of the 3DWindow and press the LMB. Blender should split the 3DWindow into two identical views of the 3-D scene as shown here.

9. Now, move your mouse over the right window and press SHIFT-F10. The window will change to an ImageWindow, where we will work with images and textures to color our real-time models.

NOTE   *All key presses in Blender are executed in the active window (the window with the mouse over it). There is no need to click a window to activate it.*

10. Move your mouse back to the plane in the left 3DWindow and select it again if it is no longer selected (i.e., not pink). Now press ALT-Z; the plane should now be drawn in solid black.

11. Press FKEY, and the plane should turn white, with the edges drawn as dotted lines. FKEY brings us into FaceSelectMode, used for selecting a face and applying textures to models.

12. Move your mouse to the right window and locate and press the Load button with the LMB. An ImageSelectWindow (Figure 5-4) opens.

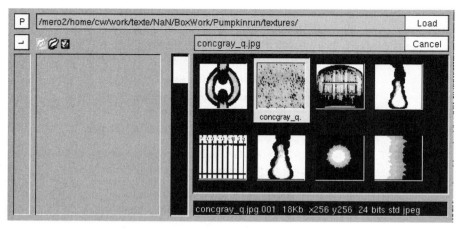

Figure 5-4: Thumbnail images in the ImageFileWindow

Pressing and holding the MenuButton ⬛ with the LMB will give you a choice of recently browsed paths and, on Windows operating systems, a list of your drives. The directory you are currently in, is shown in the top text field. The ParentDir button 🅿 allows you to go up one directory.

Using these methods, go to your CD-ROM drive and browse for the folder Tutorials/Pumpkinrun/textures/ and locate the concgray_q.jpg thumbnail. Click it with the LMB and then choose Load from top right of the ImageSelectWindow.

Figure 5-5: Textured plane in 3DWindow

13. The texture now shows up in the 3DWindow to the left. If you see some strange colors in the texture, press CTRL-K over the 3DWindow. Now leave FaceSelectMode by pressing FKEY.

We have just created a very simple environment, but we used many of the steps needed to create more complex game levels.

It is now time to save your scene. To ease the process we will include the texture in the saved scene. To do so, choose Pack Data from the ToolsMenu. A little parcel icon will appear in the menu bar to indicate that this scene is packed. Now use the FileMenu to browse to your hard disk (as described above), enter a name in the file name field (currently untitled.blend), and click the SAVE FILE button in the FileWindow. You can read more about saving and loading in Section 4.3.

6

APPENDING AN OBJECT FROM ANOTHER SCENE

Because it's beyond the scope of this book to cover modeling and the general use of Blender as a tool to create entire worlds, we'll load ready-made objects for use as examples. Because Blender doesn't use a special file format to store objects, all scenes can be used as archives and objects can be pulled from them. Thus, you can browse and reuse all the nice scenes on the CD-ROM.

Let's look at how to append an object from another scene. (That's our hero, above.) To begin:

1. First, we need more views into 3-D space. Mouse over the ImageWindow (the right one from the last step) and press SHIFT-F5 to change it to a 3DWindow.

2. Mouse over one of the 3DWindows and Press SHIFT-F1; a FileWindow appears in Append mode, as shown in Figure 6-1, which allows us to load any Blender object from a scene into the current scene.

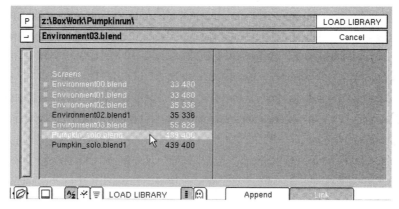

Figure 6-1: FileWindow in append mode

NOTE *You can also use Blender's FileMenu to access the Append function, but key presses are usually faster.*

3. Press and hold the MenuButton ⬒ with the left mouse button (LMB) to see a list of recently browsed paths and, on Windows operating systems, a list of

your drives, as shown in Figure 6-2. The directory you are currently in is shown in the top text field. The ParentDir button 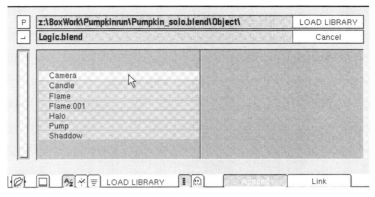 allows you to move up one directory.

Figure 6-2: Browsing in a .blend file

4. Now go to your CD-ROM drive and browse for the folder Tutorials/ Pumpkinrun/. Click Pumpkin_Solo.blend with the LMB. The file should open immediately.

5. Once you have opened the file, the FileWindow will present you with all the parts of the scene as in any file browser. LMB-click Objects, and you should see the objects contained in that scene, as shown in Figure 6-3. Select all objects by pressing AKEY; then confirm by pressing ENTER or LMB-clicking the LOAD LIBRARY button.

6. You should now see the pumpkin as an orange spot, sitting in the middle of the plane in the left 3DWindow, as shown in Figure 6-3. Switch the right window to a second 3DWindow by pressing SHIFT-F5 with the mouse over the window. You will get the same TopView as in the left 3DWindow but drawn in wireframe.

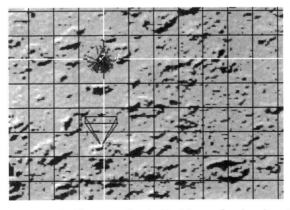

Figure 6-3: The pumpkin in TopView after loading it into the environment

We've appended a camera together with our appended objects. Now use RMB to select the camera that is closer to the pumpkin. (This is best done in the wireframe view.) Move your mouse back to the left (textured) 3DWindow and press CTRL-PAD0 to change to the selected camera and get a nice view of the character.

7

START YOUR (GAME) ENGINES

We can now start the Blender game engine! To begin, mouse over the CameraView and press PKEY. You should see the pumpkin on our textured ground. The pumpkin character has an animated candle inside it that should flicker. (To stop the game engine and return to BlenderCreator, press ESC.)

I hear you saying, "That's nice, but where is the animation?" Well, just one minute.

1. Mouse over the right 3DWindow and press PAD3 for a view from the side. Zoom into the view by pressing PAD+ a few times or hold CTRL-MMB and move the mouse up, which will give you a smooth zoom. (You also can move the view with the MMB and mouse movements while holding SHIFT.) We're preparing the view to move the pumpkin up.

2. Select the character with the RMB (click somewhere on the wireframe of the pumpkin), and it will turn pink to indicate that it is selected.

3. We will now enter the main command center for interactive 3-D in Blender. To do so press F8 or click the RealtimeButtons icon in the icon bar, as shown here.

4. Locate the Actor button at the left in the RealtimeButtons (shown in Figure 7-1) and click it with the LMB. This makes our character in essence an actor.

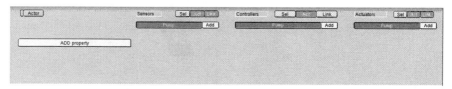

Figure 7-1: The RealtimeButtons

5. Two more buttons should appear. Click the Dynamic button, as shown below, to change the object so that it reacts to physical properties like gravity, bounce, or forces applied to it. (For now, we won't bother with the bunch of buttons that appeared when you clicked Dynamic.)

(If you now start the game engine you will not see much difference, but we will change that in a minute.)

6. Zoom the right 3DWindow out a bit using CTRL-MMB or PAD+/PAD-.

7. Make sure that the pumpkin is still selected (it should be pink; if it isn't then reselect with the RMB) and press GKEY over the right 3DWindow and move the mouse to start the so-called GrabMode which allows you to move objects within the 3-D space. The character should follow your mouse movements in the 3DWindow.

8. Move the object straight up until it disappears on the top of the CameraView (left 3DWindow), as shown in Figure 7-2, and confirm the new position with LMB. (If you are unsure you can always cancel the operation with ESC or RMB and try again.)

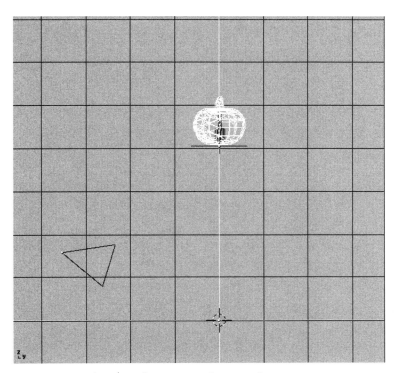

Figure 7-2: SideView after moving the pumpkin up

9. Now move the mouse to the left 3DWindow (the CameraView) and press
   PKEY to start the game engine. The pumpkin should fall and bounce nicely
   until it rests on the ground. Press ESC to exit the game engine.

8

INTERACTIVITY

 In this tutorial we'll look at how to make our character interactive. The pumpkin is our character, and we'll make it move in response to our requests.

8.1. Using the RealtimeButtons

The RealtimeButtons (F8) are logically divided into four columns. We have already used the leftmost column to set up the object parameters to make the pumpkin fall. We'll use the three right columns for building interactivity into our game.

The columns are labeled Sensors, Controllers, and Actuators. You can think of sensors as the senses of a life form, the controllers as the brain, and the actuators as the muscles.

1. Press the Add button once for each row with the LMB to make one LogicBrick for the Sensors, Controllers, and Actuators, as shown in Figure 8-1.

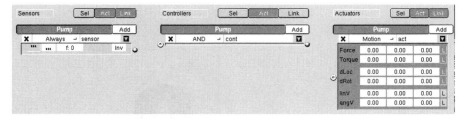

Figure 8-1: Newly created LogicBricks

The types of added LogicBricks are nearly correct for our first task, but we need to change the first one.

2. Press and hold the MenuButton (now labeled with Always) and choose Keyboard from the pop-up menu, as shown in Figure 8-2.

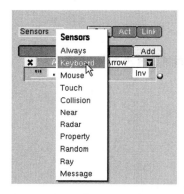

Figure 8-2: Changing the LogicBrick type

3. Now LMB-click in the Key field of the Keyboard Sensor. The text "Press any key" appears. Press the key you want to use to move the player forward (I suggest UPARROW).

8.2. Defining Movement with the Motion Controller

Now have a closer look at the Motion Controller where we will define how the player moves. The first line of numbers, labeled Force, defines how much force will be applied when the Motion Controller is active. The three numbers stand for the forces in X-, Y-, and Z-axis direction.

If you look closely at the wireframe view of the player you can see that its X-axis is pointing forward. This means that to move forward we need to apply a positive force along the X-axis. To do so, click and hold on the first number in the Force row with the LMB and drag the mouse to the right to increment the value to 80.00. You can hold the CTRL key to snap the values to decimal values or, to enter an exact value, hold SHIFT while clicking the field with the LMB and then enter a value from the keyboard.

We've nearly created the configuration shown in Figure 8-3, but we need to "wire" or connect the LogicBricks. The wires will pass the information from LogicBrick to LogicBrick — i.e., from a sensor to a controller.

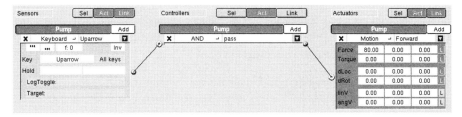

Figure 8-3: LogicBricks to move the player forward

Click and hold the LMB on the yellow ball attached to the Keyboard Sensor and drag the line that appears to the yellow ring on the AND Controller. Release the mouse, and the LogicBricks should be connected.

Now connect the yellow ball on the right side of the AND Controller with the ring on the Motion Controller.

To delete a connection, move the mouse over the connection. The line is now highlighted and can be deleted with an XKEY or DEL key press.

NOTE *Always name your Objects and LogicBricks to help you find your way through your scenes and refer to specific LogicBricks later. To name a LogicBrick click in the name field with the LMB (see figure below) and enter the name from the keyboard. Blender automatically generates unique names for objects and LogicBricks, like "sensor1", "sensor2" or "act", "act1" and so on, so you don't have to worry about name collisions.*

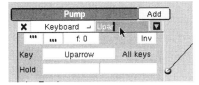

Now press PKEY to start the game engine. When you press the UPARROW key briefly, the player should move toward the camera.

8.3. Adding a Jump

To make the movement more interesting, let's add a jump. The following is an easy way to add logic to your interactive scenes. But before we try it, enter **20.0** in the third (Z-axis, up) field of the Motion Controller. Now, if you try moving the pumpkin again in the game engine, you can see that there is a problem: If you hold the key pressed, the pumpkin takes off into space. This is because the forces are also applied when the pumpkin is in the air.

To solve this problem we have to ensure that the forces are only applied when the pumpkin touches the ground. That's where the Touch Sensor comes in, like so.

1. Add a new sensor by clicking Add in the Sensors row.
2. Change the type to Touch as you did for the Keyboard Sensor (Figure 8-2).
3. Now wire the Touch Sensor to the AND Controller; both the Keyboard and the Touch Sensor should now be connected to that controller.

The type "AND" of the controller will trigger the Motion Actuator only when the key is pressed *and* the player touches the ground. (In addition to the AND Controller, the OR, Expression, and Python Controllers will help to make your game logic even more flexible.)

TIP *At the moment, space in the RealtimeButtons is tight, so let's collapse the LogicBricks. To do so press the little orange arrow □ right beneath the brick's name (so that you are still able to see the connections, though the content is hidden).*

8.3.1. Adding a constant jump

To make the movement more dynamic, we'll add LogicBricks to make the pumpkin jump constantly.

Add a new controller and a new actuator by clicking Add in the appropriate row. Name the new actuator AlwaysJump.

Wire the Touch Sensor with the new AND Controller input and the output of the controller to the new Motion Actuator, Always Jump, as shown in Figure 8-4.

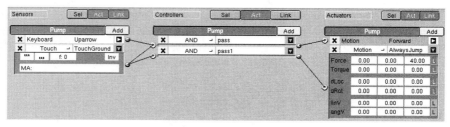

Figure 8-4: LogicBricks for adding a constant jump

As you can see, not only can one controller be connected to two sensors, but a sensor can also "feed" two or more controllers.

Now start the game again with PKEY; the pumpkin jumps, and UPARROW moves it forward.

8.4. Still More Control

Now we'll add more LogicBricks to steer the player with the Cursorkeys.

Add a new sensor, controller, and actuator by clicking the Add buttons. Change the sensor type to Keyboard with the MenuButton. (Don't forget to name the LogicBricks by clicking on the name field in the bricks.)

Wire the sensor ("Leftarrow") with the controller (pass2) and the controller output with the actuator (Left).

Enter **10.0** in the third field (Z-axis) of the Torque row. (*Torque* is the force that turns the object; in this case it will turn the actor around its longitudinal axis.)

Now try the change in the game engine. The pumpkin should turn left when you press LEFTARROW. Repeat the steps but change it to turn right by using RIGHTARROW and entering a torque of **-10.0**, as shown in Figure 8-5.

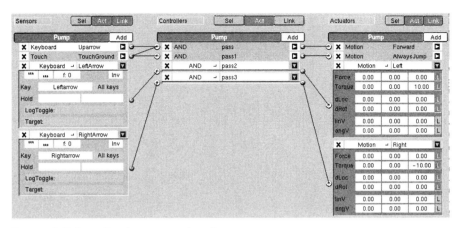

Figure 8-5: LogicBricks to steer the player

9

CAMERA CONTROL

In this section, we show you how to set up a camera that follows the actor — our attempt to mimic a real cameraman.

1. Move your mouse over the right 3DWindow (the wireframe view) and zoom out with PAD- or CTRL-MMB movements. Now locate the second camera (the one farther away from the player) and select it with RMB.

2. With your mouse over the left, textured 3DWindow press CTRL-PAD0 to change the view to the selected camera.

3. The view is now a bit strange because the camera lays exactly in the ground plane. To change this, move your mouse above the right 3DWindow and press GKEY to enter the Grab mode. Move your mouse up a bit until the pumpkin is in about the middle of the camera view.

4. Ensure that the RealtimeButtons are still open (F8) then add a sensor, controller, and an actuator as you learned in Chapter 8.

5. Wire the LogicBricks and change the Actuator into a Camera Actuator, as shown in Figure 9-1. The Camera Actuator will follow the object in a flexible way that gives smooth motions.

Figure 9-1: Adding a Camera Actuator

6. Click the OB field in the Camara Actuator and enter the name of the pumpkin object (here, Pump). The camera will follow this object. Then click and hold the Height field with the LMB and move the mouse to the right to increase the value to about 4.0 to set a fixed height for the camera (Figure 9-2).

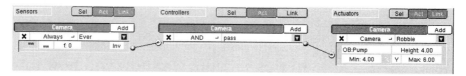

Figure 9-2: Logic Bricks for the following camera

TIP   *Holding CTRL while adjusting a NumberButton changes the value in stages, which makes it easier to adjust the value. SHIFT-LMB on a NumberButton lets you use the keyboard to enter values.*

The Min and Max fields determine the camera's minimum or maximum distance from the object. We've chosen Min: 4.00 and Max: 6.00.

Now that everything is all set, start the game engine to test the Camera Actuator. Experiment a bit with the values.

10

REAL-TIME LIGHT

This tutorial will take you on a brief tour through Blender's real-time lighting. Real-time lighting in Blender's game engine is performed by the OpenGL subsystem, which takes advantage of hardware-accelerated *transform and lighting* (T&L) if your graphics card offers it.

1. Place the 3D-Cursor with the LMB in the right 3DWindow approximately three grid units above the cameras. Press the spacebar to use the Toolbox, and then ADD a Lamp to add a lamp, as shown next.

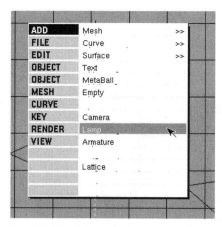

2. While adding the lamp, watch the effect on the pumpkin in the left textured view. (For reference, the pumpkin on the left in Figure 10-1 is lit, while the one on the right is not.) Select the light (it should be pink; use the RMB to select), and move it around a bit in the 3DWindow. Press GKEY to see how the textured view is updated in real time. (See how moving the light under the pumpkin gives a scary look, for example?)

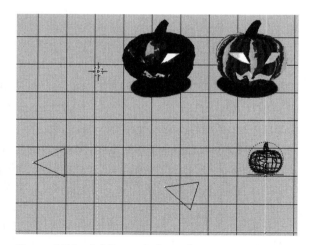

Figure 10-1: Adding a light to the scene

NOTE *The real-time lighting in Blender doesn't cast shadows. The pumpkin's shadow is created differently (with a single plane and a transparent structure). Also, bear in mind that the use of real-time lights will slow down your games. So try to keep the number of objects with real-time light as low as possible.*

We'll look at more options for lamps and real-time lighting in Section 26.7.

11

OBJECT ANIMATION

In this tutorial we'll cover the basics of combining Blender's animation system with the game engine. Blender's animation curves (Ipos) are fully integrated and give you full control of animations both in conventional (linear) animation and in the interactive 3-D graphics covered by this book.

Here we go:

1. Press SHIFT-F1 or choose Append from the FileMenu.
2. Browse the book's CD and choose Tutorials/Pumpkinrun/Door.blend.
3. Now click Object, select all objects with AKEY, and confirm with ENTER. This will append a wall with a wooden door to the scene, and the pumpkin should bump against the walls and the door. Blender's game engine handles the collision detection automatically.

4. Switch the right 3DWindow to a TopView (PAD7) and zoom (PAD+ or PAD-) as needed to see the appended door completely. (The door has the name and the axis enabled, so it should be visible.) Select the door with the RMB (it should turn pink).

We will now make a simple key frame animation:

1. Ensure that the FrameSlider (the current animation frame, shown below) is at frame 1 by pressing SHIFT-LEFTARROW.

2. Press IKEY and select Rot from the menu.

3. Now advance the animation time by pressing UPARROW five times to frame 51. With the game engine playing 50 frames per second our animation will now play for two seconds.

4. Press RKEY (be sure to have your mouse over the TopView) and rotate the door 150 degrees clockwise. (You can see the degree of rotation in the 3DWindow Header.) To make it easier to rotate exactly, hold CTRL while rotating. (See Figure 11-1.)

5. Now insert a second key by pressing IKEY and again choosing Rot.

6. Move to frame 1 by pressing SHIFT-LEFTARROW and press SHIFT-ALT-A; you should see the animation of the door being replayed. After 51 frames the animation should run to frame 250 and then repeat.

7. Press ESC to stop the animation.

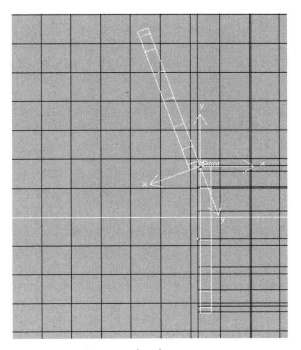

Figure 11-1: Rotating the door

Now we will add the game logic to control the animation that we've just created.

1. With the door still selected press F8 to switch the ButtonsWindow to the RealtimeButtons. Now add a sensor, controller, and actuator.

2. Next, wire your new sensor, controller, and actuator and name them (see Chapter 8).

3. Change the Sensor to a Keyboard Sensor and the Actuator to Ipo type, as shown on the following page.

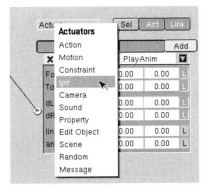

4. Change the type of the Ipo Actuator to Ping Pong mode (see Figure 11-2) using the MenuButton.

5. SHIFT-LMB Sta and change the value to **1**, then change End to **51** (see Figure 11-2). Thus, the Ipo Actuator will play the door animation from frame 1 to 51, thereby opening the door. A new invocation of the Ipo Actuator will then close the door because of playing it Ping Pong. This actuator type plays an animation forward; then, on its next call, it plays the animation backward.

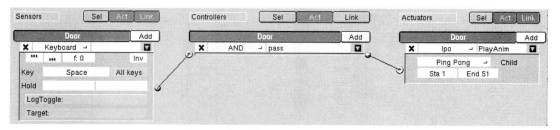

Figure 11-2: LogicBricks for playing an Ipo in Ping Pong mode

6. Finally, play the scene (PKEY) in the textured view, and the door should open and close when you press the spacebar. The door should also push the actor around if he gets hit by it.

NOTE *To visualize the animation curves (Ipos) switch one window to an IpoWindow by pressing SHIFT-F6 (see Section 24.2).*

12

REFINING THE SCENE

You may have noticed that there is a problem with the current file: The actor can climb the wall because he can jump whenever he touches an object, including the wall itself. Why is that?

Select the pumpkin and look at the Touch Sensor. The MA field is empty, as shown below. (*MA* is short for a material name.)

If you fill in a material name in the MA field, the Touch Sensor will react only to objects with this material. (In our scene this would be the ground we created at the beginning.) But what is the material name? We haven't defined a material, and we need to do so to refine our scene. To make things easier we will use Blender's ability to append ready-made elements from a different scene (see Chapter 6).

1. Mouse over one of the 3DWindows and press SHIFT-F1; a FileWindow will appear in Append mode, which allows us to load any Blender object into an open scene.

2. Browse this book's CD for the folder Tutorials/Pumpkinrun/ containing the file GroundMaterial.blend and then click with the MMB on the file name GroundMaterial.blend to open it. Or click it with the LMB and then confirm your selection with ENTER.

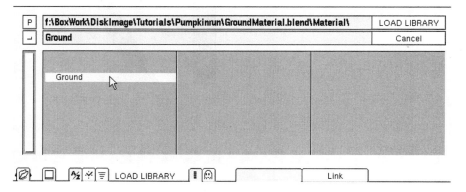

Figure 12-1: Browsing the GroundMaterial

3. Once you have entered the file, the FileWindow will show you all the parts of the scene as in a file browser. Now LMB-click Material and you will see the Materials contained in that scene (see Figure 12-1). Select the Ground material with the RMB and click LOAD LIBRARY.

4. Move back to the 3DWindow, select the ground plane, and press F5 to call the MaterialButtons.

5. Locate the MenuButton ⊡ in the ButtonsWindow Header, and click and hold it with the LMB. Choose "0 Ground" from the menu. (The zero in the name tells us that there were no objects already using the material.)

Now, select the pumpkin again, switch back to the RealtimeButtons (F8), and enter **Ground** into the MA field of the Touch Sensor, as shown below.

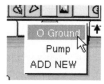

NOTE *Whether a name is capitalized makes a difference in Blender; a material called "ground" is not the same as "Ground." Blender will blank a button when you enter an object name that does not exist. This may sound frustrating, but it really helps while debugging, because it prevents you from overlooking simple typos.*

Now try to hop around again. You should find that you cannot climb the wall anymore.

Adding a Near Sensor

Wouldn't it be nice if the door would only open when the actor is close to it? The Near Sensor will help us here.

To add a Near Sensor, add a new sensor to the door and change the sensor type to Near; then wire it to the existing AND Controller (see Figure 12-2).

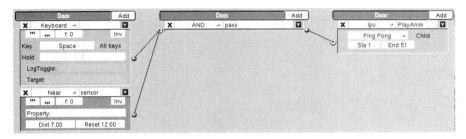

Figure 12-2: Near Sensor

The Dist 7.00 field (shown in the figure) gives the distance at which the Near Sensor starts to react to the actor. (It will react to every actor if we leave the Property field empty.) The Reset 12.00 field sets the distance between the Near Sensor and the object where the Near Sensor "forgets" the actor.

13

ADDING SOUND TO OUR SCENE

What is a game without sound? Let's add sound to our game by adding sound to an event in Blender. The following steps will introduce you to the basics.

1. Locate the SoundButtons icon ◀ in the ButtonsWindow, then click it with the LMB to switch to the SoundButtons. Because there is no sound in the scene the window will be empty.

2. Use the MenuButton ▫ (click and hold) to choose OPEN NEW; a FileWindow opens. Browse to the CD-ROM and load DoorOpen.wav from the directory Tutorials/Pumpkinrun/samples/, as shown in Figure 13-1.

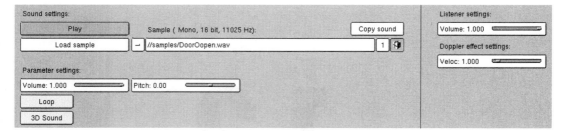

Figure 13-1: The SoundButtons with a sound loaded

NOTE   *Blender is capable of creating 3-D sound (sound located spatially in the scene) and provides many ways to affect the sound. For the moment, though, we'll go with the defaults and not touch any of these buttons. Of course, you can play the sound by clicking the big Play button.*

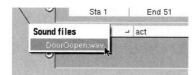

3.   Select the door object (RMB) and switch to the RealtimeButtons with F8.

4.   Add a new actuator and change the type to Sound; then wire it to the controller as shown in Figure 13-2.

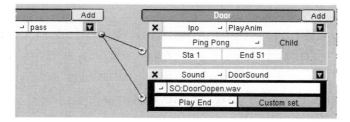

Figure 13-2: Sound Actuator for the door

5.   Click and hold the solitary MenuButton in the Sound Actuator and choose the sound file DoorOpen.wav from the pop-up menu. Change the mode Play Stop to Play End (this will mean the whole sound is played without stopping too early) and give it a try!

14

LAST WORDS

By this point, you should have a good basic idea of what it takes to make a game with Blender. We've taken you through some of the basic steps, and you are now prepared to follow other tutorials or to start playing with ready-made scenes or your own ideas.

Before beginning the following tutorials, you may find it helpful to reread Chapter 4 to review the basics. Also don't hesitate to use our support (see Section 29.4).

PART THREE
BEGINNER TUTORIALS

These beginner tutorials are aimed at beginners in interactive 3-D graphics. We tried to make the tutorials as self-contained as possible, but if you experience problems, please go to the Chapter 4 or use our support or that of the Blender Community (Section 29.4).

In the following tutorials, we use the "hands-on" approach to give you quick results, so make sure you follow the words and screenshots closely, and an explanation will follow later. Of course, you are invited to experiment!

15

TUBE CLEANER: A SIMPLE SHOOTING GAME

Tube Cleaner was designed by Freid Lachnowicz. It is a simple shooter game that takes place in a tube. There are three kinds of enemies, and your goal is to collect as many points and bullets as you can as you travel up the tube. (To play the finished game, you can load the scene Games/TubeCleaner.blend from the CD. Instructions are included.)

Here's a look at the opening screen:

This tutorial will not to teach you how to create your own version of Tube Cleaner from scratch. Instead, it will teach you how to create interactivity. And, of course, you are encouraged to change and extend the game to your liking!

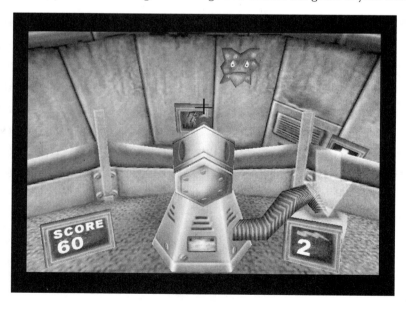

The Tube Cleaner game controls are rather simple:

Table 15-1: Tube Cleaner Game Controls

Controls	Description
Arrow keys	Rotate the cannon left, right, up, and down
Spacebar	Shoot

15.1. Loading the Models

To begin this tutorial, start Blender and load Tutorials/TubeCleaner/
TubeCleaner_00.blend from the CD. This scene contains all of the models that
you'll need to start with. We'll show you how to make the scene interactive by
showing you how to:

- Add game logic to the gun, allowing it to move up, turn, and shoot
- Add game logic to the enemies
- Create the score system including a display
- Provide extra bullets

As shown in Figure 15-1, the scene contains a CameraView on the left, a wireframe view (view from top, TopView) on the right, and the RealtimeButtons on
the bottom. In the TopView you can see that the Base object is already selected
and active (it is purple in the wireframe).

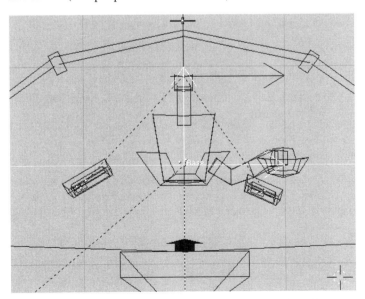

Figure 15-1: Wireframe TopView in the loaded Tube Cleaner scene

The Base object will carry the gun and will contain some of the game's global
logic. The cannon itself is parented to this base, creating a hierarchy that will
make our later work easier because we won't have to worry about composite
movements.

15.2. Controls for the Base and Cannon

We will begin by adding a control for rotation around the vertical axis of the base. This will also rotate the gun and the camera because they are parented to the base.

1. Make sure that the Base object is selected (it should be purple; use the RMB to select it if it is not already selected) and click the Add buttons in the RealtimeButtons for each row of sensors, controllers, and actuators. In every row a new LogicBrick will appear, as shown in Figure 15-2.

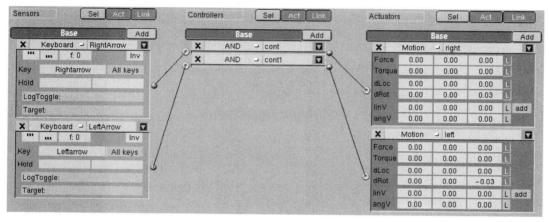

Figure 15-2: LogicBricks to rotate the gun

2. Now link (wire) the LogicBricks by clicking and drawing a line from the little yellow balls (output) to the yellow donuts (input) of the LogicBricks. These connections will pass the information between the LogicBricks.

3. Change the first LogicBrick to a Keyboard Sensor by clicking and holding its MenuButton with the LMB and selecting Keyboard from the pop-up menu.

NOTE   *If you have problems with the creating, changing, and linking of LogicBricks, please see the tutorial in Part II.*

4. Now, click the Key field with the LMB and press the RIGHTARROW key when prompted to "Press any key" in the Keyboard Sensor. The Key field should now display "Rightarrow," and the Keyboard Sensor will now react to this key only.

5. Change the third number in the dRot row of the Motion Actuator to **0.03** by using SHIFT-LMB on the number and entering the value with the keyboard. The three fields always denote the three axes (X,Y,Z) of an object; we will rotate around the Z-axis.

6. Move your mouse over the CameraView and press PKEY to start the game. You should now be able to rotate the gun with the RIGHTARROW key.

NOTE *You should always name your LogicBricks and other newly created elements in your scenes (click the default name and enter a new one) to help you to find and understand your game logic later. See the way we've named our LogicBricks in Figure 15-4, for example.*

7. Use the same procedure as above to add LogicBricks to rotate the gun to the left. Use LEFTARROW as the key in the Keyboard Sensor and enter **-0.03** in the third dLoc field of the Motion Actuator.

As you can see, the space in the RealtimeButtons is getting sparse even though we have only six LogicBricks. To clean up your screen area, use the ⬇ Icon in the LogicBricks to collapse the LogicBricks to just a title. (Here's another good reason to properly name your LogicBricks.)

15.2.1. Upward Movement

We want Tube Cleaner to have continuous upward movement within the tube. We could copy the effect we used for the rotation of the gun, but there is an alternative that will give us much more control over the movement and that will also allow the player to move to a specific level of the tube. The method we'll employ uses the capabilities of Blender's game engine and its powerful animation system in tandem.

1. Move your mouse over the CameraView and press ALT-A to have Blender play back all the animations defined in the scene. (Press ESC to stop the play-back.) Now you've seen the animations, but so far none of these animations is played by the game engine. We have to tell the objects to play the anima-tion. In this way we can interactively control animations with, for example, play, stop, or suspend.

2. Mouse over the wireframe view and press SHIFT-F6. The window will change to an IpoWindow (see Figure 15-3), meant for displaying and editing Blender's animation curves.

The IpoWindow is organized into axes: the horizontal X-axis shows the time in Blender's animation frames, and the vertical Y-axis shows Blender units. The diagonal line (which shows as yellow in the program) is the animation curve for the movement along the Z-axis of the Base object, representing upward move-ment for our object. Thus, to move the object 10 units up you could move the Ipo cursor (the vertical line just to the right of the Y-axis, shown as green in Blender) with an LMB-click on frame 10. (The CameraView will reflect this movement immediately.)

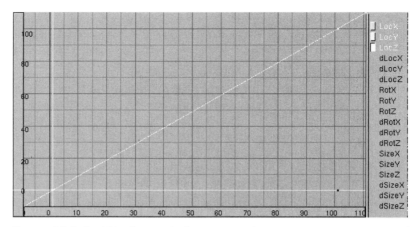

Figure 15-3: IpoWindow with the animation curve representing upward movement

To play this animation in the game engine, we use the "Ipo Actuator" LogicBrick, set to Property type. A *property* is a variable owned by a game object, which can store values or strings.

1. Create a new property to hold the height (zLoc(ation)) of the Base object by clicking "ADD property" in the RealtimeButtons for the Base object.

2. Click on Name and change the default name "prop" to "zLoc" as shown below. This property will hold the height of the gun in the tube.

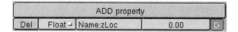

NOTE   *Blender uses capitalization to distinguish between names of objects and properties; "zloc" is not the same as "zLoc."*

Continue creating the LogicBricks shown in Figure 15-4. The Always Sensor triggers the logic for every frame of the game engine animation, ensuring constant movement. The AND Controller simply passes the pulses to two actuators, both of which are connected to the controller and will be activated at the same time.

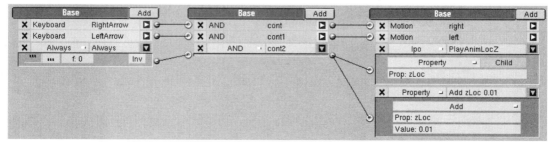

Figure 15-4: LogicBricks for the upward movement

The Ipo Actuator will play the Ipo animation according to the value in the property zLoc. To produce constant motion we increase the zLoc property every frame with the Property Actuator. Here it is from the type Add, which adds Value (here 0.01) to the zLoc property.

Try different entries in the Value field to get a feel for the speed of the animation. If you'd like to move the cannon downward try entering **-0.01** into the Value field. Once you've finished experimenting a bit enter **0.01** for the value field, as shown in Figure 15-6.

To play the game as it stands so far, move your mouse to the CameraView and press PKEY.

TIP *Blender can show you the Properties in use and their values while the game runs. To do so, choose "Show debug properties" from the Game menu and activate the D button (debug) for every property you'd like to have displayed on screen.*

15.3. Shooting

Let's now add the ability to shoot.

1. Switch the IpoWindow back to a 3DWindow by pressing SHIFT-F5 over the IpoWindow; then select the Gun object with the RMB.

NOTE *You can click every wire from the Gun object but only appropriate selections will be reflected in the ButtonsWindow Header (OB:Gun) and in the RealTime Buttons where Gun will appear in the columns for the LogicBricks.*

2. Now add a sensor, controller, and actuator to the Gun object and wire them as discussed earlier in this tutorial.

3. Change the Sensor to a Keyboard Sensor (name it "Space") and choose (click the Key field) Space as trigger for the gun.

4. Change the Actuator to an Edit Object Actuator. (The default type, Add Object, adds an object dynamically when the actuator is triggered.)

5. Enter **bullet** into the OB field (see Figure 15-5) by clicking it with the LMB and then entering a name from the keyboard. This adds the object "bullet," a premade object, to a hidden layer of the scene.

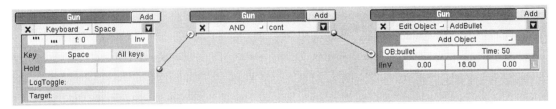

Figure 15-5: LogicBricks to fire the gun

6. Now enter **18.00** (Figure 15-5) as the second number in the linV fields to give the bullet an initial speed.

7. Activate (press) the little L button behind the linV row. This ensures that the bullets will always leave the gun in the direction aimed. Enter **50** in the Time

field to limit the lifetime of the bullets to 50 frames, which will prevent rico-chets from bouncing around forever.

Now try to run the game and shoot a bit.

15.3.1. Limiting Our Ammunition

So far we have unlimited ammunition. To change this we again add a property; this time one that stores the number of bullets left.

1. Add a new property by clicking ADD property (as shown in Figure 15-6), then name this property "bullets" and change its type to Int with the MenuButton now labeled Float (the standard type for new properties). (An Int[eger] property only holds whole numbers; this is ideal for our bullets as we don't want half-bullets.) SHIFT-LMB on the field to the right of the Name field and enter **10** to set the number of bullets available at the start of the game to 10.

Figure 15-6: Add property

To decrease the number of bullets with every shot we use the same Property Add Actuator that we used to make the base of the cannon move up.

2. Add another actuator by clicking Add in the Gun column of the Actuator, then wire it to the AND Controller we created in the previous step. Change the actuator type to Property and choose Add as the action, then enter **bullets** in the Prop field and **-1** in the Value field. This will subtract 1 (or add -1) from the property "bullets" with every shot triggered by the spacebar.

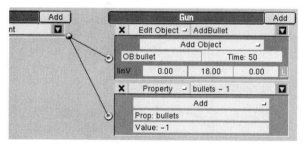

So far the gun doesn't take any notice of the number of bullets. To change this we use an Expression Controller, which allows us to add single line expressions to process game logic.

3. Change the AND Controller with the MenuButton to an Expression Controller. Then click on the Exp field and enter **Space AND bullets>0** and press ENTER (as shown below). Here "Space" is the name (exactly as you typed it in the LogicBrick) of the Keyboard Sensor and "bullets" is the property. The Controller now only activates the following actuators if the sensor Space is active (meaning that the spacebar is pressed) *and* bullets is bigger than zero.

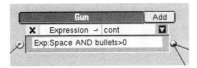

Try running the game again. You should find that you can only shoot ten times. (Read more about expressions in Section 26.9.)

15.3.2. Making the Bullets Display Function

The last step we need to take to make the gun work is to make the bullets display functional.

Select the display (the right one with the flash on it) with the RMB. It is best to hit the little dot on the 1. The name BulletsDisplay should appear in the RealtimeButtons and in its header as OB:BulletsDisplay. Alternatively, you can zoom into the wireframe view to make the selection easier (see Section 4.10).

Properties

You can see in the RealtimeButtons that there is already a property called Text for the display object. The object has a special text-texture assigned which will display any information in the property called Text that is on it. To test this change the value **10** in the property; the change should be displayed immediately in the CameraView.

Because properties are local to the object that owns them, we have to find a way to pass the value of properties between objects. This is done inside a scene (but will not work across scene borders) with the Property Copy Actuator.

1. Add a line of LogicBricks to the BulletsDisplay like you did before and wire them. Change the Actuator to a Property Actuator, type Copy. See Figure 15-7.

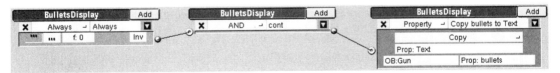

Figure 15-7: LogicBricks to display the number of bullets

2. Enter **Text** into the first Prop field as the name of the property we copy into. Enter **Gun** into the OB field using correct capitalization. (Blender will blank the input field if you enter a nonexistent object.)
3. We will get the value for the number of bullets from the Gun object. Enter **bullets** into field Prop beneath OB as the property name from which we get the value.

Now start the game again and shoot until you have no more bullets.

15.4. More Control for the Gun

Adding the ability to tilt the gun adds more freedom of movement and makes the game more dynamic. We will use a technique similar to the one we used to create upward movement, by combining animation curves with LogicBricks.

1. Select the gun again, and collapse the LogicBricks by clicking their ▼ arrow icons. (This gives us more space for the logic to come.)

2. The upward movement of the gun already contains a motion curve that we can use, but we need to add a property that contains the actual rotation (tilt, rotation around the x-axis). Add a new property by clicking "ADD property" and name it **rotgun**.

3. Use the Add buttons to add a sensor, controller, and one . . . no, two actuators. (You should remember this from the upward movement.) We need one actuator to change the property and one to play the Ipo.

4. Now wire the new LogicBricks as shown in Figure 15-8. The collapsed LogicBricks are the ones you've created for shooting. Change the Bricks as shown in Figure 15-8 and enter all the necessary information.

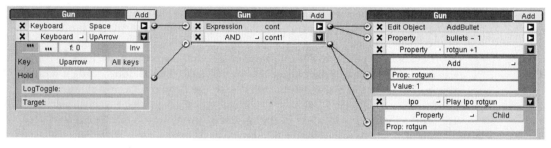

Figure 15-8: LogicBricks to rotate the gun upward

We use the property Add Actuator to increase rotgun by one every time UPARROW is pressed, and we play the Ipo according to the rotgun property to rotate the gun up.

NOTE   *I activated the pulse mode* ▦ *icon for the Keyboard Sensor to give a keyboard repeat here. This allows us to keep the gun rotating as long as we have the key pressed, without having to release it.*

Now test the rotation. You should see that the gun rotates only a specific distance and then stops.

We control this movement with the animation curve (Ipo). You can see the curve when you switch a window to an IpoWindow with SHIFT-F6 (use SHIFT-F5 to return to the 3DWindow). Note how the curves go horizontally from frame 21 (horizontal axis). This means that no further rotation is possible.

You can also see that we need to make the rotgun negative to rotate it down. Again, add a sensor, controller, and one (yes, this time, it's really only one) actuator. Then wire and name them, as shown in Figure 15-9.

We use the Ipo Actuator for the tilting down too. This is perfectly okay, and it allows us to save on creating another LogicBrick. It would also be okay to use a second Ipo Actuator here.

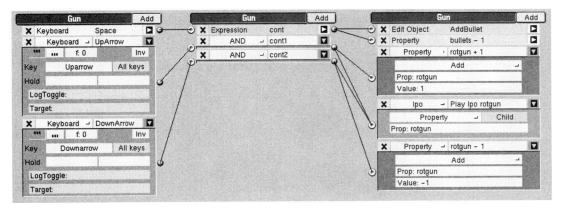

Figure 15-9: Completed LogicBricks allowing us to tilt the gun

TIP *If you prefer "pilot-controls" just swap the Uparrow and Downarrow input in the keyboard sensors.*

There is one drawback to all of this: If you press UPARROW for too long the gun will stop rotating though rotgun is still incremented. This will cause a delay in the gun's rotation back, when you press DOWNARROW again. To correct this we can use expressions again. (See Figure 15-10 for the correct expressions.) These expressions will stop changing rotgun when rotgun is already greater than 21 or less than -21.

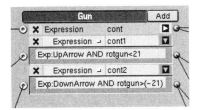

Figure 15-10: Expressions that correctly stop the rotation

CAUTION *It is time to save your project now! Blender scenes are usually very compact, so saving only takes seconds. But first you need to pack (include in the Blender file) the textures, using Pack Data from the ToolsMenu to keep everything together and allow us to send the file to someone. Once your scene is packed, use the FileMenu or save with the keyboard command F2. (See Section 4.3.)*

15.5. Add an Enemy to Shoot

It is now time to add something to shoot at. We want our enemy to:

- React to hits (collisions) with the bullets
- Make a silly face when hit, and die
- Add some points to the player's score

These are all tasks to build into the enemy's game logic.

1. Select the Target object with the RMB. Notice how we've tried to keep the game logic on the target itself? Although we could have added this game logic to the player or any other central element, doing so would make our logic very complex and difficult to maintain. By keeping this game logic local we simplify the logic, make it easier to maintain, and make it much easier to reuse the objects and the logic, even in other scenes.

    We begin again by adding a sensor, controller, and actuator and wiring them. (You should be familiar with this procedure by now.)

    To have our enemy react to a collision, change the Sensor to a Collision Sensor. Enter **bullet** into the Property field to define the name of the property carried by the bullet. In this way the Collision Sensor will only react to collisions with bullets.

2. Change the Actuator to Edit Object and choose Replace Mesh as the type, then enter **TargetDead** into the ME field, as shown in Figure 15-11. This mesh shows the dead target and will be shown from now on when you hit the target. The dead target is on a hidden layer which you can see when you switch layer 11 on and off by pressing SHIFT-ALT-1KEY (see Section 24.1.1).

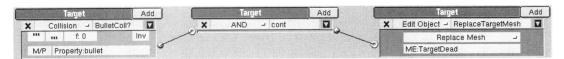

Figure 15-11: LogicBricks to make the target look silly

15.5.1. Scoring

To score our hit we will use Blender's messaging system, which allows us to send messages from objects to objects. In this case we tell the score display to add some points to our score.

1. Add a second actuator to the target then wire it with the existing controller and change it to a Message Actuator. Leave the To and Body fields blank (as shown below); just fill in the Subject field with **10points**. (This is equivalent to shouting the score into a room at the scorekeeper.)

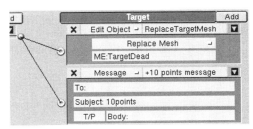

We now need to set up the score display to react to the score messages.

2. Select the Score-display object and add LogicBricks, as shown in Figure 15-12.

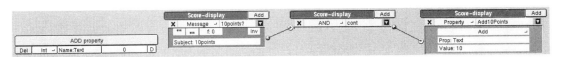

Figure 15-12: LogicBricks to count the score

The Score-display is again an object with a special texture on it showing the content of the Text property (as explained for the bullets display). Be sure to change the 999 to zero or the score will start with 999 points.

The Message Sensor will only hear messages with the 10points subject and then trigger the Property Actuator to add 10 to the Text property, which is then displayed. This makes it very easy to add different scores to different actions simply by adding a new line of LogicBricks to listen for different subjects, then adding the appropriate number of points.

Now try out the game so far and shoot at the enemy. Hits should add 10 points to your score. If anything fails to work, check for correct wiring, and check that the names and capitalization of properties and message subjects are as they should be.

In the final game the targets start to slide down the tube (see Figure 15-13 for a possible solution). The simple target that we've created here also has the drawback that even hitting a dead target will add to your score.

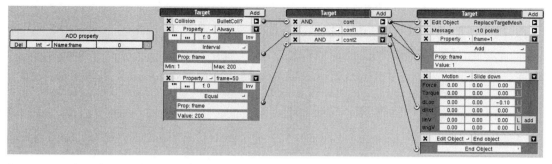

Figure 15-13: Advanced animation for dead targets

We have already used most of the LogicBricks shown in Figure 15-13. Together with the reference (see Chapter 27) and the final game on the CD you can now try to extend the file or just enjoy playing the game.

Whatever you do, don't despair and be sure to keep experimenting. By breaking the task into small steps, you'll be able to tackle even complex logic without getting lost.

16

LOW POLY MODELING

by W.P. Van Overbruggen

In this tutorial, we're going to model a low polygon car (a 1950s-style car to be exact). Because our goal is to produce a real-time model for use in games, we'll set a polygon limit of 1,000 triangles for the entire car. Even though most recent console and PC racing games have cars of up to 4,000 triangles, the 1,000-triangle limit should give us enough space to add nice details while still keeping playability acceptable on almost any recent computer with a 3-D graphics card.

You can load and play a complete game with the car shown in Figure 16-1 from the CD: Games/55hotwheels.blend.

Figure 16-1: Racer game

16.1. Loading an Image for Reference

To make the process easier we will use an image displayed in Blender's back buffer as a guide.

1. Load the image into the image back buffer by pressing SHIFT-F7 in the 3DWindow to reach the back buffer window, as shown here.

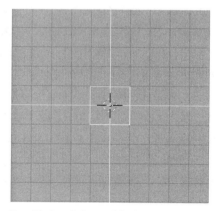

2. To load the guide image press the big BackGroundPic button to open up a new set of buttons including the Load button. Press the Load button.

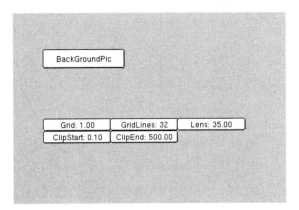

3. The image window (shown below) is normally used for loading textures, but we will now use it to select the image we will be using for reference. Go to the folder Tutorials/Carmodelling/, which contains the three images, called front.jpg, back.jpg, and side.jpg. Load side.jpg by LMB-clicking on the image and pressing ENTER to confirm.

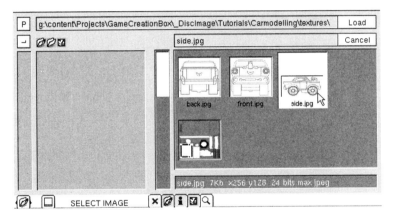

4. Once the image is loaded head back to the 3DWindow by pressing SHIFT-F5.

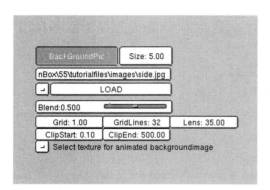

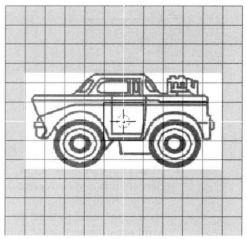

16.2. Using the Reference Image

All right — let's start modeling this car.

1. Make sure you are in FrontView by pressing PAD1. Select the default plane with the RMB, then press XKEY to delete it. Next, add a new plane by pressing the spacebar and selecting Mesh > Plane from the menu.

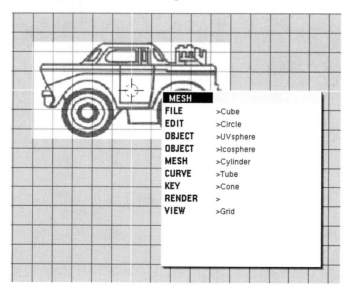

2. Now that we have a plane in FrontView delete the bottom two vertices.

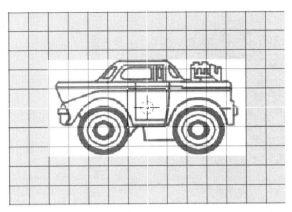

3. To delete the vertices you can either select them by holding SHIFT and select-ing them with the RMB or by pressing BKEY for BorderSelect and, while hold-ing down the LMB, dragging a border around the two bottom vertices. Once selected, delete them by pressing XKEY.

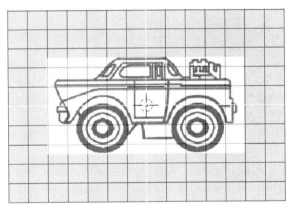

4. Now select the other two vertices in the same manner and line them up with the back of the body of the car by pressing GKEY and moving them. Confirm the new position by clicking the LMB.

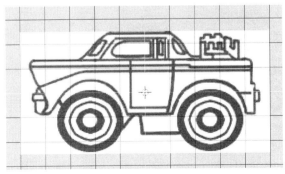

5. Select the right vertex with the RMB and move (GKEY) it to the front of the car.

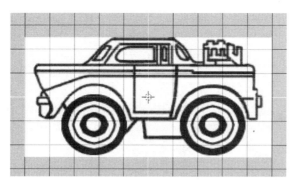

6. Now we'll start adding additional vertices to complete the side view of the car. Make sure you have the right vertex selected, and press EKEY to extrude the vertex into a new vertex. Press ENTER to confirm the pop-up request. To create a smooth front, move the new vertex a little to the right and little lower. Press the LMB when you are satisfied with the position.

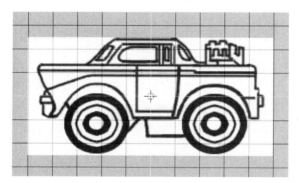

7. Now use these same methods to trace the entire side of the body of the car with as few vertices as possible. To connect the last two vertices to each other, select them both (hold SHIFT to select the second one with the RMB), then press FKEY to connect them. When you are finished leave EditMode (TAB) to complete the outline.

8. Use this same method to trace the other parts of the car, like the top and the bumpers. Use the image above as a reference.

16.3. Outlining the Wheels

1. To outline the wheels, first place the 3D-Cursor ⊕ in the middle of the wheel on the reference image by pressing the LMB over the wheel's center.

NOTE *New objects are always added at the exact position of the 3D-Cursor. You can always zoom the view by holding CTRL-MMB and moving the mouse up and down. To pan the view hold down SHIFT-MMB and move the mouse.*

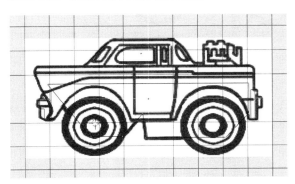

2. Press the spacebar and choose Mesh > Circle from the top entry of the Toolbox. When a menu pops up asking how many vertices you want the circle to consist of, set this to 10 by holding SHIFT, pressing the LMB at the value and entering **10**. To confirm click the OK button.

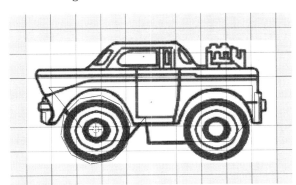

3. The circle might not be the same size as the wheel, so we fix this by pressing SKEY (for scale) and moving the mouse closer to the center of the circle. When you are pleased with the result press the LMB and leave EditMode (TAB).

NOTE *When scaling the wheel to the approximate size of the image, you can hold down CTRL to scale down in steps of 1.0, or scale in even smaller steps by holding SHIFT.*

4. The last thing we will do before leaving SideView is select the wheel and press SHIFT-D to duplicate it. Next, move it into place as the front wheel and press the LMB to confirm the new location.

16.4. Loading the Front Image

Using what we have learned so far in this tutorial we will now load the front.jpg of the car into the back buffer and use it to create the front of the car.

1. Press SHIFT-F7 over the 3DWindow to begin.

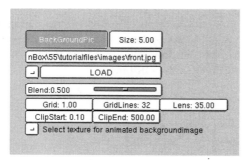

2. First go into SideView by pressing PAD3. You may notice that the scale of the front image and our traced model differ. To fix this quickly select all of the objects by pressing BKEY and draw a border around them. Then press SKEY to scale our tracing to match the front image. Press the LMB to confirm the new scale.

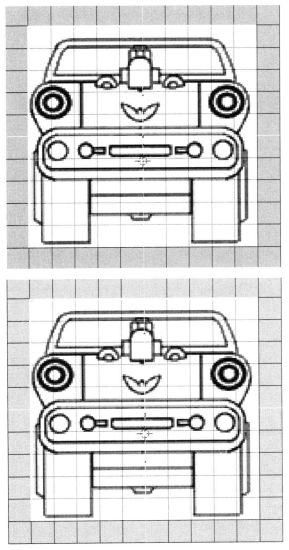

3. Now select the top of the car with the RMB.

4. Press TAB to go into EditMode and select all the vertices with AKEY.

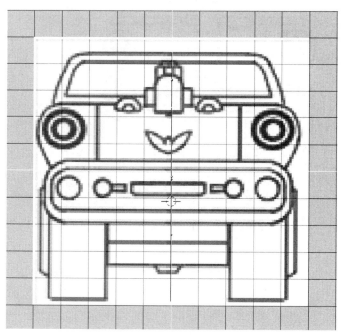

5. Now press EKEY to extrude the selected vertices alongside the image and position them just before the top starts to curve (as shown in the following image). Press the LMB to confirm the extrude.

6. Now extrude it a second time to create a smoother top.

7. Once the third row of vertices is in place, select the top vertices and move them to the right to follow the shape a bit more closely.

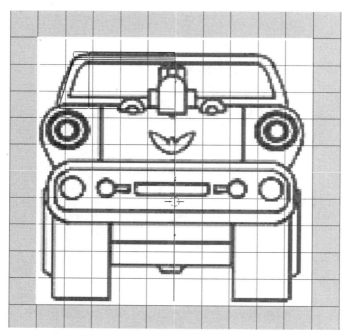

8. Extrude all other parts as in step 6 above.

As you can see, we're only building one side of the car. This saves us a considerable amount of time because a car is usually symmetrical: we can easily duplicate this side later on, flip it, and re-attach it to the original side of the car to create the complete model.

Now, when you select the wheels, make sure you first place them correctly in the FrontView in relation to the image. Because we originally traced them in FrontView, Blender positioned them along the same line as the other parts of the car.

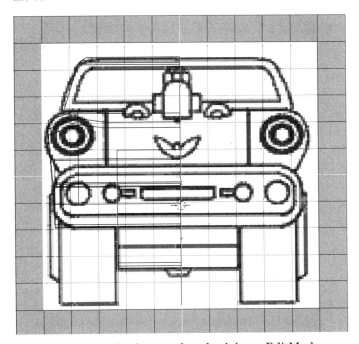

9. Extrude the wheels once, but don't leave EditMode yet.

10. To create the hubcaps press EKEY once more to extrude them, but don't move them this time. Instead press SKEY to scale them inward to the size of the hubcaps, then confirm with the LMB.

11. Press EKEY once more and move the extruded vertices to the left to create the hubcap. Once positioned, confirm again with the LMB.

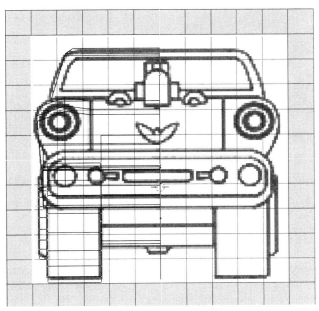

12. Press SKEY one more time and make them a bit smaller so that they are not at a 90-degree angle.

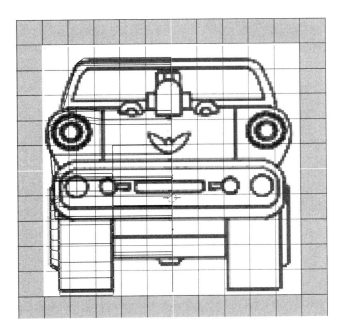

16.5. A Quick Break

Let's have a quick look at how our model looks in 3-D. To do so, press the MMB and move the mouse into a 3-D view. We're getting there.

1. Press ZKEY to see the car in shaded mode. Now don't be alarmed: there are some holes in the model, but they will be closed up soon. But first we have to finish up a little work on the rear of the car.

2. Go intoTopView by pressing PAD7 and switch back to wireframe with ZKEY. A classic car like this needs those classic fins on its back.

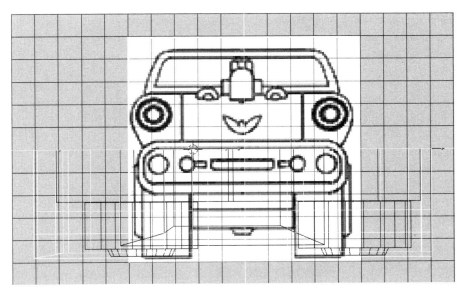

3. Select the body of the car and go into EditMode (TAB). Select the last two rows of vertices and then deselect the two vertices from the side of the car, as shown in the image.

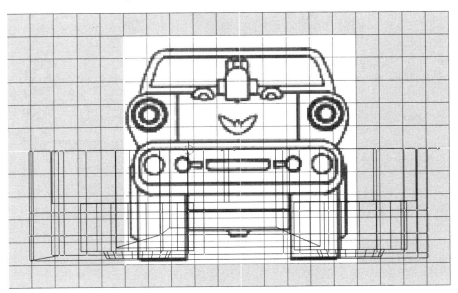

4. Grab the vertices with GKEY and while holding CTRL move them one grid unit to the right.

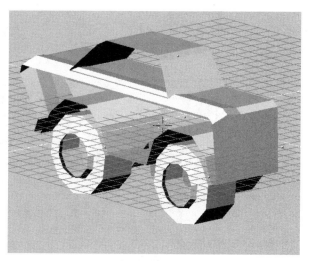

5. Return to FrontView (PAD1) and smooth out the trunk of the car by moving the vertices to make a smoother curve.

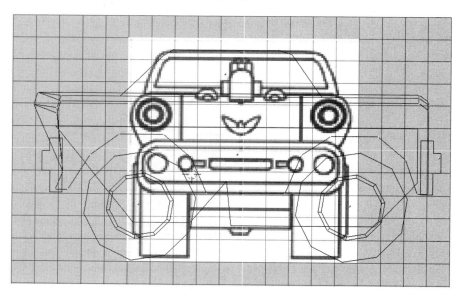

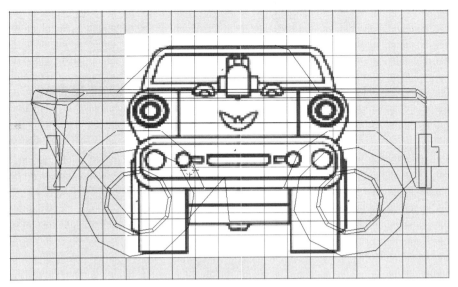

6. Now while still in FrontView, you may notice that the chassis is poking through the back of the car.

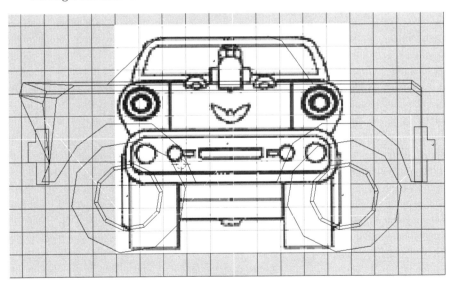

7. This is quickly fixed by moving the chassis's back vertices more to the right, as shown in the images.

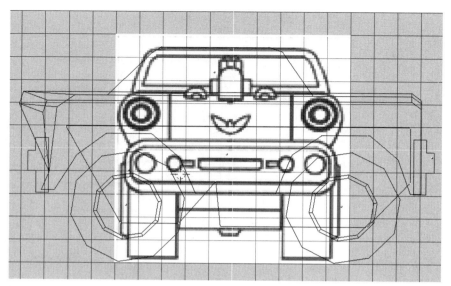

8. To finish this section, return to FrontView to add the bumpers to the car with the same extrude method used previously.

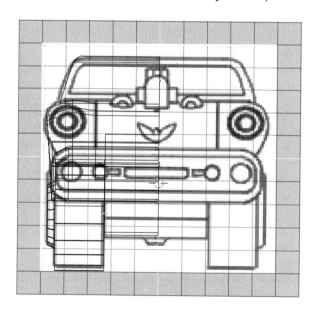

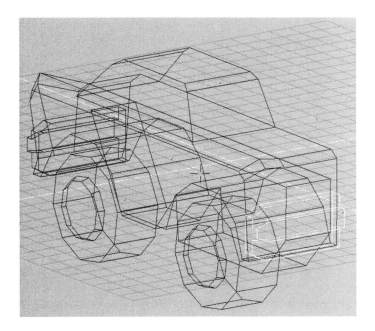

16.6. Closing Up the Holes

Now it's time to close those holes in the side of the car.

1. Select the top of the car and go into LocalView by pressing PAD/ . LocalView allows you to work on a single object without the clutter of other objects in your view.

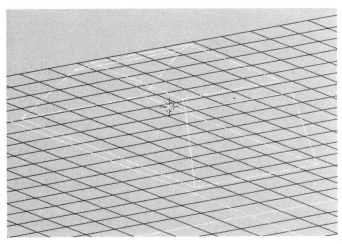

2. This view is especially handy for more complex models, but it will be quite useful here too. Go into SideView (PAD3) once more and enter EditMode by pressing TAB.

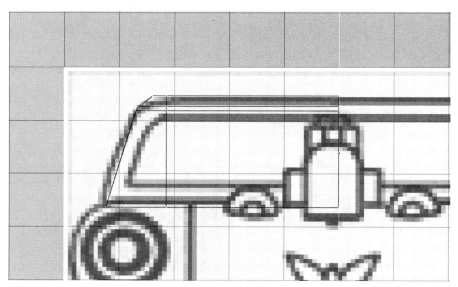

3. Select the top row of vertices on the outside, then press FKEY to create a face to close it up. After that, select the bottom four vertices and press FKEY to close the first part of the side.

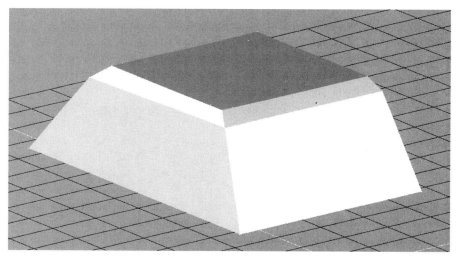

You need three or four vertices to create a face in Blender. Faces or polygons can be squares (otherwise known as *quads*) or triangles in Blender. If you get an error, "Can't make edge/face", make sure that you don't have more than four vertices selected.

TIP   *Blender can also help you to fill faces with more than four vertices using SHIFT-F. However, when the vertices are not in one level this may result in ugly fills and unwanted triangular faces.*

4. Switch back to TopView, and we'll smooth the edges of the top by moving the vertices at the edges slightly inward.

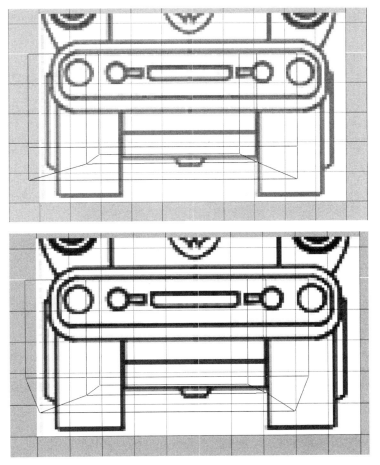

NOTE *Try to keep the faces you create as clean as possible — quads are preferred — to save a lot of time when it comes to texturing the model. Follow these steps and close the sides of the model using these techniques.*

5. Once every hole is closed up you should have something like this:

16.7. Flip It

Now it's time to flip this half car over to create a complete one.

1. Make sure you're in SideView (PAD3), select the top of the car and go into EditMode.

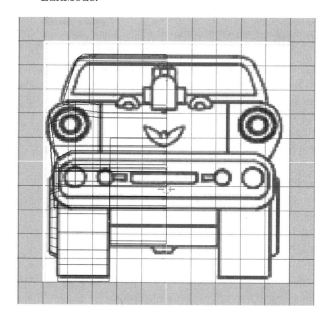

2. Select everything by pressing AKEY, then press SHIFT-D to duplicate it. Now to actually flip the car: First press SKEY and then XKEY without touching the mouse, because were going to flip the model over the X-axis. Press ENTER to confirm the action. (You can flip objects across the Y-axis with YKEY.)

3. To connect the two parts, line up the middle row of vertices by moving the new part to the right and selecting the middle line of vertices (best done with Border Select BKEY).

4. Because we now have two rows of identical vertices we can remove the vertices that are covering each other. Press F9 to go into the EditButtons, and click the Remove Doubles button to remove the double vertices.

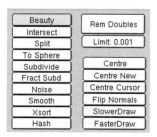

If the vertices are close enough to each other you should get a pop-up stating, "removed: 6". Good job: You now have removed 6 vertices and the model is now joined together. (If you get a lower number increase the Limit value a bit and try again to remove the remaining doubles.)

16.8. Finishing Things Off

Once this is all done we should have a very nice low poly car, if I do say so myself!

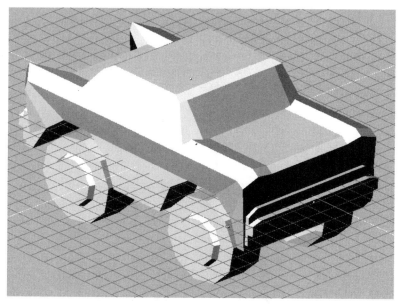

As you should see at the top right of your Blender screen, the model consists of 406 faces, and quite a lot of them are quads. (A graphics card can only handle triangle polygons, but it will sort this out by itself.) But that count of 406 faces doesn't mean we have 406 polygons: the real polygon count should be around 800 triangles, which is pretty decent.

If you want to, you can add extra detail to the car like headlights, taillights, and a big ol' engine block on the hood to make it a bit more interesting.

As a final note, once the model is finished you might look for hidden faces to optimize it. A useful tip for this is to turn on the "Draw faces" button in the EditButtons. For example, take the top of the car. In the screenshot, I have selected the faces that can't be seen and that are just a waste of polygons.

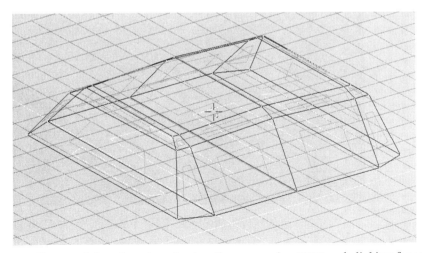

You can delete faces by selecting them, pressing XKEY and clicking faces. And voila — another eight polygons saved.

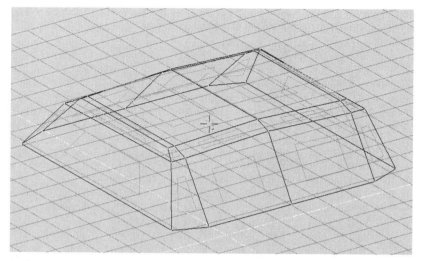

I hope you've enjoyed this introduction to Blender's powerful modeling tools and fast interface for modeling objects.

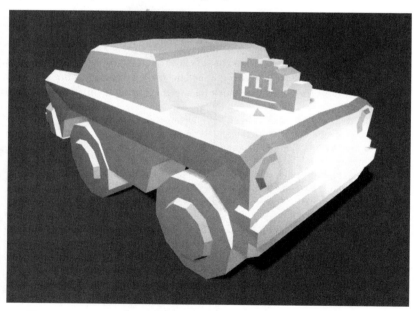

You can get the final model from the CD as Tutorials/Carmodelling/lowpolycar.blend.

PART FOUR
INTERMEDIATE TUTORIALS

The intermediate tutorials explain various aspects of making interactive 3-D graphics with Blender. This includes level design, the physics provided by the game engine, and special effects like smoke and fire or making real-time displays for simulations or games.

The tutorials teach each of these aspects using ready-made scenes to speed up your learning, but they have been designed to be adapted by you for your own scenes.

17

SUPER-G

In this chapter we'll take you through the process of level creation and design. As our vehicle, we use the sport of Super-G — an Olympic discipline that mixes alpine downhill with slalom. We've chosen to use this combination of skills in our game because it gives a nice mix between mayhem speed and sharp curves.

To play the game (shown in Figure 17-1), load the file Games/SuperG.blend from the CD. You get a point every time you pass between two goals and your completion time is measured. As it stands, this game is already enough to create a little competition between friends, although it is not yet a complete game.

Figure 17-1: Super-G ski racing

Here are the game's basic controls.

Table 17-1: Super-G Game Controls

Controls	Description
LEFTARROW/RIGHTARROW	Steer
UPARROW	Accelerate
DOWNARROW	Decelerate (a bit, drive a half-circle to really stop)

17.1. Adding Objects to the Level

Let's look at how to add objects to a level. To begin, load Tutorials/SuperG/
SuperG_00.blend from the CD. As you'll see, this file is pretty bare: it has no
objects like trees or flags. You can race it (press CTRL-LEFTARROW for a full-screen
view), but it is a bit boring and it won't keep score. Let's fix that.

The file Tutorials/SuperG/LevelElements.blend contains some ready-made
objects that we can include in our game (see Figure 17-2), like a tree and a fence.

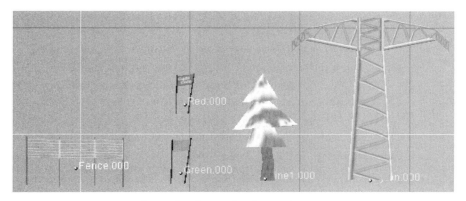

Figure 17-2: Some ready-made objects for Super-G

You can load these objects to the level by appending them to the level scene with SHIFT-F1 or by choosing Append from the FileMenu. Append all or only some objects, but if you want to append the flags Green.000 and Red.000 you must also append Red_dyna and Green_dyna, which are needed for proper functionality.

We'll place the flags first using the object TrackPath in the scene as our guide and the window layout shown in Figure 17-3. This layout inludes a TopView (at left) for the placement in the X-Y plane, a SideView to adjust the height, and a CameraView to control the height of the elements.

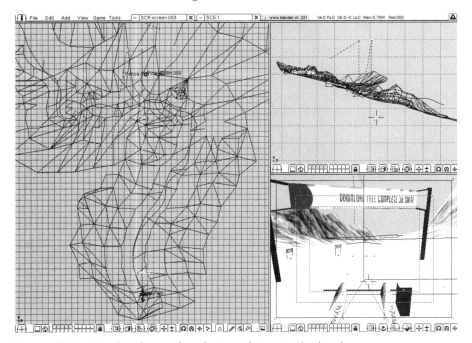

Figure 17-3: Window layout for placing objects in the level

1. Select the red flag (RMB), and then extend the selection to the green flag with SHIFT-RMB.

2. Use the grabber (GKEY) in the TopView to move both flags to the beginning of the track, then confirm the position with the LMB.

3. Without deselecting, move your mouse to the SideView and move both flags until you can see them sticking out of the snow in the CameraView.

4. Now, with the first flag set, we can continue adding more.

5. With the first two flags still selected, mouse over the TopView, then copy the two flags with ALT-D. The copied flags are in GrabMode, so move them along the path and confirm their position with the LMB.

TIP *ALT-D here makes a linked copy, which means that the dozens of objects we will create will share their mesh, saving in file size. (See Section 4.12.)*

6. Mouse over the SideView to set the height of the new flags.

NOTE *It's starting to become difficult to see whether the position is correct in the CameraView, depending on how far you placed the new flags, because the level is quite large compared with the size of the flags. This makes it difficult to locate the flags at precisely the right spot. One way to solve this problem is to change the CameraView to a PerspectiveView and then navigate to the new flag position by rotating, panning, and zooming the view. Another way would be to create a new camera and move this camera along the track while creating new objects.*

17.1.1. FlyMode

Blender's FlyMode offers a very convenient and fun way to place a camera. To use FlyMode:

1. Create a new camera with the Toolbox in the old CameraView. This newly created camera will have the same point of view as the old one, so you can't see a difference straight away, but it is now the active camera.

2. With your mouse over the CameraView, press SHIFT-F to start FlyMode. Move your mouse, and you should see the camera rotating and banking with your movements. Speed up by repeatedly pressing the LMB and slow down with the MMB. End FlyMode with ESC (which stops the camera and resets it to its old position) or by pressing the spacebar (which stops FlyMode and keeps the current position).

3. After repositioning the camera you can select the flags again and continue with the copy and place cycle until all objects are placed on track. Place the other objects in the same way.

4. To switch back to the player view, select the camera attached to the player and make it active by pressing CTRL-ALT-PAD0.

17.2. Placing Objects with Python

Even when you've become adept with navigating in a 3-D world, the task of placing numerous objects gets a bit boring and becomes distracting. To avoid this, this tutorial will introduce an advanced technique that uses Python scripting inside Blender's game engine and Blender Creator.

NOTE *This tutorial will give you an idea of how to use and combine Blender's tools to achieve complex tasks in a short time, but it requires a basic understanding of Python.*

Blender's game engine can be used to let objects fall onto the level ground, but these positions will only be valid as long as the game engine runs.

Although it is possible to have hundreds of objects with game logic needed to achieve this task, it will slow down the game and make it unplayable on slower computers. The solution is to store the position in a file on disk and the use the positions out of this file in Blender Creator to place objects without the game logic.

1. Load the scene Tutorials/SuperG/SuperG_00.blend as a base for this tutorial, then append all objects from Tutorials/SuperG/LevelElements.blend to this scene.

2. Place all the elements you want to have in your level in TopView, using the procedures for copying and moving as described in the previous chapter, but this time make sure that all elements are placed above the ground.

    The object DesignHelper contains the LogicBricks and Python script we need.

3. Now we need to select the objects we want to place. Switch to ObjectBrowse with SHIFT-F4, then select multiple objects with the RMB. Press ENTER when you are satisfied with your selections.

4. Switch back to the 3DWindow with SHIFT-F5 and extend the selection with the DesignHelper object. Now copy the LogicBricks of the helper to all other selected objects with CTRL-C and choose Logic Bricks from the menu.

5. Open a TextWindow with SHIFT-F11 and browse to the WritePositions Python script, shown in Figure 17-4.

Figure 17-4: Script to write object positions

```
1 import GameLogic
2
3 # CHANGE the file/path name!  (e.g. c:\temp\objs.txt)
4 FILE="tmp/objs.txt"
5
6 f = open(FILE,"a",8192)   # opening for appending
7
8 contr = GameLogic.getCurrentController()
9 owner = contr.getOwner()
10
11 # get position
```

```
12 pos = owner.getPosition()
13
14 f.write(owner.getName()[2:]+" "+str(pos[0])+" "+str(pos[1])+"
   "+str(pos[2])+" \n")
15
16 f.close()
```

6. Change the file name in line 4 to reflect your hard disk directory layout and your needs. Now start the game engine, wait until all objects are settled on the ground, and then stop the game engine.

NOTE   *You can examine the file created by the script in any text editor; it is a regular text file containing the names and positions of the objects line by line. To read back the positions, change the filename in the "ReadPosition" script and press ALT-P with your mouse over the TextWindow.*

Figure 17-5: Script to apply the object positions

```
1 import Blender
2
3 # CHANGE the file/path name!  (e.g. c:/temp/objs.txt)
4 FILE="/tmp/objs.txt"
5 f = open(FILE,"r",8192)
6
7 lines = f.readlines()
8
9 for line in lines:
10    words=line.split(" ")[:-1]
11    obj=Blender.Object.Get(words[0])
12    obj.LocX=float(words[1])
13    obj.LocY=float(words[2])
14    obj.LocZ=float(words[3])
15
16    Blender.Redraw()
17
```

Throughout this tutorial I have shown you the most common ways to build levels during the design phase of a game. When developing any bigger games or interactive 3-D applications, you would need to write a set of tools or scripts to help you with your work. These tools will take some effort initially to write, but they will help you in the future when you wish to further develop or change your games. Also, the tools or scripts can be reused in future projects.

Blender's combination of 3-D content creation tools with the ability to use Python scripting gives you a fast and flexible tool set for performing nearly all aspects of your work.

18

POWER BOATS

The tutorials in this chapter deal with methods of making real-time cockpit instruments and how to pass information between game elements, using the Power Boats game as the base. I (Carsten Wartmann) designed the Power Boats game (shown in Figures 18-1 and 18-2) with the idea of making a fun game that would have the character driving around in a powerful boat. I tried to make it a bit more of a simulation than an arcade game, but because I have never driven a real power boat, I doubt I was very successful. :)

I added some basic game elements, like the counting and timing of laps. However, to make it a real game it needs more, like an intro, more levels, and of course other boats (CPU controlled) to race against. I'll leave that part up to you.

Figure 18-1: Power Boats — third-person perspective

So enjoy driving around. Explore my scene and of course expand or change it! I am very curious to see what people can do with it in terms of making it a game or creating new levels.

Figure 18-2: Power Boats — first-person perspective

Here are the basic game controls:

Table 18-1: Power Boats Game Controls

Controls	Description
LEFTARROW/RIGHTARROW	Steering; you need to have some speed to steer
QKEY	Increase throttle
AKEY	Decrease throttle
F1	First-person perspective
F2	Camera behind boat
F3	Third-person perspective
F4	Helicopter camera

18.1. Engine Control

The engine control (shown in Figure 18-3) is designed mainly for showing the throttle position, so it is in fact an instrument.

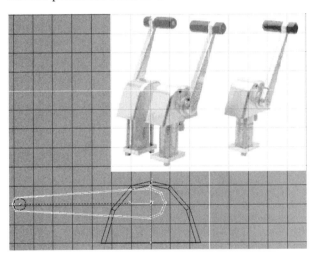

Figure 18-3: Engine control in the 3DWindow with modeling help

1. Load the file EngineControl_00.blend from the Tutorial/Powerboats/ directory on the CD or model one yourself.

2. Select the lever (EngineCArm) with the RMB; we are going to create an animation curve for this object. The object should not be rotated, so that we can use one main axis for rotating the lever.

NOTE   *Ipo animation curves in Blender are global to the scene (world) axis. To overcome this we can use object hierarchies by parenting them. After parenting we can rotate or move the parent object, and the Ipos on the child will get their reference from the parent object.*

3. Rotate the lever around the Y-axis about 15 degrees to determine the neutral position. Once you reach this position, insert a keyframe with IKEY and choose Rot from the pop-up menu. (You should have an IpoWindow (SHIFT-F6) open so you can see the horizontal lines of the newly generated Ipos.)

4. Advance the current frame by pressing UPARROW ten times.

5. Rotate the lever another 20 degrees and insert another Rot keyframe by pressing IKEY.

NOTE *We can't rotate the lever completely to the end position because Blender would try to interpolate the key positions (Ipo is short for interpolation curves), which would lead to an unwanted result: Ipos for more than one axis.*

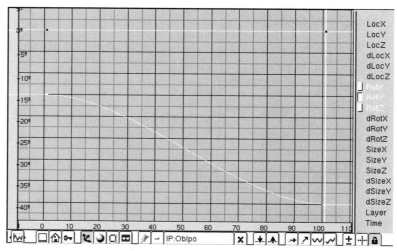

Figure 18-4: Animation curves (Ipo) for all three axes

6. Mouse over the IpoWindow and select the curved line (RotY when you use the prepared scene) with the RMB. Now enter EditMode (TAB) for this curve. The right key should be selected (yellow, RMB-click to select).

7. With your mouse over the IpoWindow press NKEY and enter **-160** in the LocY field, as shown here.

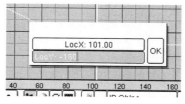

8. You can test the Ipo by pressing ALT-A over any 3DWindow. Save the file now.

9. Load Powerboats_00.blend. Because this file does not have the engine control and instruments for the FPS perspective we can use it for this tutorial.

10. Use SHIFT-F1 or Append from the FileMenu and browse to the prepared engine control file (your file or EngineControl_02.blend from the CD). Enter Objects and select all three objects (RMB), then press ENTER or click the LOAD LIBRARY button. The engine control is now appended to the actual scene together with the animation curve, while preserving the object hierarchies.

11. Zoom out until you see the mountain size engine control. Now select the base of the control and use rotate, scale, and move until it fits to the boat and is positioned nicely on the dashboard.

12. Extend the selection with SHIFT-RMB on the boat mesh (Hull), and parent the engine control to the boat with CTRL-P. Now the control is mounted to the boat (as shown in Figure 18-5), but it needs to be made functional.

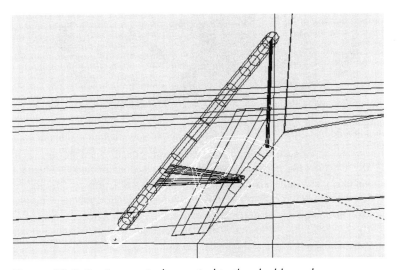

Figure 18-5: Engine control mounted to the dashboard

13. Select the conrol lever (EngineCArm) with the RMB and switch to the Real-timeButtons (F8). Create the LogicBricks as shown in Figure 18-6.

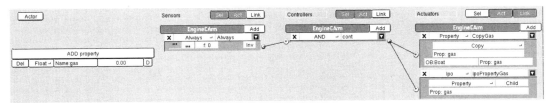

Figure 18-6: Engine control LogicBricks

These LogicBricks copy the gas property (the throttle position) from the boat object to the local gas property of the lever object. The values of gas reach from 0 percent to 100 percent, and we play the Ipo with the Property Ipo Actuator according to this value so that the lever will always reflect the gas property.

18.2. Cockpit Instruments

The procedure we'll use to create cockpit instruments is very similar to one we used above for the engine control. In fact, the engine control is not a control here but also an instrument.

The instruments are first modeled in Blender (as shown in Figure 18-7), then the rendered image is used as texture in the Power Boats scene. (You can see and change the instruments in the scene Tutorials/Powerboats/Instruments.blend.)

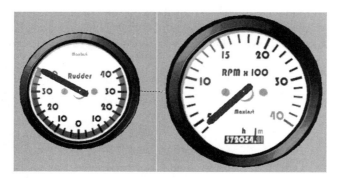

Figure 18-7: Intruments

Note that the scale of the revolution counter is not linear. To make it display the revolutions correctly, we need to use a complicated formula. Or even better, we can use Blender's Ipo curves to visually calibrate any displays simply by moving Ipo handles (Figure 18-8). Unlike the method we used for the engine control, we pass the value for the revolutions to the cockpit instruments. (We used the Copy Property Actuator for the engine control, which is an easy way to do it, although it will not work across scene borders.)

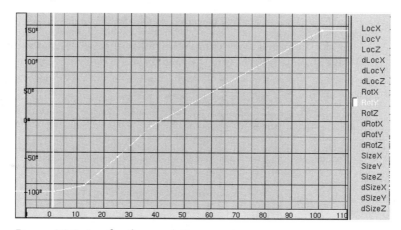

Figure 18-8: Ipo for the revolution counter

When you switch to a third-person view in the Power Boats game, you see the instruments as an overlay, which is accomplished by rendering an overlay scene onto the main scene. In this case we need to send the rpm value from two instruments across a scene border. We use Blender's messaging system to send the rpm value from the engine, and every instrument can listen to this message and process it. This makes it very easy to add a new instrument (in this case, for example, a warning when the rpm gets too high), which is also tied to changes in the rpm value.

You can see in Figure 18-9 that we receive messages with the subject RPM, which triggers the MessageBody script (Figure 18-10). This script extracts the message body into the property (which needs to exist on the object) "mbody." The Property Ipo Actuator then plays the Ipo according to the value in mbody.

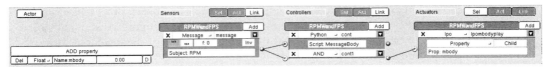

Figure 18-9: LogicBricks to receive rpm messages and play the Ipo

To make this script work the Message Sensor has to be named "message" and there needs to be a property, mbody. The script will convert the message body into the correct type (string or integer) of the property.

Figure 18-10: Script to extract message bodies

```
1 # Extracts message bodies
2 from types import *
3
4 cont = GameLogic.getCurrentController()
5 mess = cont.getSensor("message")
6 me   = cont.getOwner()
7
8 bodies = mess.getBodies()
9 if bodies!=None:
10    for body in bodies:
11        if type(me.mbody) is StringType:
12            me.mbody = body
13        else:
14            me.mbody = float(body)
```

TIP *To take full advantage of Python, we recommend installing a complete Python distribution, which also comes with a very good guide to Python. Because Python's development is very fast, we suggest using Python 2.0 for the best compatibility with this version of Blender. All games in the Games directory on the CD work without a full Python installation.*

But how are the messages sent? That's where the Message Actuator comes in, as shown here.

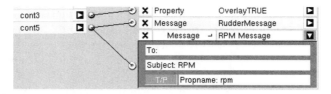

NOTE   *The Subject field contains RPM, and the T/P button is activated.*

You can apply the lessons learned in this tutorial to many different games and interactive 3-D applications in which you need controls or displays. We've shown you two possibilities: how to pass information between objects and how to use Blender as a tool to produce textures for the game engine. And of course, Blender's animation curves allow us to change and adjust the displayed information graphically.

19

BALLERCOASTER

by Martin Strubel

The Blender game engine can simulate the natural behavior of rolling balls quite nicely, which makes it perfect for building a roller coaster, or rather, a BallerCoaster!

This tutorial will go into some detail about natural behavior, so fasten your seat belts for some physics in the last section. (But please don't skip to the next chapter yet: It's not all that bad, and of course we will start with the fun stuff first.)

To save you, dear reader, a good bit of time, we provide you with a kit of prefabricated elements such as curves, slopes, and other path types that you can simply plug together. We will also show you how to generate your own path elements using Blender's bevel curves. (And now, a thank-you to my dear mate Freid, who modeled the room environment and let me use it as the background.)

19.1. Assembling a Track

To get an idea of what your finished BallerCoaster will look like, see the demo file Games/BallerCoaster.blend and Figure 19-1.

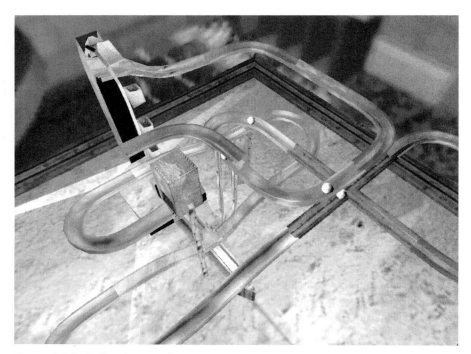

Figure 19-1: BallerCoaster demo

To begin, start Blender and load the demo file using F1. To start the demo, move the mouse over Blender's 3DWindow and press PKEY. I have also added some extras, accessible using the following hotkeys:

Table 19-1: BallerCoaster Game Controls

Controls	Description
NKEY	Make the ball dispenser spawn some fresh balls
SKEY	Switch track elements (just try!)
Spacebar	Toggle between the ball camera (following red ball) and the observer's perspective
AKEY	Switch fixed camera view
ENTER	Restart demo

Because you've probably become a little dizzy after looking through the crazy ball camera, it's probably time to make your own track now. (We will look at the demo again later when discussing some game logic: a bit of intelligence attached to the objects.) Go ahead and switch to the screen "elements" with CTRL-RIGHTARROW, and you should see a bunch of path elements waiting to be grabbed and moved with your mouse (see Figure 19-2).

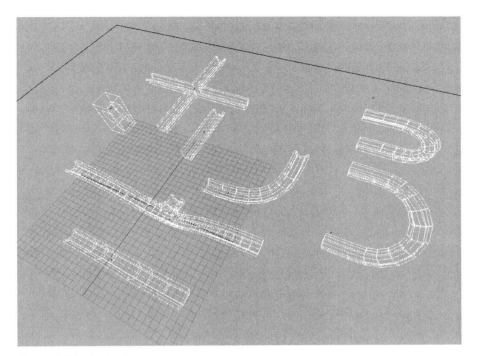

Figure 19-2: Path elements

To grab them:

1. Switch to TopView using PAD7.
2. Select an element with the RMB.
3. Press ALT-D to make a linked copy of the object (see Section 4.12).
4. Press GKEY to move the element, while holding CTRL. This will snap the position of the object to the grid, helping you with the alignment of the elements. The same works with rotation: press R, then rotate with the mouse while holding down CTRL.
5. Switch to FrontView or SideView using PAD1 resp. PAD3 and move your object to the desired place (with CTRL-hold).

NOTE *If you accidentally forgot to hold CTRL while moving the object, you can always snap it to the grid again by pressing SHIFT-S, Sel > Grid.*

Assuming that you have plugged together some elements to create a decent track, let's test it! Grab the ball dispenser (the little rusty box) and place it above the track, then press PKEY to run the demo and NKEY to add some balls. You should see the balls disappear when they hit the ground plane. This is intentional, because we don't want to crowd the scene with too many dynamic objects. (Notice how if you add a lot of balls at once by firing NKEY, the whole animation gets quite slow. This is because the dynamics calculations take quite a bit of CPU time.)

19.2. Game Logic

At this point we've got the makings of only a very simple game. To get a nice cycle to work as in the demo, we need to add some more logic. Here's the logic we've used so far:

Ball dispenser: Pressing NKEY produces a new ball.

Balls: Balls that hit the ground are destroyed.

In Figure 19-3 you can see the LogicBricks for the object "dispenser," as displayed in the RealtimeButtons (F8). The keyboard event simply adds a new object, "ball," at its position, marked by the little pink PivotPoint. This ball object is located in layer 10 (0KEY). Now change to layer 10 by pressing 0KEY and selecting the ball to check its attached logic. The ball logic is simple: When the ball collides with an object with the property "death," it will cause its own end.

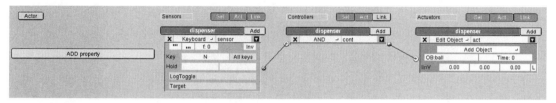

Figure 19-3: LogicBricks for the dispenser

NOTE *Objects to be added inside the game engine must always be in a nonvisible (inactive) layer! Read more about layers in Section 24.1.1.*

Now return to layer 6 and select the ground plane. You should see that it does indeed have the property "death", as shown on the left side of the Realtime-Buttons. It's that easy! (In layer 10 you will also see the bucket object, which we've used to fake the ball elevator. Its logic is more complex and not too elegant, but it's still simpler than defining an animation for each single bucket. We will not go into the details of its logic, though, we leave that to you.)

TIP *Press HOMEKEY in the 3DWindow if you feel lost in 3-D space — this will help you to locate your objects.*

19.3. Making Track Elements

Because assembling all this prefabricated stuff may get a little boring, we will now show you how to make track elements yourself.

Bevel curves

In the demo file, select the screen "elements" from the screen menu (or press CTRL-RIGHTARROW). Here you will find all the element prototypes, in the form of beveled curves.

This curve type consists of a path (a 3-D curve) and a diameter curve, which is extruded and oriented along the path. Let's take a closer look at these (see Figure 19-4).

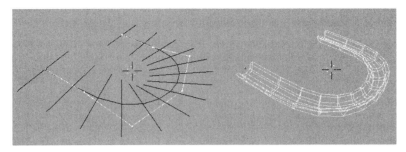

Figure 19-4: Beveling a track

1. Select one of the bevel curves with the RMB and press TAB to switch into EditMode.

2. You can now move the control vertices of the path as usual, and change the local orientation with TKEY and by moving the mouse. The orientation of the path is immediately reflected in the railway-like representation.

3. Pressing TAB again will recalculate the extrusion of the diameter curve.

The easiest way to create new tracks is to make a true duplicate of an existing track element (using SHIFT-DKEY) and to modify its curve. If you'd rather start from the scratch though, here's how:

1. Activate the EditButtons by pressing F9.

2. Add a Bezier Curve by pressing the spacebar and then Curve > Bezier Curve (a NURBS curve works too).

3. Add a second, preferably closed curve (Bezier Circle), then modify it so that it is U-shaped. Rename this object **dia** by entering the name in the OB field (Figure 19-5).

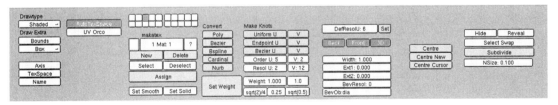

Figure 19-5: EditButtons for the bevel curve

4. Select the first path curve again, activate the 3D setting in the EditButtons, and enter the name of the U-shaped curve (**dia**) in the field BevOb.

5. Adapt the resolution of both of the curves to the most acceptable low polygon count. You might want to convert the diameter curve into a polygon curve by clicking the Convert Poly button (Figure 19-5) to get the best control over the shape.

6. Finally, convert the bevel object into a mesh for the game engine by selecting the object and pressing ALT-C for Convert Curve To: Mesh. But careful! You should make a duplicate copy (SHIFT-DKEY) of the curve objects before conversion, because the original curve object will be lost otherwise.

When editing curves:

- If the resolution of a curve near a control vertex is too great, change its weight by selecting the vertex, then choosing the weight from the weight button group (or enter the weight manually by holding SHIFT while clicking the Weight button) and apply Set Weight.

- If you want to play with the order setting of the curve to modify the bending shape, remember that the minimum number of control vertices must be greater than the order. For our needs, the Endpoint option might be the best one.

19.3.1. Plastic surgery — some mesh beautification

With our conversion to the mesh complete, we may need to align the vertices to the path element's ends, as shown in Figure 19-6. If we don't, we may end up with ugly effects as a result of joining slightly intersecting path elements.

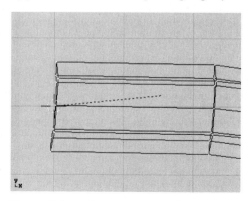

Figure 19-6: Aligning vertices

1. To align the vertices, use the BorderSelect tool BKEY to select all the end vertices, then do the following:

2. Set the 3D-Cursor to a grid point using the LMB and pressing SHIFT-SKEY, then 3KEY (Curs > Grid) to snap the cursor to the grid.

3. Press DOTKEY to use the 3D-Cursor as a scaling center.

4. Place the mouse cursor on the right of the 3D-Cursor to indicate the direc-

tion for the scale constraint, then press SKEY followed by the MMB to constrain the scaling in X direction. Hold down CTRL and scale the vertex group's X components to 0.0, yielding a perfect alignment in X.

19.3.2. Texturing

We will give you only a quick introduction to texturing here, as we show you how to glue a texture on to your newly created track element:

1. Select the desired mesh and press FKEY to enter FaceSelect mode. Press AKEY to select all faces.
2. Open an ImageWindow (SHIFT-F10) and either choose an image from the MenuButton or load a new image by clicking Load Image.
3. Move your mouse pointer over the 3-D view and press UKEY to pop up a mapping menu. Use the Cube mapping option; as a result, you should see the so-called UV mapping of all selected faces in the ImageWindow.
4. You can edit these mappings by selecting the vertices and transforming them as you did earlier in the 3DWindow.

19.4. The Real-World Physics Behind BallerCoaster

This section is included here for those who want to know why this demo seems so realistic. We'll tell you how it works.

19.4.1. Gravity

Most of the environmental phenomena we observe daily is based on forces. We are all aware of the mystic force that exists between any entity in space, especially between earth and ourselves — the force of gravity.

In the simplified world of our BallerCoaster, you can observe several types of motion: free fall, the static touch of an object with the ground, rolling, sliding, and collisions. All of this motion is handled by Blender's built-in physics engine, so that in this simple demo there is no need to take over control of the motion: Gravity does that work.

19.4.2. Dimensions

Blender users often ask us what Blender grid units equate to in the real world. Meters? Inches? Feet? The answer is that the equivalent is what you want it to be. Not very helpful, is it? Let us find a better answer.

The default setting for the gravity settings in the WorldButtons is 9.81. This means that, when this setting is used, one Blender unit is equivalent to one meter in the real world. But you could just as easily calculate and set the gravity acceleration in inches, setting the Blender unit as one inch, and produce the same physical behavior.

If you want to build a consistent world with the same scaling, but different physics, it really helps to model everything in its absolute size (say, if you want to model a two-meter-tall ogre, you would use two Blender units). It also helps to use the default gravity, if you're keen on producing true natural behavior. (You can always tweak the gravity factor, or even use different worlds with different gravities, later.)

Figure 19-7 shows an example of "human" (172 cm height) dimensions. The grid units are set in the current 3DWindow by pressing SHIFT-F7.

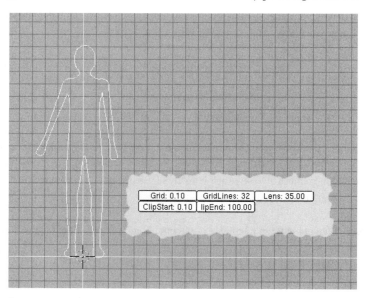

Figure 19-7: Dimensions

In our demo, the balls have a size of 0.04 units, which is equal to 4 cm. We use a gravity lower than 9.81 to slow down the motion a bit. (We don't want to get too seasick from the crazy ball camera view.) Moreover, a displayed grid unit is equal to 0.05 Blender units, as set in the ViewButtons (press SHIFT-F7 in the active 3DWindow).

19.4.3. Rolling, rolling, rolling

Rolling is the most common state of motion in our BallerCoaster. Without going into the scientific details (you may already be sick of these from physics class), what causes the rolling motion? Friction!

If you pull your balky donkey (who is of course refusing to walk) by its leash, you will need to expend quite some force to get him moving. You need to overcome the force of the friction between his feet and the ground. By the same token, if you put a nonrolling object on an inclined plane, you encounter different types of motion, depending on the friction between the object and the ground as well as the inclination of the plane:

Sticking: The external force on the object is not great enough to overcome the force of friction, and the object does not move. This is called *static friction*.

Sliding: The applied force is greater than the static friction force threshold, and the external force produces *kinetic* or *dynamic friction*.

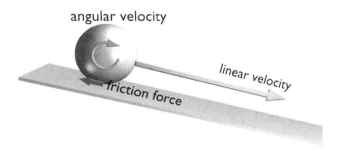

angular velocity

linear velocity

friction force

Figure 19-8: Forces on a rolling object

The same states of friction apply to a rolling object, but the effect is different. In both cases, the force of friction will apply a torque to the object and make it roll (as illustrated in Figure 19-8).Therefore, no matter how great the amount of friction, the rolling object is not decelerated (unless it's sliding). But sliding can occur in different ways:

- The ball does not move very fast, but spins on the ground below it. For physicists, this means that its rotational energy is about to be converted into a linear kinetic energy (some part of the energy is burned in the friction process).

- There is little rotation, but a lot of linear motion. The ball will get a rotational acceleration by the kinetic friction, and some energy will be lost in the sliding process (your donkey's feet can get HOT!).

So, our simple conclusion from our exploration into the physics of motion: If your donkey refuses to move, put it into a barrel and roll it!

What do we have left to worry about then? The case of sliding or sticking is handled by Blender's physics engine. We need only specify the material parameters of the objects involved, meaning their friction coefficients.

NOTE   *Friction normally describes the interaction of two materials. Blender simplifies this a bit and expresses friction as a value for each material. When two materials intersect, Blender uses the lower of both of the involved friction values.*

19.4.4. Setting dynamic material parameters

This is a quick guide to dynamic materials (also see the demo and see Section 26.6):

1.   Select the object, then switch to the MaterialButtons (F5) and choose a material per object.

NOTE *Normally, materials are assigned to a mesh, but we want to assign the material to the object itself, so that we can use several objects with a shared mesh, but not shared materials. Material assignment per object is selected using the OB button (Figure 19-9).*

2. Click the DYN button to switch to the dynamic parameters of the material.

3. Use a low restitution (elasticity) of the materials to avoid too much jumping. For the two materials' interaction, the maximum restitution value is taken.

4. Use a relatively high friction on the balls and a lower friction on the track elements. Remember, the lowest of the friction values is used.

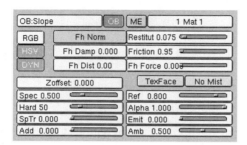

Figure 19-9: Dynamic settings in the MaterialButtons

19.4.5. Final remarks

When you run this demo on an older 3-D graphics accelerator or computer, the demo will probably run at a slow frame rate. As a result, the balls may get lost because they don't respect collisions at all above a certain speed (quantum physics people call this effect *tunneling*). This is, of course, an undesired effect in a game engine, but because we've chosen speed over accuracy, you will have to live with that fact (or consider upgrading your PC). Happy rolling!

20

SQUISH THE BUNNY — CREATING WEAPON EFFECTS FOR A FIRST-PERSON SHOOTER

by Randall Rickert

This tutorial outlines an approach to creating weapon effects in Blender, using the file Tutorials/SquishBunny/stb-tutorial.blend as an example of the techniques. You will learn to add a smoke trail effect to a rocket as well as more sophisticated techniques, as demonstrated in the game scene when the player fires a rocket.

Table 20-1: Squish the Bunny Game Controls

Controls	Description
WKEY	Move forward
SKEY	Move backward
AKEY	Sidestep left
DKEY	Sidestep right
Spacebar	Jump
LMB	Shoot a rocket
Mouse movement	Rotate and look

Figure 20-1: Squish the Bunny demo file

Table 20-2 lists the people who made the Squish the Bunny demo file.

Table 20-2: The Squish the Bunny Demo File Makers

Artist	Role
Randall Rickert	Design and logic
Randall Rickert and Reevan McKay	Eye candy
Janco Verduin	Ear candy

20.1. Introduction

This tutorial will outline an approach to creating weapon effects in Blender. We will be editing a simple first-person shooter game scene as our example. In this scene you can run around in an immersive environment, firing a rocket launcher that makes fiery explosions and leaves scorch marks on the walls. This scene could form the basis for a game in which you fight your way out of a fortress, carry out a mercenary mission, or test your mettle in a gladiator-style tournament.

The goal of this tutorial is to show you how to make some of the eye candy that is essential to making such a game engaging. A scene showing the effects in action is Games/Squish-the-Bunny.blend (Figure 20-2).

Figure 20-2: The generator room

20.2. Getting Started

To begin, start Blender and open the file Tutorials/SquishBunny/stb-tutorial.blend. This file has an environment model and a human-perspective camera with enough game logic to allow the player to navigate using the keyboard and mouse in the style of some popular first-person shooter games, and to shoot a rocket from the rocket launcher.

To see it in action, press PKEY. Use WKEY, SKEY, AKEY, and DKEY to move around, and the spacebar to jump. Move the mouse to turn and to look up and down. The LMB will shoot a rocket. Press ESC when you are ready to exit the game.

20.3. A Trail of Smoke

Our first step toward spicing up the action will be to add a smoke trail behind the rocket. A trail of smoke will make the fast-moving rocket more visible, and it will add a lot of visual depth to the scene, giving the player a better sense of the space.

After exiting the game, press CTRL-LEFTARROW to switch from the current screen to one better suited to editing the scene. You will see a 3DWindow on the left side of the screen with a wireframe view of the scene, an ImageWindow on the right, and a ButtonsWindow at the bottom showing the EditButtons (Figure 20-3).

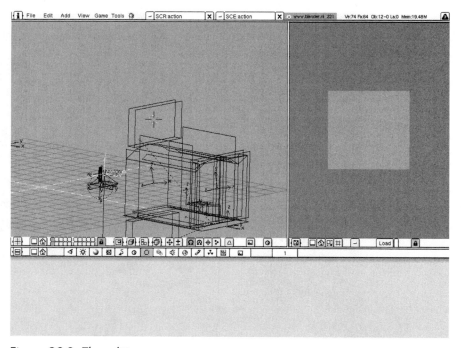

Figure 20-3: The editing screen

20.4. Building a Puff of Smoke

To represent the puffs of smoke that make up the trail of the rocket, we will use a special kind of polygon called a *halo*. A halo face is a polygon that always faces the camera. When used with a texture containing transparency information in an alpha channel this type of polygon can create the illusion of volume, because the camera's perspective won't flatten the polygon by viewing it from the edge.

1. With your mouse in the 3DWindow, press PAD7 to switch to TopView (make sure you have PAD-NUM LOCK turned on).

2. Press the spacebar and from the pop-up menu select ADD > Mesh > Plane (see Figure 20-4).

Figure 20-4: Add a plane mesh

3. A plane is added to the scene and automatically placed in EditMode (as shown in Figure 20-5). Press PAD1 to switch to FrontView.

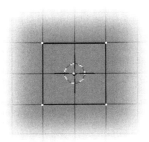

Figure 20-5: The plane in EditMode

For each polygon, one side is considered to be the face side. For the sake of speed, the game engine renders only the face and not the back of each polygon.

We need to orient the face of the plane toward the negative end of the X-axis (the left side of the window), because this is the side of an alpha face that will face the camera.

4. Press RKEY to begin rotating the vertices. Hold CTRL to constrain the rotation to five-degree increments as you rotate the vertices -90 degrees (counterclockwise). You can see the degrees of rotation in the WindowHeader at the bottom of the 3DWindow (as shown in Figure 20-6).

5. When the rotation reaches -90 degrees LMB-click to apply the rotation and end RotationMode. Press TAB to leave EditMode.

Figure 20-6: Amount of rotation

6. Press RKEY again. You are now changing the basic orientation of the object (not just moving the vertices of the polygon). Rotate the object 90 degrees (clockwise), facing upward so that you will be able to see the texture on the plane once you apply it.

7. Now turn your attention to the EditButtons (F9). Change the name of the object to "smoke" (Figure 20-7) by clicking in the OB field and entering the new name. This will allow you to refer to the smoke object in the game LogicBricks, which will be necessary a little bit later.

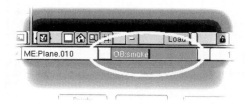

Figure 20-7: Change the name of the smoke object

8. In the 3DWindow, press PAD7 to return to TopView, then press ALT-Z to change the DrawMode of the 3DWindow from wireframe to OpenGL textured. The smoke object will turn black.

9. Press FKEY to enter FaceSelectMode. The smoke object will turn white. This mode lets you modify settings for each face of a mesh object. The single face of the mesh is automatically selected.

10. With your mouse in the ButtonsWindow at the bottom of the screen, change the view from EditButtons to the PaintFaceButtons by selecting the PaintFaceButtons icon (Figure 20-8).

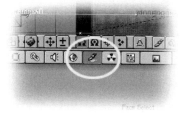

Figure 20-8: PaintButtons

11. Select the Tex, Halo, and Alpha buttons, and deselect the Collision button (see Figure 20-9). This tells Blender to display a texture on the face, to rotate the face toward the camera, to use the alpha channel of the texture for transparency, and not to calculate collisions with this face.

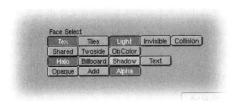

Figure 20-9: Face settings for the smoke plane

12. Apply a smoke texture to the face by LMB-clicking the Load button in the header of the ImageWindow, navigating to Tutorials/SquishBunny/texture/ smoke.tga, and MMB-clicking it.

13. You will see the texture appear in the ImageWindow. It is completely white, but the transparency in the alpha channel will make it look like a puff of smoke or steam, as you can see in the 3DWindow (Figure 20-10). Press FKEY to exit FaceSelectMode.

Figure 20-10: Smoke texture applied to the plane

20.5. Adding Game Logic to the Smoke

You now have a smoke puff object. The next step is to create the pieces of logic that tell Blender how to use this object.

1. With your mouse in the 3DWindow, press SHIFT-0 to turn on layer 10, where the rocket object is located. You will see a very small object labeled rocket. Select it with the RMB (Figure 20-11).

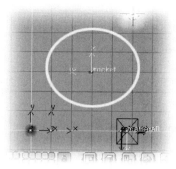

Figure 20-11: Selecting the rocket object

2. Change the view in the ButtonsWindow from PaintButtons to RealtimeButtons by selecting the RealtimeButtons icon in the ButtonsWindow Header. The RealtimeButtons display the game logic for the rocket.

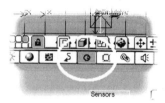

3. LMB-click the Add button at the top of the Sensors column to add a sensor. Add a controller and an actuator in a similar way. Be sure to add the actuator by using the Add button beside the rocket object and not the one for the hit-effect object.

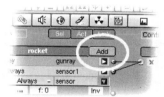

4. Connect the newly created LogicBricks together in a chain by holding the LMB and dragging the mouse from the ball of the sensor to the doughnut of the controller, and from the ball of the controller to the doughnut of the actuator (see Figure 20-12).

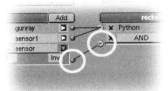

Figure 20-12: Connecting LogicBricks

5. Change the type of actuator from Motion to Edit Object by selecting it from the MenuButton at the top of the brick (Figure 20-13). In the OB button, enter the name of the object to be added (which is "smoke" in this case).

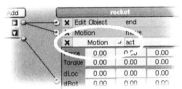

Figure 20-13: Changing the actuator type

6. Change the value in the Time field to 32 (Figure 20-14). This step tells Blender that each smoke puff added to the scene by this actuator should be removed from the scene after 32 cycles of the game engine. In other words, each smoke puff lives for 32 game cycles. The game engine makes 50 cycles per second, so our smoke puffs live about two-thirds of a second. We could give them a longer life, but having a lot of additional objects in the scene simultaneously can cause a big decrease in speed. (You might be thinking that the number 32 still sounds a bit arbitrary. It was chosen because it fits the animation we will apply to the smoke in the next section.)

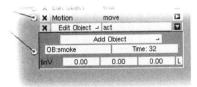

Figure 20-14: Settings in the Edit Object Actuator

7. After seeing the size of the rocket in comparison to the size of the smoke object, it might be apparent that this smoke object is too big. Select the smoke object again, then press SKEY to begin changing its size. Continue reducing the size of the smoke object by moving your mouse toward the center of the object until it is about one-fourth of its original size. As in

RotationMode, you can monitor the exact value by watching the Header of the 3DWindow.

8. Objects must be on a hidden layer in order for the Add Object Actuator to add them to the scene. Press MKEY to move the smoke object to a different layer. You will see a grid representing the available layers.

9. Press 0KEY to specify that it should be moved to layer 10, and press ENTER. Hide layer 10 again by pressing SHIFT-0.

10. You don't have to return to the full-screen window to test the smoke trails. You can run the game engine in this screen to see the results without viewing the title screens again. Press PAD0 in the 3DWindow to view the scene through the camera (CameraView), then press PKEY as before to start the game engine. You should see a trail of white smoke when you fire a rocket.

20.6. Animating the Smoke

The smoke puffs will look a lot better if they expand and fade away rather than simply sitting still until they vanish suddenly.

1. Exit the game, return to a wireframe view, turn on layer 10 again, and select the smoke object (if it's not still selected).

2. Change the ImageWindow to an IpoWindow by moving your mouse into the ImageWindow and pressing SHIFT-F6 or selecting the IpoWindow icon from the WindowType drop-down menu. This menu is accessed by clicking on the WindowType icon at the far left side of the WindowHeader (Figure 20-15). If you don't see the WindowType icon, you may need to scroll the header by holding the MMB and dragging it to the right.

Figure 20-15: Changing the window type to IpoWindow

We will animate the smoke object's size by specifying key sizes at certain points in the object's timeline. Blender will plot a smooth transition between these values (called *keys* or *keyframes*), and this transition will be visualized as an IpoCurve. The IpoWindow will allow you to see and edit the IpoCurves, which describe how the smoke object changes over time. The vertical axis of the IpoWindow represents the value being animated. The horizontal axis represents time in animation frames, each of which is equal to 1/25 of a second.

1. Look at the CurrentFrame button in the header of the ButtonsWindow (Figure 20-16) to be sure the current frame is frame 1. If it is not, press SHIFT-LEFTARROW to cause Blender to jump to frame 1. In the 3DWindow press IKEY to call the InsertKey menu, and select Size. Press RIGHTARROW until the CurrentFrame button shows that you are on frame 16.

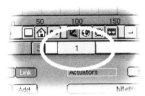

Figure 20-16: The CurrentFrame button

2. Using the same technique you used before, increase the size of the smoke object to about two and a half times its current size. Insert another size key as before. As you insert these keys, you can see curves being plotted in the IpoWindow. To frame the IpoCurves so that they are easier to see, press HOME with your mouse in the IpoWindow (Figure 20-17).

We will animate the color and opacity of the smoke object by drawing IpoCurves for the object color channels directly into the IpoWindow. In order for these curves to take effect, we must return to FaceSelectMode (FKEY) and select one additional setting for the face in the FacePaintButtons. Activate the button labeled ObColor. When you select this button you will see the smoke turn black because there are no values yet for the object color.

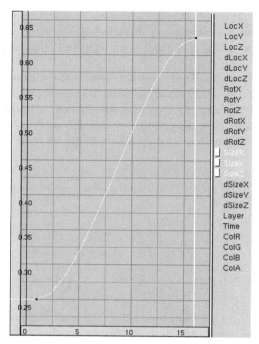

Figure 20-17: Ipo Curves for the size of the smoke object

1. Leave FaceSelectMode and return your attention to the IpoWindow. The labels ColR, ColG, ColB, and ColA refer to the red, green, blue, and alpha object color channels, respectively (Figure 20-18). Useful values for these channels will are in the range from 0.0 to 1.0.

Figure 20-18: Object color channels

2. Select the ColA channel by LMB-clicking it. It will turn white. Add the first key with CTRL-LMB in the IpoWindow at frame 1.0 and value 1.0, and the second key by repeating the procedure at frame 16 and value 0.0 (Figure 20-19).

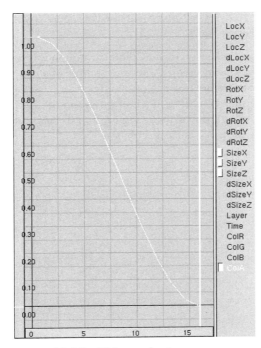

Figure 20-19: Object color Ipos

3. In a similar fashion, select each of the ColR, ColG, and ColB channels in turn, and to each one add a key at frame 1.0 with a value of about 0.8, giving the smoke a light gray color.

We have created some animation data for the object, and now we must add the logic, which will activate the animation:

1. Return the ButtonsWindow to the RealtimeButtons view.
2. In the same manner we used for adding logic to the rocket, add a sensor, actuator, and controller to the smoke object and connect them together as before. This time we will change the actuator type to Ipo. Set the Sta (starting frame) button to 1 and the End (end frame) button to 16, because that is the frame range covered by our animation (Figure 20-20).

Figure 20-20: Ipo Actuator settings

NOTE *Remember to hide layer 10 before switching to CameraView again and starting the game engine to see the results of your work.*

Try animating the ColR, ColG, and ColB channels in interesting ways. The file Games/Squish-the-Bunny.blend shows an example of a completed smoke effect. It also demonstrates how an explosion effect can be achieved. The explosion effect uses a complex mixture of Python programming, animation, and the LogicBricks in Blender's graphical game logic editor. Dissection of this file is left as an exercise for the more adventurous reader.

PART FIVE
ADVANCED TUTORIALS

The advanced tutorials in this section require a
deeper understanding of the techniques behind
Blender's scenes. For example, some basic knowledge
of a programming language or character animation is
strongly recommended. The character animation
tutorial teaches you how to use Blender's powerful
and also gives some useful tips. However, to create
natural movements you will need to practice and
observe nature as well.

As in the intermediate tutorials Blender scenes are
provided to give a framework for your experiments.
Two of the scenes are puzzle type games which
contain complex Python scripts.

21

FLYING BUDDHA MEMORY GAME

Flying Buddha is a game designed by Freid Lachnowicz (artwork, models, textures) and me (Carsten Wartmann, Python and game logic). The goal of the game is to find pairs of gongs, like in the good old game Memory. It also includes some action elements, like a dragonfly that becomes angry (note the indicator at the top right) if you jump too high. Also, it requires good timing to use the controls of the Buddha effectively.

The Buddha's goal is to reach Zen. His goal is complete when he has found all pairs. When playing competitively, the time needed to find all pairs is displayed on screen.

Figure 21-1: Buddha in action

Load the game Games/FlyingBuddha.blend from the CD and have fun playing it! Here are the controls.

Table 21-1: Flying Buddha Game Controls

Controls	Description
Arrow keys	Movement; you can steer in the air and slow down your fall
SKEY	Select a gong

21.1. Accessing Game Objects

Accessing individual objects from Blender's game engine is not trivial. In this game, I needed to be able to randomly shuffle the gongs at game start.

In general, it is a good to have as much game logic as possible contained on the object that needs that logic, which helps when reusing this object in the same or even different (Blender) scenes. Thus, my first thought was to let the gongs choose a new position themselves. But this soon turned out to be too complicated, because of problems with synchronization and the challenge of working with the complex logic in the gongs.

I decided instead to use an object to control the shuffling process and to have a Near Sensor gather the information about the other objects, including their positions. This approach has many advantages. For example, it allows us to filter out entire groups of objects with the Property field, it does not bind us to a fixed number of objects, and so on.

21.1.1. LogicBricks

Load the file Tutorials/Buddha/FlyingBuddha_simple.blend from the CD. This file contains a fully functional but simplified version of the Flying Buddha game, without all the intro scenes (press CTRL-LEFTARROW for a full-screen view). We'll use this file to explore the game logic.

The difference between the full game and this tutorial file is the built-in debugging and testing logic. Most notably, you can test the reshuffling of the gongs every time by pressing the spacebar. You'll find the logic for this on the Flamethrower object (on layer 4).

Have a look at Figure 21-2. The relevant parts for this example are the sensors "mixitbaby" and "near," both of which are connected to a Python controller, which is then connected to a message actuator. Also note the "shuffle" property, which controls the number of swapped pairs. (The other bricks are not related to the shuffling; they are needed for other game parts.)

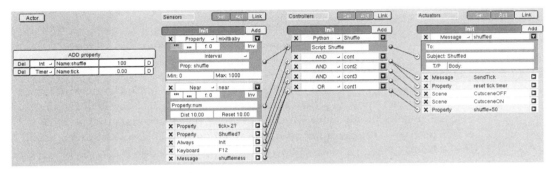

Figure 21-2: LogicBricks for shuffling the gongs

As you can. see, the Near Sensor looks only for objects carrying a property with the name "num" Make sure that the Dist setting is high enough for the Near Sensor to cover all objects. The Python controller will be called by the Property Sensor as long as the property "num" is in the range of 0 to 1000.

21.1.2. Shuffle Python script

Open a TextWindow (SHIFT-F11, see Section 28.1) and choose the script Shuffle with the MenuButton. You'll see the script shown in Figure 21-3.

Figure 21-3: Script to shuffle the gongs

```
1 # Shuffle script, swaps positions of two gongs
2
3 import GameLogic
4
5 def ranint(min,max):
6 return(int(GameLogic.getRandomFloat()*(max+1-min)+min))
7
8 contr = GameLogic.getCurrentController()
9 owner = contr.getOwner()
```

```
10 key = contr.getSensor("mixitbaby")
11 near = contr.getSensor("near")
12 mess = contr.getActuator("shuffled")
13
14 # collects all gongs
15 objs=near.getHitObjectList()
16
17 owner.shuffle = owner.shuffle - 1
18 if owner.shuffle<0:
19 GameLogic.addActiveActuator(mess,1)
20 else:
21 g1 = ranint(0,19)
22 g2 = ranint(0,19)
23
24 pos1 = objs[g1].getPosition()
25 pos2 = objs[g2].getPosition()
26 objs[g1].setPosition(pos2)
27 objs[g2].setPosition(pos1)
```

Let's have a look at the script.

- The lines 1 through 12 initialize the script and get information about the controller, sensors, actuators, and the owner needed to access properties. The definition of a new function in line 5 makes a random function that returns an integer number in a specified range. (This will save much typing later.)

- Line 15 has the first important step. Using the method getHitObjectList() of the near object we collect all game objects with the near sensor into the list objs.

- In line 17 we decrement the property shuffle by one.

- The if block, which begins in line 18, executes the message sensor connected to the Python controller if the property shuffle is less then zero. The message can then be used to start the game.

- The else block is executed when owner.shuffle is bigger than zero. This means that gongs need to be swapped.

- In lines 21 and 22 we get two random numbers into the variables g1 and g2. The numbers will be in a range from 0 to 19 because we have 4x5=20 gongs. g1 and g2 are the indices of the gongs we want to swap in the next lines. (Note that lists in Python start with the element 0.)

- In lines 24 and 25 the script reads the positions of the gong-objects using the random indices. The method used here is `getPosition()`. You can insert a `print pos1,pos2` statement after line 25 to actually see the gong positions while running the game.

TIP   *Python is an autodocumenting language. Use a* `print dir(object)` *statement to find out what methods an object provides.*

- The final two lines then swap the positions of the two gongs. The first obj indexed as objs[g1] is set to pos2, which is the position of the first gong. The same goes for the other gong. You can see the shuffling process in the game itself by looking at the gongs from the back.

In this tutorial I have shown you how to use Python in the game engine to access and change objects in a scene. We used this approach to keep the game logic local on the objects.

If you are familiar with non–object-oriented programming languages or systems, this may appear strange to you at first, but this approach has many advantages. For one, when using it you don't need to change the logic while editing your scenes or adding objects. In fact, the script will even work when adding objects while running the game. Also, it makes it much easier to reuse the logic in other scenes this way.

22

GAME CHARACTER ANIMATION USING ARMATURES

by Reevan McKay

The new armature system opens up new possibilities for character animation in the Blender game engine, but can be somewhat intimidating for new users. This tutorial guides you through the steps involved in building an armature and creating actions that can be used for smooth character animation in the game engine. Check the file Games/ePolice.blend for a decent example using the character from this tutorial.

Figure 22-1: Character animation in the game engine

22.1. Preparing the Mesh

This tutorial assumes you have already modeled a character that you want to use in an animation. Due to the high cost of calculating skeletal deformation, you will get better performance by using fewer vertices in your meshes. Thus, it pays to spend some time optimizing your models before continuing. You can use the file Tutorials/CharacterAnimation/animation_tut.blend as a basis for this tutorial.

Many aspects of Blender's game and animation engines depend on the fact that you have modeled your character and armature using the correct coordinate system. The FrontView (PAD1) should show the front of your character and armature. If this is not the case, rotate your mesh so that the front of the character is displayed in the FrontView, and apply the rotations as described in the next step.

NOTE   *Before adding bones and animating a mesh, it's a good idea to make sure that the base mesh object does not have any rotation or scaling on it. The easiest way to do this is to select the mesh and apply any existing transformations with CTRL-A > Apply size/rot.*

22.2. Working with Bones

The next step is to build the skeleton or *armature* that will be used to deform the character.

A single armature object can contain an entire hierarchy of bones, which makes editing animations easier. Add an armature object from the Toolbox by pressing the spacebar and then ADD > Armature as shown at right.

ADD	Mesh	>>
FILE	Curve	>>
EDIT	Surface	>>
OBJECT	Text	
OBJECT	MetaBall	
MESH	Empty	
CURVE		
KEY	Camera	
RENDER	Lamp	
VIEW	Armature	
	Lattice	

You will see a yellow bone appear. You can reposition its endpoint by moving the mouse. When you are more or less satisfied with its position (you can still edit it later), use the LMB to finalize the bone. At this point a new yellow bone will appear, attached to the end of the first bone.

You can continue to add connected bones in this fashion (see Figure 22-2). If you do not want to create another bone, press ESC to cancel the current (yellow) bone. The bones you added previously will not be affected.

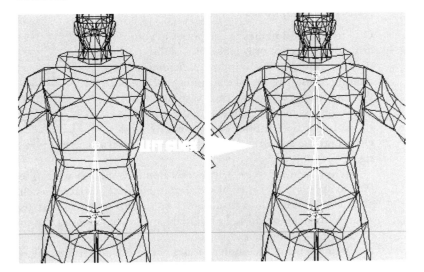

Figure 22-2: Adding bones

Armatures have an EditMode similar to meshes. You can determine whether you are in EditMode by looking at the EditMode icon in the 3DWindow Header. As with meshes, you can toggle in and out of EditMode using TAB.

While in EditMode, you can add and remove bones or adjust the rest position of existing bones. The rest position of your armature should correspond to the untransformed position of the mesh you want to deform, and you should build the armature inside the mesh, like a skeleton inside a human body.

While you are in EditMode, you can reposition a bone by selecting one or more of its endpoints and using the standard transformation tools such as scaling (SKEY), rotation (RKEY), and translation (GKEY). You can also extrude selected points to form new bones with EKEY.

You can choose one or more bones by selecting their startpoints and end-points. Like meshes, you can select all bone points within a region by using BKEY or deselect all bones in an armature with AKEY. You can also select an entire bone chain at once by moving the mouse over any one of the chain's points and pressing LKEY.

Delete selected bones with XKEY or duplicate them with SHIFT-D.

22.3. Creating Hierarchy and Setting Rest Positions

Now we'll create the hierarchy and set the rest positions. We begin by naming bones.

22.3.1. Naming bones

Give meaningful names to the bones in your armature. This not only makes it easier to navigate the hierarchy, but if you follow a few simple naming rules, you can take advantage of the pose-flipping features. You can then display the bone names on the model by selecting the armature, switching to the EditButtons window (F9) and clicking the green Draw Names button, as shown at right.

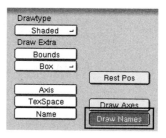

When naming symmetrical body elements such as arms or legs, it is a good idea to append .left or .right (or simply .l and .r) suffixes to each part. For example, name the right arm Arm.Right and the left one Arm.Left. Nonpaired limbs such as the head or chest do not need any special naming. This information is used when flipping poses.

When reusing the same action on different armatures, the engine looks at the names of the bones in the armature and the names of the animation channels in the action. When there is a perfect match (capitalization matters), the animation data in the action is applied to the appropriate bone.

NOTE   *To take advantage of action reuse, make sure that all your skeletons use the same naming convention.*

22.3.2. Parenting bones

To establish parenting relationships within an armature, you must first make sure the armature is in EditMode. To do so, select only the bones you wish to modify (or select all bones with AKEY) and switch to the EditButtons with F9. You will see a list (as shown in Figure 22-3) of the selected bones, and next to each bone in the list you will see a "child of" label and a pull-down menu.

NOTE   *Parenting is much easier if you have already named your bones, though it is not necessary.*

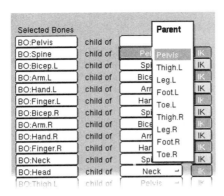

Figure 22-3: Parenting bones in the EditButtons

To make a bone the child of another bone, simply select the appropriate parent from the pull-down menu. To clear a parenting relationship, set the "child of" menu to the first (empty) choice in the menu.

NOTE *This menu contains only the names of bones that could be valid parents. This prevents you from accidentally making a loop in parents (such as making an arm the parent of the chest, which should be parent of the arm).*

Press the IK button (IK stands for *inverse kinematics*) next to the parenting menu to ensure that the root of the child is connected to the tip of the parent. This is not so important for game models (because the IK solver is not active in the game engine), it can be a useful way to define a bone "chain" that can be selected with LKEY.

22.3.3. Basic layout

For a typical humanoid character, the hierarchy shown in Figure 22-4 is recommended. Some characters may benefit from additional bones for elements such as flowing skirts or hair.

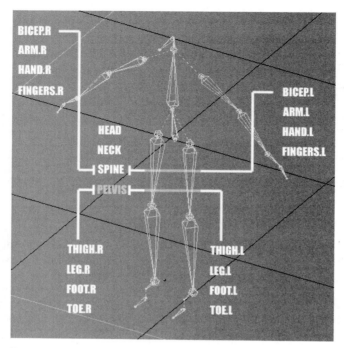

Figure 22-4: Typical bone layout for a humanoid character

22.3.4. Coordinate system conventions

Before continuing, it is a good idea to clear any rotation or scaling that you may have assigned to the armature. To do so, leave EditMode and with the armature object selected, apply the transformations with CTRL-A.

The center point of the armature (represented by a small yellow or purple dot) should be on the ground, between the character's feet. If it is not, enter EditMode for the armature, select all bones with AKEY, and move the bones so that the center point is at the correct location.

The final step before preparing the mesh for deformation is to ensure that the bones in the armature have consistent orientations. Each bone is like an individual object with its own coordinate system. You can see these coordinate systems by selecting the armature object, switching to the EditButtons with F9, and clicking the green Draw Axes button, shown at right.

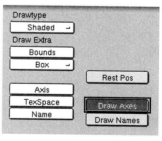

NOTE   *Generally you should make sure that the Z-axis for each bone points in a consistent direction. In most cases this means having the Z-axis point upward. You can adjust the roll angle of a bone by selecting it in EditMode, pressing NKEY, and adjusting the roll field.*

If you will be reusing actions on different armatures, it is very important that both armatures have their bones oriented in the same way. If they are not, you will see a lot of strange flipping when you assign the action.

22.4. Establishing Mesh Deformation Vertex Groups

22.4.1. Creating groups

Once your armature is established, it is time to specify which bones will affect which vertices of the mesh by using vertex groups. To access the vertex grouping features, select the mesh you will be deforming and enter EditMode. Switch to the EditButtons and find the Group column (shown in Figure 22-5).

Figure 22-5: Group buttons in the EditButtons

Normally you will have one vertex group for each bone in the armature. A vertex can belong to more than one group, which is how smooth deformation is achieved. In order to be recognized by the armature, the vertex groups must have exactly the same names as the bones they are associated with (capitalization matters).

To create a new vertex group, click the New button and edit the name in the text button that will appear. You can see a list of all of the current deformation groups by clicking the menu next to the group name button (Figure 22-6). Selecting an item from this menu changes the active deformation group.

Figure 22-6: Deformation groups

You can assign vertices to the currently active deformation group by selecting vertices and clicking the Assign button. The selected vertices will be assigned to the active group with the weight specified in the Weight slider. You can remove vertices from the current deformation group by selecting them and clicking the Remove button (shown at right).

Create vertex groups for all of the bones in your armature (making sure the names of the groups and bones match) and assign vertices to the appropriate groups. Make sure that every vertex is affected by at least one bone. For this "first pass" of the deformation process, try to keep things simple by leaving the weight set to 1.000, and avoid having vertices being assigned to more than one group.

22.4.2. Attaching the mesh to the armature

At this point, you are ready to attach the mesh to the armature. Make sure that the mesh and the armature are correctly aligned and that you are not in EditMode (Figure 22-7). Then, select the mesh first, and while holding SHIFT, select the armature and press CTRL-P > Use Armature.

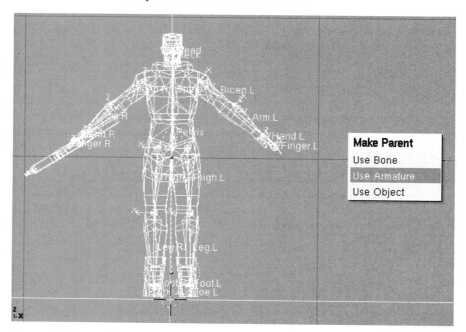

Figure 22-7: Lined up mesh and armature

22.4.3. Testing the skinning

Once you have attached the mesh to the armature, you are ready to start testing the deformation. It often takes a fair amount of tweaking to get satisfying results.

You want to avoid the excessive pinching or stretching that can occur when vertices are not assigned to the right bones. We'll spend more time on that later though. For now, we'll take a look at how to pose the armature, which is a skill needed for testing the deformation.

22.4.4. PoseMode

In addition to EditMode, armatures have a PoseMode (shown at right). This is used to position bones within the armature. Setting keyframes in PoseMode defines an "action" for the armature, and the game engine will use these actions to animate the character.

NOTE *Only transformations performed in PoseMode will be incorporated into the action (and therefore the game engine). Rotations, scalings, and translations performed in ObjectMode cannot be recorded in actions.*

You can toggle in and out of PoseMode by selecting an armature and pressing CTRL-TAB or by clicking on the PoseMode icon in the 3DWindow Header bar. When in PoseMode, the armature will be drawn in blue, with selected bones drawn in a lighter shade, as shown in Figure 22-8.

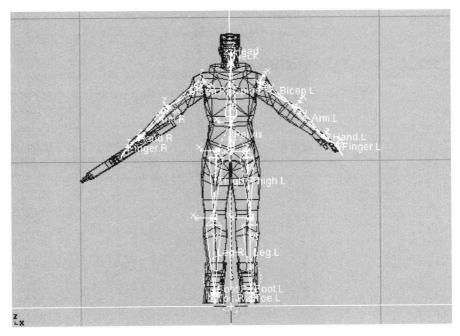

Figure 22-8: Armature in PoseMode

To manipulate bones in PoseMode, select bones with the RMB and use the standard transformation keys for scaling, rotation, and translation.

NOTE *You cannot add or remove bones in PoseMode, and you cannot edit the armature's hierarchy.*

At any time, you can clear the pose you have made and return to the armature's rest position by clearing the rotation, scaling, and translation components using ALT-R, ALT-S, and ALT-G respectively.

You can set keyframes for a pose by selecting one or more bones and pressing IKEY, and choosing one of the transformation channels to key from the pop-up menu (shown in Figure 22-9).

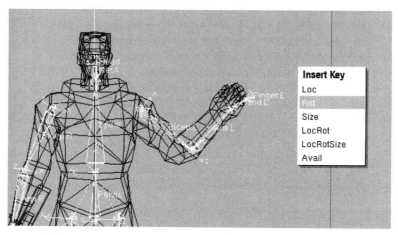

Figure 22-9: Selected Arm.L bone

22.5. Weight Editing

In PoseMode, manipulate the limbs of the armature through their typical range of motion and watch carefully to see how the mesh deforms. You should watch out for deformation artifacts caused by any of the following:

- Vertices that are not assigned to any bones can be easily detected by moving the root of the character's hierarchy (usually the hips or pelvis) and seeing if any vertices are left behind (see the following image).

- Vertices that are not connected to the correct bones. If you move a limb (such as the arm) and notice vertex "spikes" protruding from other parts on the body, you will have to enter EditMode for the mesh and remove the offending vertices from the vertex group (see below).

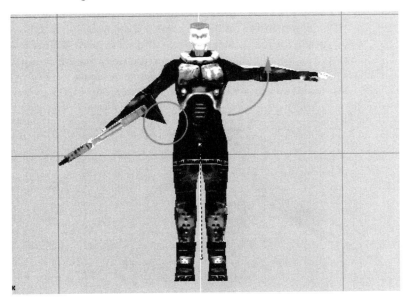

- Pinching or creasing caused by inappropriate vertex weighting. This effect is most visible in the joints of limbs such as arms and legs. Often it is a symptom of vertices that are members of too many groups. The easiest way to fix this is to use the weight painting tool (see the following page).

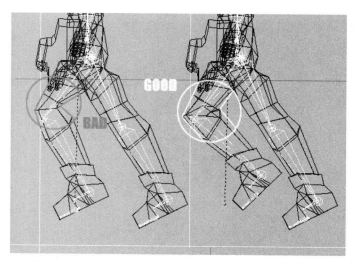

To adjust vertex weights, you have the choice of manually assigning weights using the method outlined above, or you can use the weight painting tool (shown at right). This feature lets you "paint" bone influence onto the mesh and see the resulting deformation in real time.

To use this feature, make sure you are in wireframe or untextured mode with ZKEY or SHIFT-Z. Then, access the weight-painting mode by selecting the mesh and clicking the weight-paint icon in the 3DWindow Header.

In weight-painting mode the mesh is displayed with a "false color" intensity spectrum similar to the view from an infrared camera (Figure 22-10). Blue areas have little or no influence from the current deformation group, while red areas have full influence. As you change the active deformation group in the EditButtons, you will see the coloring on the model change.

Figure 22-10: Weight-painted character

Painting weights onto the model works somewhat like vertex painting. The LMB paints onto the area beneath the cursor. Pressing UKEY undoes the last painting operation. The cursor size and opacity settings in the VertexPaintButtons determine your brush settings and the Weight field in the EditButtons (below) determines the color you are using (0.000 is the blue end of the spectrum, and 1.000 is red).

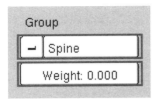

To remove weight from a group of vertices, set the vertex weight to 0.000 and paint over the area.

NOTE   *You do not need to have the mesh in EditMode to change the active deformation group or to change the weight.*

22.6. Animation

Animation is very important for conveying the impression of life in a game world and for giving the player an immediate reward for his or her decisions. Game characters typically have a set of animated actions they can perform, such as walking, running, crawling, making attacks, or suffering damage. With the armature system, you can design each animation in a separate action and define which actions play at which times using LogicBricks.

NOTE   *At this writing, animation constraints (including the IK Solver) do not work in the game engine. This means that game animation must be done using forward kinematics exclusively.*

22.6.1. Multiple actions and fake users

If you want to create multiple actions in a Blender file, remember that only one action can be assigned to an armature at a time; if the other actions do not have any users, they will not be saved when the file is saved. To prevent additional actions from disappearing, you can add fake users.

To create a fake user for an action, press SHIFT-F4 to browse the various objects and data blocks in the Blender file. You may need to click the P button once or twice to find the root of the file's structure, which should look like Figure 22-11.

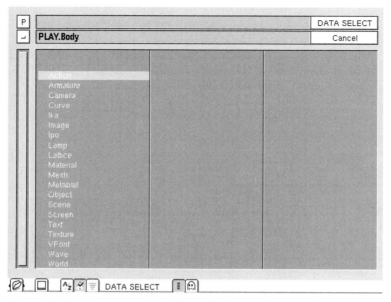

Figure 22-11: Structure of the file in the DataSelectWindow

From there, descend into the Action directory, and select the actions you want to protect with the RMB. Pressing FKEY will add a fake user to the selected items (indicated by the capital **F** that appears next to the action name), preventing them from being accidentally removed from the file.

22.6.2. Creating an idle cycle

The simplest action to create for a character is the idle or rest position. This action can be played when the character is not doing any other action. A good idle animation gives the game's character the illusion of life by keeping it moving even when the player is not actively issuing any control commands. (Since the character is not moving through the level while playing the idle animation, we don't have to worry about syncing the animation with the physics system.)

1. To create a new action, split the view by MMB-clicking one of the window borders, selecting Split Area, and LMB-clicking to set where the split will appear.
2. Change the type of the newly created window to ActionWindow by LMB-clicking the WindowType icon in the header and choosing the topmost icon (Figure 22-12).

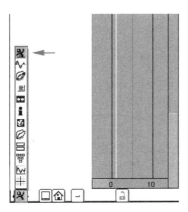

Figure 22-12: Switch to ActionWindow

3. Go to a 3DWindow and select the armature you wish to animate. Enter
    PoseMode and make sure that Blender is on frame 1 by changing the num-
    ber in the frame counter button in the header of the ButtonsWindow, or by
    using LEFTARROW and DOWNARROW.

You are now ready to make the first frame of the idle animation, using the
PoseMode techniques described earlier. What this pose looks like will depend
largely on the personality of your character and the type of game you are making.

Consider which actions might immediately follow the rest position. If the
character is supposed to be able to fire a weapon quickly, the rest position might
involve holding the weapon in a ready-to-fire stance. A less fast-paced game might
have the character adopt a more relaxed, at-ease pose.

1. When you are satisfied with the first frame, select all of the bones in Pose-
    Mode and insert a rotation key by pressing IKEY > Rot.

2. Next, deselect all bones and select only the character's root bone (usually
    the pelvis or hips) and insert a Loc key. Normally only the root bone gets
    location keys, while all bones get rotation keys.

When you insert keys, notice that new channels appear in the ActionWindow
(Figure 22-13). The yellow rectangles represent selected keyframes and grey
rectangles represent unselected keyframes. You can move keyframes in the
ActionWindow by selecting them and grabbing them with GKEY.

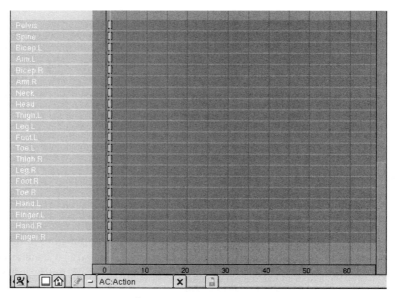

Figure 22-13: Keys in the ActionWindow

To delete keyframes select them and press XKEY > "Erase selected keys" (see below).

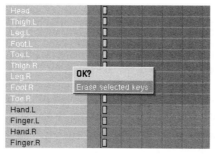

You can erase an entire action channel (all keyframes for a particular bone) by selecting one or more action channels by pressing SHIFT-RMB on the channel names in the column at the left. Selected channels are displayed in blue, while unselected channels are displayed in red. Pressing XKEY > "Erase selected channels" with the mouse over the channel list deletes the selected channels (see the following image).

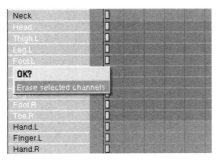

In order to create an action that loops smoothly, you will need to copy the first frame and duplicate it as the last frame of the animation. There are two main ways of doing this.

The first way is to select all of the bones in PoseMode and click the Copy Pose button. This will copy the transformations from the selected bones into a temporary buffer. You can paste the pose at another keyframe by changing the frame and clicking the Paste Pose button.

NOTE   *This doesn't necessarily set keyframes at the new point in time, unless you have activated the KeyAC option in the info window. If you have not activated KeyAC and you want to make keyframes after pasting the pose, you can press IKEY > Avail.*

The second way to copy a block of keyframes is even easier (see the following image). In the ActionWindow, select the vertical column of keyframes for all channels (hint: use BKEY to select with a bounding rectangle). Pressing SHIFT-D will duplicate the keyframes. You can move the block to a new point in the timeline and drop them by clicking the LMB. To ensure that the keyframes stay on whole frame increments, hold down CTRL while dragging.

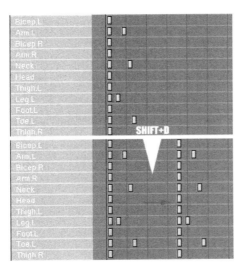

NOTE *Idle animations tend to be fairly long, because the motion involved is typically subtle and shouldn't be seen to loop too often. The last frame should be at least 100 or higher.*

While animating, you can "scrub" through the animation by holding the LMB and dragging the mouse in the ActionWindow. This will move the position of the green "current frame" indicator. In this way you can test parts of the animation to make sure they play smoothly. You can also play the whole animation by moving to the first frame and pressing ALT-A with the mouse over a 3DWindow. To see the animation in a loop, set the Sta and End values in the DisplayButtons (F10) window to match the start and end frames of your loop.

At this point you can go back in and add additional keyframes between the start and end. Remember to keep the motion reasonably subtle so that the player doesn't notice the repetitive nature of the action. Good elements to add are breathing effects, having the character adjust its grip on any weapons or equipment, and slight head turns.

When you are satisfied with the action, give it a name by editing the name field in the ActionWindow Header (below). Also make sure to create a fake user for the action to prevent it from disappearing from the file when you create your next action.

22.6.3. Creating a walk cycle

Another very important action is the character's walk cycle. This animation will be used when the character is moving through the level. This animation is somewhat more complicated, because we have to consider how the animation will interact with the physics system.

When creating the walk cycle, it is generally best to animate it in such a way that the character seems to be walking on a treadmill. The forward motion will be provided by the game's physics system at run time.

A walk cycle actually consists of two steps: one for the left foot and one for the right foot. For each step there are two main keyframes: the striking pose and the crossing pose (Figure 22-14).

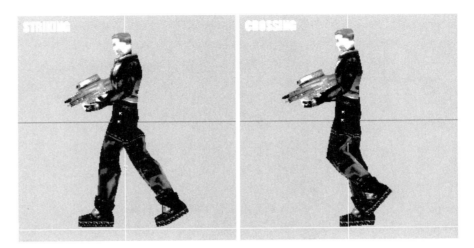

Figure 22-14: Striking and crossing

The striking pose represents the moment when one foot has just been planted on the ground and the other is about to be lifted. The crossing pose represents the moment when the two legs cross each other under the character's center of gravity: One foot is on the ground and moving backward, while the other is lifted and is moving forward.

Create the striking pose

To start creating this animation, switch to the ActionWindow and create a new blank action by clicking the Action menu and choosing Add New. This will create a copy of any action that may have already been on the character. Name the action and make sure the animation is blank by moving the mouse over the channel list, selecting all channels with AKEY, and deleting them with XKEY > "Erase selected channels".

For this animation, we'll make a 24-frame walk cycle. We'll set five keyframes to get a basic walking motion established. Once that's done you can go back and add additional keyframes to smooth out the motion and improve the animation (Figure 22-15).

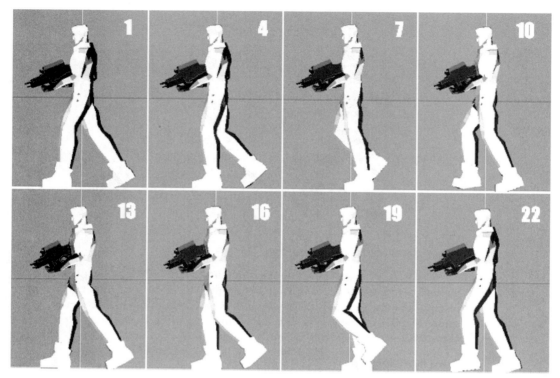

Figure 22-15: Keyframes for the walk cycle

We first set the striking pose for the left foot. This pose will be copied and pasted as the last frame of the action to ensure the animation loops smoothly.

NOTE   *If you later make changes to this first frame, copy those changes to the last frame again.*

The striking pose has the following characteristics:

- The leading leg is extended, and the foot is firmly on the floor.
- The trailing foot has the toes on the floor, and the heel has just left the ground.
- The pelvis is lowered to bring the feet down to the level of the floor.
- If the walk cycle incorporates arm swinging, the arms oppose the legs. If the left leg is advanced, the left arm will be swung back and vice versa.

When you are satisfied with the pose, insert rotation keyframes for all bones, and insert an additional location keyframe for the pelvis bone. Copy this pose to the end of the animation loop, which will be frame 25. (Frame 25 will not actually be played, however; we will end the loop at frame 24 when playing.) Since frame 25 is a duplicate of frame 1, the animation should play back seamlessly.

If you built the character's armature using the naming conventions and coordinate systems recommended earlier in the tutorial, you can take advantage of the character's axial symmetry by copying the striking pose and pasting it flipped. To do this, go to the first frame, and select all bones in PoseMode. Click the Copy Pose button and set the active frame to the middle of the animation (in this case, frame 13). To paste the pose, click the Paste Flipped button (shown below).

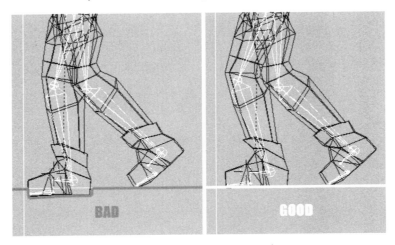

Set Avail keyframes for the appropriate bones.

NOTE *If your animation does not incorporate arm swinging (for example, if the character is carrying a weapon), you might choose to select the pelvis and legs only when copying and pasting the pose. Otherwise, the character will seem to switch the weapon from one hand to the other.*

Create the crossing pose

The next task is to create the crossing pose. The first one will occur halfway between the first frame of the animation and the flipped pose you just created, at frame 7. The crossing pose has the following characteristics:

- The planted foot is underneath the character's center of gravity.
- The lifted foot is crossing past the planted leg.
- The pelvis is raised to bring the feet up to the level of the floor.
- If the arms are swinging, the elbows will be crossing each other at this point.

Set Avail keyframes for all bones on this frame and copy the pose. Advance the active frame to halfway between the end of the animation and the second striking pose (frame 19) and paste the pose flipped.

At this point test your animation loop. It is a good idea to go in and look at it frame by frame with LEFTARROW and RIGHTARROW. If you see frames where the feet seem to push through the floor, adjust the height of the pelvis accordingly and set Loc keyframes, or adjust the rotation of the bones in the offending leg and set Rot keyframes for them (Figure 22-16).

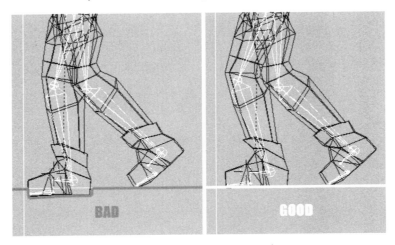

Figure 22-16: Bad positions of the character's legs

If you prefer working with IpoWindows, you can edit action channel Ipos directly, though this is not always required. To do this, select an action channel in the ActionWindow, make a window into an IpoWindow with SHIFT-F6 and click the ActionIpo icon in the IpoWindow Header (below).

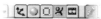

NOTE   *Action Ipos display rotations in quaternions instead of Euler angles. This gives nice, predictable results when working with complex combinations of rotations, but can be a bit unusual to work with. The best tactic is to set the action value of the quaternions by inserting Rot keyframes in PoseMode, and only using the IpoWindow to adjust the way the curves are interpolated.*

To view several different Ipos in different windows, you can use the pin icon in the IpoWindow Header buttons to prevent the displayed Ipo from changing when you change object selection (below).

When you are finished, make sure to add a fake user for this action to prevent it from getting lost when the file is saved.

22.7. Game Logic

When adding game logic to your character, make sure to put it on the armature object itself, rather than on the mesh.

If you are making your character a dynamic physics object, you may need to adjust the center point of the armature based on the size of the dynamic object to make sure that the character's feet touch the floor. The character's feet should touch the bottom of the dotted dynamic object sphere, as shown in Figure 22-17.

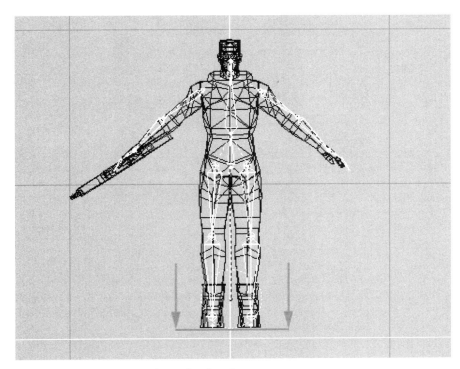

Figure 22-17: Dynamic object for the character

Generally speaking, you will need to add an action actuator for each different action that your character can perform. For each actuator, you will need to set the start and end frames of the animation, as well as the name of the action.

Since version 2.21, Blender has had the ability to create smooth transitions or to blend between different game actions. This makes the motion of game characters appear much more natural and avoids motion "popping." To access this functionality, all you have to do is adjust the Blending parameter in the action actuator. This field specifies how long it will take to blend from the previous action to the current one and is measured in animation frames. A value of 0 indicates that no blending should occur. Note that this blending effect is only visible in the game engine when the game is run (Figure 22-18).

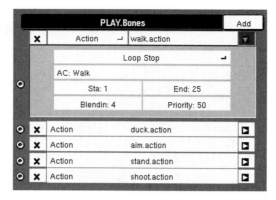

Figure 22-18: Blending actions

Action actuators have many of the same playback modes as Ipo actuators, including looping, playing, flippers, and property- driven playback.

You should try to design your game logic so that only one action is triggered at a time. When multiple actions are active at the same time, the game engine can display only one of them on any given frame. To help resolve ambiguity, you can use the Priority field in the action actuator. Actions with lower numbers will override actions with higher numbers.

23

BLENDERBALL

Blenderball is made by Joeri Kassenaar, based on an idea by W.P. van Overbruggen. It is an action puzzle game in which you have to guide a ball through a dangerous maze. The game play can extend from the original puzzle to a two-player game, or just an image puzzle.

In the Blenderball game (see Figure 23-1) you have to guide the balls through a maze, avoiding traps and dead ends. The goal is to fill all pockets at the end ring with balls.

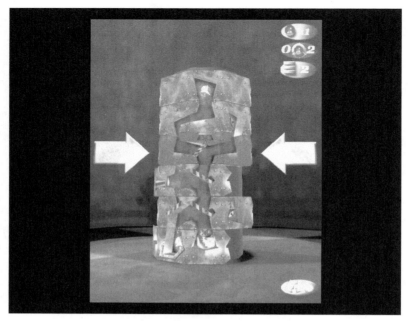

Figure 23-1: Blenderball game

Table 23-1 lists Blenderball's controls.

Table 23-1: Blenderball Controls

Controls	Description
LEFTARROW	Turn ring segment left
RIGHTARROW	Turn ring segment right
UPARROW	Go one ring segment up
DOWNARROW	Go one ring segment down
DEL	Turn camera left
PgDn	Turn camera right
AKEY	Toggle automatic camera tracking
CTRL	Track camera new

Table 23-2 lists the game's displays.

Table 23-2: Blenderball Displays

Display	Description
	Balls left to solve level
	Balls collected/balls needed to solve level

Table 23-2: Blenderball Displays

Display	Description
	Current level
	Auto camera/manual camera indicator

On the CD there are many assets you can use to start your own games based on Blenderball. Look in the folder Tutorials/Assets/Blenderball/ for commented sources of the Blender scenes, new images, and sounds.

23.1. Customize the Blenderball Image Puzzle

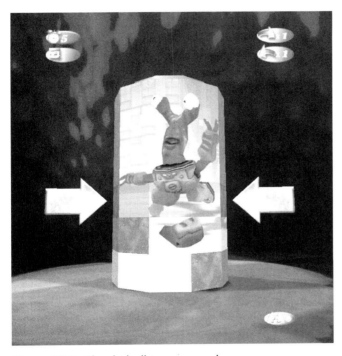

Figure 23-2: Blenderball image puzzle

Table 23-3 lists the Blenderball image puzzle controls.

Table 23-3: Blenderball Image Puzzle Controls

Controls	Description
LEFTARROW	Turn ring segment left
RIGHTARROW	Turn ring segment right
UPARROW	Go one ring segment up

Table 23-3: Blenderball Image Puzzle Controls

Controls	Description
DOWNARROW	Go one ring segment down
DEL	Turn camera left
PGDN	Turn camera right
AKEY	Toggle automatic camera tracking
CTRL	Track camera new

Table 23-4: Blenderball Image Puzzle Displays

Display	Description
	Time left to solve puzzle
	Current level
	Left turns available
	Right turns available
	Auto camera/manual camera indicator

Load Tutorials/Blenderball/Blenderball_imagegame_00.blend. This scene is ready for changing the images.

NOTE   *To play a game first, switch to the full-screen view by pressing CTRL-LEFTARROW and the start the game engine with PKEY. After that return to the editing layout by pressing CTRL-RIGHTARROW.*

Try to get all rings in a position that the image is shown correctly. Use the arrow keys to select the ring and rotate the ring's segment. There is a hard time limit.

Now, prepare the images you want to use in your favorite 2-D image manipulation program. Here are the guidelines to make images that fit into the game:

- Images have to be square, containing two images side by side, as shown here.

- For performance reasons you should not use textures bigger than 512 by 512 pixels in size.
- Blender can use Targa (.tga) and JPEG (.jpg) images.

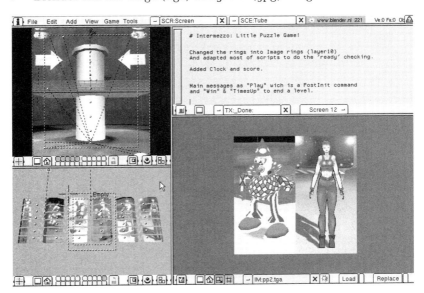

Figure 23-3: Screen to change images

Select one of the ring segments with the RMB in the lower left window. Now press FKEY to enter FaceSelectMode; the image to the right will update according to your selection. Now press the Replace button in the ImageWindow to choose a different image from the disk.

If your image meets the requirements mentioned before, it should now be on the rings and you can play your customized game.

23.2. Changing the Levels of the Blenderball Game

The Blenderball tutorials are in the advanced section for a good reason. If you have already had a look at the files, you saw that the game logic is very complex and mostly done with Python. It would have been possible to use the normal LogicBricks for most tasks, but this would have led to a file being very inflexible, hard to overlook, and difficult to change. Python gives us the option to create new levels by changing a few lines of code.

Load the Tutorials/Blenderball/Blenderball_00.blend file. Its window layout is configured to work on new levels. Use CTRL-RIGHTARROW and CTRL-LEFTARROW to switch between the folowing screens:

ChooseRings A screen to select and choose the rings. It also contains the Python script to where you can change the levels.

Play This is the full-screen view to play Blenderball.

Work A screen to play and change the Python level.

Switch to the screen Work and have a look at the TextWindow containing the InitRingRotation.py script, shown below.

Figure 23-4: Python list holding initial ring rotations

```
 1 # List that holds initial rotations (L=left, R=right), Level number, balls,
number of pockets
 2 mixed= [ "L0 R0 L0 R0 R0 R0 :01 :03 01",
 3          "R0 R0 R0 R0 R0 R1 :02 :03 02",
 4          "R1 R1 R1 L0 R1 R2 :03 :03 03",
 5          "R2 R2 R1 R2 L0 R2 :04 :05 03",
 6          "R3 R3 R1 R2 L1 L0 :05 :03 03",
 7          "L1 L1 L1 R2 R1 R2 :06 :05 03",
 8          "R4 L4 R4 L4 R4 L3 :07 :07 05",
 9          "L1 L1 R0 L2 L1 R2 :08 :06 05",
10          "L0 R0 L1 R2 L0 L2 :09 :05 05",
11          "R1 R1 R1 R2 L1 R2 :10 :07 05",
12          "L4 R4 L2 R2 R1 R2 :11 :07 06",
13        "R2 L2 L5 L1 R0 R1 :12 :07 07" ]
```

Look at the list called "mixed." It contains the initial rotations of the rings in the levels line by line. So line 2 in the script (first line of the list) is used for the first level. An L means rotation to the left, and an R to the right. The number behind the letter determines how many steps the ring is rotated.

Now change the first R0 in the first line to R1 and press PKEY with the mouse in the textured CameraView to start the game engine. Unlike with the unmodified game (there are no rotation of rings in the first level), the second ring is now rotated to the right one step (looking from top to base).

The numbers at the end of each line are: the level number, the number of balls you have available to solve the level and how many pockets in the last ring have to be filled to solve the level.

Figure 23-5: Python list for the ring layout

```
 1 # make a list of rings to spawn, originals are hidden in layer 8
 2 ring_name= [
 3     ["3RingIn",      "3RingWarpOut",  "3RingFlipIn",    "3RingFlipOut", "3Ring2FlipWarp",
"3RingEndM"],
 4     ["3RingIn",      "3RingWarpOut",  "3RingFlipIn",    "3RingKick",    "3Ring2FlipWarp",
"3RingEnd2"],
 5     ["3RingIn",      "3RingWarpOut",  "3RingExtraBall", "3RingFlipOut", "3RingWarpIn",
"3RingEnd3"],
 6     ["3RingIn",      "3RingWarpOut",  "3RingForceBall", "4RingSturn",   "3Ring2FlipWarp",
"3RingEnd3"],
 7     ["3RingIn",      "3RingFlipIn",   "3RingExtraForce","2RingSturn",   "3RingForceBall",
"5RingEnd3"],
 8     ["3RingInWarp",  "3RingForceBall","3RingKick",      "3RingFlipOut", "3RingWarpIn",
"3RingEnd3"],
 9     ["3RingIn",      "3RingKick",     "3RingFlipIn",    "3RingTruw",    "3RingSideFlip",
"8RingEnd5"],
10     ["3RingIn",      "3RingForceBall","3RingFlipIn",    "1RingTruw",    "3RingSturn",
"8RingEnd5"],
11     ["3RingIn",      "3RingKick",     "3RingFlipIn",    "3RingTruw",    "3RingSideFlip",
"8RingEnd5"],
12     ["3RingIn",      "3RingWarpOut",  "3RingFlipIn",    "1RingTruw",    "3RingWarpIn",
"8RingEnd7"],
13     ["3RingIn",      "3RingWarpOut",  "3RingExtraForce","3RingTruw",    "3Ring2FlipWarp",
"8RingEnd7"],
14     ["3RingWarpOut","3RingFlipIn",    "1RingTruw",      "3RingIn",      "3RingWarpIn",
"8RingEnd7"],
15     ["3RingIn",      "3RingFlipIn",   "3RingWarpOut",   "3RingTruw",    "3RingWarpIn",
"8RingEnd7"]
16         ]
17
```

The list in Figure 23-5 shows how the levels are made. Each ring has a unique name and you can assemble new levels.

Use the ChooseRings screen to look at the rings. When you select a ring you will see the name in the Header of the ButtonWindow (e.g. OB:3RingSideFlip). Use this name in the ring_name Python list. For example, change the first line of the ring_name list to:

```
1    ["3RingIn", "3RingWarpOut", "3RingKick", "3RingSideFlip","3Ring2FlipWarp", "3RingEndM"],
```

You can add completely new levels by adding new lines to both of the Python lists.

This tutorial shows how to use advanced Python scripting to build complex game logic. However, it also shows how easy it is to edit the game levels in just a few single lines of text. This can be done by anyone who knows how to use a text editor. Plus, it also helps when loading levels from a disk or even from the Internet. Last but not least, it provides a very flexible interface for a separate level editor! You don't have to deal with a complex file structure; simply produce a simple, human-readable text file.

PART SIX
REFERENCE

The reference section will be your guide to exploring
the Blender 3-D game engine further after following
the tutorials. To learn modeling and linear
animation, refer to *The Blender Book* (No Starch Press)
or *The Official Blender 2.0 Guide* (Premier Press).

24

BLENDER WINDOWS AND BUTTONS

This section describes the most important Blender windows and buttons you need in order to create interactive content. Because Blender is a fully integrated application for creating both linear animations and stills as well as real-time 3-D content, there are numerous buttons and window types that need to be explained. (To explore the linear capabilities of Blender, please see Section 29.5.)

24.1. The 3DWindow

The 3DWindow (Figure 24-1) is the most important window for working and navigating inside 3-D scenes. It is also used to play the interactive content. As such, a good knowledge of its options and capabilities will help you create your scenes and explore scenes from the CD.

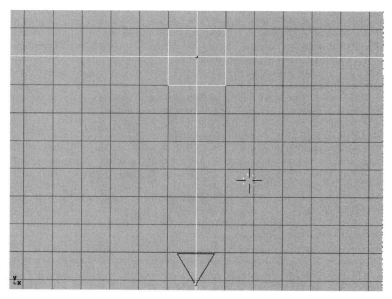

Figure 24-1: The 3DWindow canvas

The standard 3DWindow contains the following.

A grid

The dimensions (distance between the grid lines) and resolution (number of lines) can be set with the ViewButtons. This grid is drawn as infinite in the presets of ortho ViewMode (TopView, FrontView, RightView). In the other views, there is a finite "floor."

Many Blender commands are adjusted to the dimension of the grid, to function as a standard unit. Blender works best if the total "world" in which the user operates continually falls more or less within the total grid floor (whether it is a space war or a logo animation).

Axes in color codes

The reddish line is the X-axis, the green line is the Y-axis, and the blue line is the Z-axis. In the Blender universe, the "floor" is normally formed by the X- and Y-axes. The height and "depth" run along the Z-axis.

A 3D-Cursor

This is drawn as a black cross with a red and white striped circle. An LMB click moves the 3D-Cursor. Use the SnapMenu (SHIFT-S) to give the 3D-Cursor a specific location. New objects are placed at the 3D-Cursor location.

Layers (visible in the header buttons)

Objects in "hidden" layers are not displayed. All hotkey commands and tools in Blender take the layers into account: Objects in the hidden layers are treated as not selected. (See the following paragraph as well.)

ViewButtons

Separate variables can be set for each 3DWindow (e.g., for the grid or the lens). Use the SHIFT-F7 hotkey or the WindowType button in the 3DHeader. The ViewButtons are explained in detail elsewhere in this manual.

24.1.1. 3DHeader

WindowType (IconMenu)

As with every window header, the first button allows you to set the window type.

Full Window (IconTog)

Maximize the window, or return it to its original size; return to the old screen setting. Hotkey: ALT-CTRL+UPARROW.

Home (IconBut)

All objects in the visible layers are displayed completely, centered in the window. Hotkey: HOMEKEY.

Layers (TogBut)

These 20 buttons show the available layers.

In fact, a layer is nothing more than a visibility flag. This is an extremely efficient method for testing object visibility. This allows the user to divide the work functionally. For example: Cameras are placed in layer 1, temporary objects in layer 20, lamps in layers 1, 2, 3, 4 and 5, and so on. All hotkey commands and tools in Blender take the layers into account. Objects in "hidden" layers are treated as unselected.

- Use the LMB for the buttons; SHIFT-LMB for extended selecting of layers.
- Hotkeys: 1KEY, 2KEY, etc. 0KEY, MINUSKEY, EQUALKEY for layers 1,2,3,4, etc. Use ALT-(1KEY, 2KEY, ... 0KEY) for layers 11, 12, ... 20. Here, as well, use SHIFT-hotkey for extended select.

Lock (TogBut)

Every 3DWindow has its own layer setting and active camera. This is also true for a scene: Here it determines which layers — and which camera — are used to render a picture. The lock option links the layers and camera of the 3DWindow to the scene and vice versa: The layers and camera of the scene are linked to the 3DWindow.

This method passes a layer change directly to the Scene and to all other 3DWindows with the Lock option on. Turn the Lock off to set a layer or camera exclusively for the current 3DWindow. All settings are immediately restored by turning the button back on.

LocalView (IconTog)

LocalView allows the user to continue working with complex scenes. The currently selected objects are taken separately, centered, and displayed completely. The use of 3DWindow layers is temporarily disabled. Reactivating this option restores the display of the 3DWindow in its original form.

If a picture is rendered from a LocalView, only the objects present are rendered plus the visible lamps, according to the layers that have been set. Activating a new camera in LocalView does not change the camera used by the scene.

Normally, LocalView is activated with the hotkey PAD/.

ViewMode (IconMenu)

A 3DWindow offers three methods for 3-D display:

Orthonormal Blender offers this method from every view, not just from the
X-, Y-, or Z-axes.

Perspective You can toggle between orthonormal and perspective with the hotkey PAD5.

Camera This is the view as rendered. Hotkey: PAD0.

View Direction (IconMenu)

These presets can be used with either ortho or perspective. Respectively, these are the:

TopView, hotkey PAD7.

FrontView, hotkey PAD1.

RightView, hotkey PAD3.

The hotkeys combined with SHIFT or (CTRL) give the opposite view direction (DownView, BackView, LeftView).

Draw Mode (IconMenu)

Set the drawing method. Respectively:

Bounding box. The quickest method for animation previews, for example.

Wireframe. Objects are drawn with lines.

Solid. Z-buffered with the standard OpenGL lighting. Hotkey: ZKEY; this toggles between wireframe and solid.

Shaded. This is as good an approach as is possible to the manner in which Blender renders, with Gouraud shading. It displays the situation from a single frame of the camera. Hotkey: SHIFT-Z. Use CTRL-Z to force a recalculation of the view.

Textured. Real-time textures (UV textures) are shown.

Objects have their own draw type, independent of the window setting (see EditButtons > DrawType). The rule is that the minimum DrawMode is displayed.

View Move (IconBut, click-hold)

Move the mouse for a view translation. This is an alternative to SHIFT-MMB.

View Zoom (IconBut, click-hold)

Move the mouse vertically to zoom in and out of the 3DWindow. This is an alternative to CTRL-MMB.

These buttons determine the manner in which the objects (or vertices) are rotated or scaled.

Around center (IconRow) The midpoint of the bounding box is the center of rotation or scaling. Hotkey: COMMAKEY.

Around median (IconRow) The median of all objects or vertices is the center of rotation or scaling.

Around cursor (IconRow) The 3D-Cursor is the midpoint of rotation or scaling. Hotkey: DOTKEY.

Around individual centers (IconRow) All objects rotate or scale around their own midpoints. In EditMode all vertices rotate or scale around the object midpoint.

EditMode (IconTog)

This button starts or terminates EditMode. Hotkey: TAB or ALT-E.

Vertex Paint (IconTog) This button starts or terminates Vertex Paint Mode. Hotkey: VKEY.

FaceSelect (IconTog) This button starts or the FaceSelectMode. Hotkey: FKEY.

Proportional vertex editing tool (IconTog) The proportional vertex editing tool can be activated with the icon in 3DWindow Header, or OKEY.

The proportional editing tool is available in EditMode for all object types. This tool works like a magnet; you select a few vertices and while editing (grab, rotate, scale) the surrounding vertices move proportionally with it. Use the PAD+ and PAD- keys to adjust the area of influence; this can be done "live" while editing.

You can choose between a sharp falloff and a smooth falloff.

OpenGL renderer (IconTog) An LMB click renders the current view in OpenGL. CTRL-LMB renders a animation in OpenGL. The rendered pictures are saved as in the DisplayButtons indicated.

24.1.2. The mouse

The mouse provides the most direct access to the 3DWindow. Below is a complete overview:

LMB

Position the 3D-Cursor.

CTRL-LMB

In EditMode: Create a new vertex.

LMB (click-hold-draw)

These are the gestures. Blender's gesture recognition works in three ways:

- Draw a straight line: start translation mode (Grabber).
- Draw a curved line: start rotation mode.
- Draw a V-shaped line: start scaling mode.

MMB (click-hold)

Rotate the direction of view of the 3DWindow. This can be done in two ways (and can be set in the UserMenu):

- *The trackball method.* In this case, your starting position in the window when you start the mouse movement is important. The rotation can be compared to rotating a ball, as if the mouse grasps and moves a tiny miniscule point on a ball. If the movement starts in the middle of the window, the view rotates along the horizontal and vertical window axes. If the movement begins at the edge of the window, the view rotates along the axis perpendicular to the window.

- *The turntable method.* A horizontal mouse movement always results in a rotation around the global Z-axis. Vertical mouse movements are corrected for the view direction and result in a combination of (global) X- and Y-axis rotations.

SHIFT-MMB (click-hold)

Translate the 3DWindow. Mouse movements are always corrected for the view direction.

CTRL-MMB (click-hold)

Zoom in or out on the 3DWindow.

RMB

Select objects or (in EditMode) vertices. The last one selected is also the active one. This method guarantees that a maximum of one object and one vertex are always selected. This selection is based on graphics (the wireframe).

SHIFT-RMB

Extend select objects or (in EditMode) vertices. The last one selected is also the active one. Multiple objects or vertices may also be selected. This selection is based on graphics too (the wireframe).

CTRL-RMB

Select objects on the object centers. Here the wireframe drawing is not taken into account. Use this method to select a number of identical objects in succession or to make them active.

SHIFT-CTRL-RMB

Extend select objects. The last object selected is also the active one. Multiple objects can be selected.

RMB (click-hold-move)

Select and start translation mode, the Grabber. This works with all the selection methods mentioned.

24.1.3. Numeric Keypad (PAD)

The numeric keypad on the keyboard is reserved for view-related hotkeys. Below is a description of all the keys with a brief explanation.

PAD/

LocalView. The objects selected when this command is invoked are taken separately and displayed completely, centered in the window. (See the description of 3DHeader > LocalView.)

PAD*

Copy the rotation of the active object to the current 3DWindow. This works as if this object is the camera, without including the translation.

PAD-, PAD+

Zoom in, zoom out. This also works for CameraView.

PAD.

Center and zoom in on the selected objects. The view is changed in a way that can be compared to the LocalView option.

PAD5

Toggle between perspective and orthonormal mode.

PAD9

Force a complete recalculation (of the animation systems) and draw again.

PAD0

View from the current camera or from the object that is functioning as the camera.

CTRL-PAD0

Make the active object the camera. Any object can be used as the camera. Generally, a camera object is used. It can also be handy to let a spotlight function temporarily as a camera when directing and adjusting it.

ALT-PAD0 reverts to the previous camera. Only camera objects are candidates for the "previous camera" command.

PAD7

TopView. (along the negative Z-axis, Y up)

SHIFT-PAD1

DownView. (along the positive Z-axis, Y up)

PAD1

FrontView. (along the positive Y-axis, Z up)

SHIFT-PAD1

BackView. (along the negative Y-axis, Z up)

PAD3

RightView. (along the negative X-axis, Z up)

SHIFT-PAD3

LeftView. (along the positive X-axis, Z up)

PAD2, PAD8

Rotate using the turntable method. Depending on the view, this is a rotation around the X- and Y-axes.

PAD4, PAD6

Rotate using the turntable method. This is a rotation around the Z-axis.

SHIFT-(PAD2, PAD8)

Translate up or down; correct for the current view.

SHIFT-(PAD4, PAD6)

Translate up or down; correct for the view.

24.2. IpoWindow

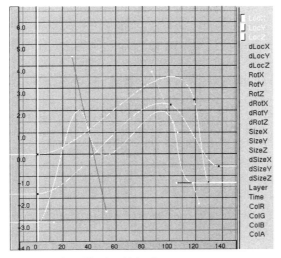

Figure 24-2: The IpoWindow

The IpoWindow allows you to visualize and manipulate animation curves that can control nearly every aspect of an animation inside Blender. For the Blender game engine, the most important aspects are the positions or rotations of objects and the color of objects.

24.2.1. IpoHeader

WindowType (IconMenu)

As with every window header, the first button enables you to set the window type.

> **Full window (IconTog)** Maximize the window or return it to the previous window display size; return to the old screen setting. Hotkey: (ALT-)CTRL-UPARROW.

> **Home (IconBut)** All visible curves are displayed completely, centered in the window. Hotkey: HOMEKEY.

IpoKeys (IconTog)

This is a drawing mode for the animation curves in the IpoWindow (the IpoCurves). Yellow vertical lines are drawn through all the vertices of the curves. Vertices of different curves at the same location in "time" are joined together and can easily be selected, moved, copied, or deleted. This method adds the ease of traditional keyframing to the animation curve system.

For object Ipos, these IpoKeys can also be drawn and transformed in the 3DWindow. Changes in the 3-D position are processed immediately in the IpoCurves.

Ipo type

Depending on the active object, the various Ipo systems can be specified with these buttons.

> **Object Ipo (IconRow)** Settings, such as the location and rotation, are animated for the active object. All objects in Blender can have this Ipo block.
>
> **Material Ipo (IconRow)** Settings of the active material are animated for the active object.
>
> A NumBut is added as an extra feature. This button indicates the number of the active texture channel. Eight textures, each with its own mapping, can be assigned per material. Thus, per material Ipo, eight curves in the row "OfsX, OfsY, . . . Var" are available.
>
> **Speed Ipo (IconRow)** If the active object is a path curve, this button can be used to display the speed Ipo.
>
> **Lamp Ipo (IconRow)** If the active object is a lamp, this button can be used to animate light settings.
>
> **World Ipo (IconRow)** This is used to animate a number of settings for the WorldButtons.
>
> **VertexKey Ipo (IconRow)** If the active object has a vertex key, the keys are drawn as horizontal lines. Only one IpoCurve is available to interpolate between the keys.
>
> **Sequence Ipo (IconRow)** The active sequence effect can have an IpoCurve.
>
> The DataButtons can be used to control the Ipo blocks themselves.

Ipo browse (MenuBut)

Choose another Ipo from the list of available Ipos. The option Add New makes a complete copy of the current Ipo. This is not visible; only the name in the adjacent button will change. Only Ipos of the same type are displayed in the menu list.

> **IP: (TextBut)** Give the current Ipo a new and unique name. After the new name is entered, it appears in the list, sorted alphabetically.
>
> **Users (NumBut)** If this button is displayed, there is more than one user for the Ipo block. Use the button to make the Ipo Single User.
>
> **Unlink Ipo (IconBut)** The current Ipo is unlinked.

Copy to buffer (IconBut)

All selected IpoCurves are copied to a temporary buffer.

Paste from buffer (IconBut)

All selected channels in the IpoWindow are assigned an IpoCurve from the temporary buffer. The rule is: the sequence in which they are copied to the buffer is the sequence in which they are pasted. A check is made to see if the number of IpoCurves is the same.

> **Extend mode constant (IconBut)** The end of selected IpoCurves are horizontally extrapolated.
>
> **Extend mode direction (IconBut)** The ends of selected IpoCurves continue extending in the direction in which they end.
>
> **Extend mode cyclic (IconBut)** Repeasts the full length of the IpoCurve cyclically.
>
> **Extend mode cyclic extrapolation (IconBut)** The full length of the IpoCurve is extrapolated cyclically.

> **View zoom (IconBut, click-hold)** Move the mouse horizontally or vertically to zoom in or out on the IpoWindow. This is an alternative to CTRL-MMB.
>
> **View border (IconBut)** Draw a rectangle to indicate what part of the IpoWindow should be displayed in the full window.

> **Lock (TogBut)** This button locks the update of the 3DWindow while editing in the IpoWindow, so you can see changes made to the Ipo in real time in the 3DWindow. This option works extremely well with relative vertex keys.

24.2.2. IpoWindow

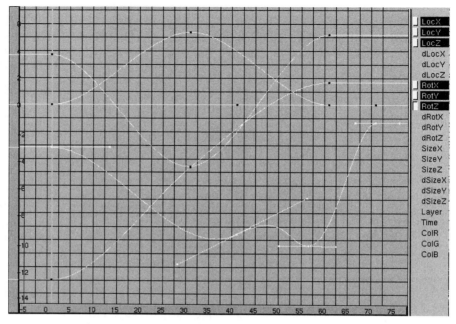

Figure 24-3: The IpoWindow

The IpoWindow shows the contents of the Ipo block. Which one depends on the Ipo type specified in the header.

The standard IpoWindow has a grid with the time expressed horizontally in frames and vertical values that depend on the channel. There are two sliders at the edge of the IpoWindow. How far the IpoWindow is zoomed in can be seen on the sliders, which can also be used to move the view. The righthand part of the window shows the available channels.

To make it easier to work with rotation IpoCurves, they are displayed in degrees (instead of in radials). The vertical scale relation is: 1.0 Blender unit = 10 degrees.

In addition to the IpoCurves, the vertex keys are also drawn here. These are horizontal blue lines; the yellow line visualizes the reference key.

Each channel can be operated with two buttons:

IpoCurve select (TogBut) This button is displayed only if the channel has an IpoCurve. The button is the same color as the IpoCurve. Use the button to select IpoCurves. Multiple buttons can be (de)selected using SHIFT-LMB.

Channel select (TogBut) A channel can be selected whether there is an IpoCurve or not. IpoCurves are drawn only for selected channels. Multiple channels can be (de)selected using SHIFT-LMB.

24.2.3. The mouse

CTRL-LMB

Create a new vertex. These are the rules:

- There is no Ipo block (in this window) and one channel is selected: a new Ipo block is created along with the first IpoCurve with one vertex.
- There is already an Ipo block, and a channel is selected without an IpoCurve: a new IpoCurve with one vertex is added.
- Otherwise a new vertex is simply added to the selected IpoCurve.

  This is not possible if multiple IpoCurves are selected or if you are in EditMode.

MMB (hold-move)

Depending on the position within the window:

- On the channels; if the window is not high enough to display them completely, the visible part can be shifted vertically.
- On the sliders; these can be moved. This only works if you are zoomed in.
- For the rest of the window; the view is translated.

CTRL-MMB (hold-move)

Zoom in or out on the IpoWindow. You can zoom horizontally or vertically using horizontal and vertical mouse movements.

RMB

Selection works the same here as in the 3DWindow: normally one item is selected. Use SHIFT to expand or reduce the selection (extend select).

- If the IpoWindow is in IpoKey mode, the IpoKeys can be selected.
- If at least one of the IpoCurves is in EditMode, only its vertices can be selected.
- Vertex keys can be selected if they are drawn (horizontal lines).
- The IpoCurves can be selected.

RMB (click-hold-move)

Select and start translation mode (i.e., the Grabber). The selection can be made using any of the four selection methods discussed above.

SHIFT-RMB

Extend the selection.

24.3. EditButtons

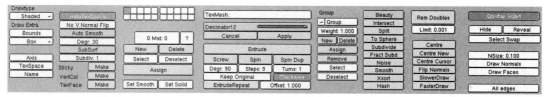

Figure 24-4: The EditButtons (F9)

The settings in this ButtonsWindow visualize the ObData blocks and provide tools for the specific EditModes. Certain buttons are redrawn depending on the type of ObData. The types that can be used in the Blender game engine are: mesh, empty, armature, lamp, and camera. Options and buttons that are not appropriate for the Blender game engine are not described here.

The DataButtons in the header specify which block is visualized. Mesh is used as an example here, but the use of the other types of ObData is identical.

Mesh Browse (MenuBut)

Selects another mesh from the list provided.

ME (TextBut)

Gives the current block a new and unique name. The new name is inserted in the list and sorted alphabetically.

Users (But)

If the block is used by more than one object, this button shows the total number of objects. Press the button to change this to Single User. An exact copy is then created.

OB (TextBut)

Gives the current object a new and unique name. The new name is inserted in the list and sorted alphabetically.

This group of buttons specifies object characteristics.

DrawType (MenuBut)

Choose a preference for the standard display method used in the 3DWindow from the list provided. The DrawType is compared with the DrawMode set in the 3DHeader; the least complex method is the one actually used. The types, listed in increasing degrees of complexity, are:

Bounds. A bounding object is drawn in the dimensions of the object.

Wire. The wire model is drawn.

Solid. Z-buffered with the standard OpenGL lighting.

Shaded. This display, which uses Gouraud shading, is the best possible way to view the manner in which Blender renders. It depicts the situation of a single frame from the camera's point of view. Use CTRL-Z to force a recalculation.

The Draw Extra options are displayed above the selected DrawType.

Bounding box (TogBut)

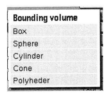

A bounding object is displayed in the dimensions of the object.

Box (MenuBut)

With this MenuButton you can choose between different bound objects.

Axis (TogBut)

The axes are drawn with X, Y, and Z indicated.

Name (TogBut)

The name of the object is printed at the object center..

Set Smooth (But)

This sets a flag that specifies that rendering must be performed with normal interpolation. In EditMode, it works on the selection. Outside EditMode everything becomes Smooth.

Set Solid (But)

This sets a flag that indicates that rendering must be Solid. In EditMode this works on the selection. Outside EditMode everything becomes Solid.

24.3.1. EditButtons, mesh

AutoTexSpace (TogBut)

This option automatically calculates the texture area, after leaving EditMode. You can also specify a texture area yourself (outside EditMode, in the 3DWindow; TKEY), in which case this option is turned off.

No V.Normal Flip (TogBut)

Because Blender normally renders faces double-sided, the direction of the normals (toward the front or the back) is automatically corrected during rendering. This option turns this automatic correction off, allowing smooth rendering of faces that have sharp angles (smaller than 100 degrees).

Be sure the face normals are consistently set in the same direction (CTRL-N in EditMode). The direction of the normals is especially important for real-time models, because the game engine renders them single-sided for reasons of speed.

Auto Smooth (TogBut)

Automatic smooth rendering (not faceted) for meshes. This is especially interesting for imported meshes created in other 3-D applications.

The button Set Smooth also has to be activated to make Auto Smooth work. The smoothing isn't displayed in the 3DWindow.

Degr: (NumBut)

Determines the degree to which faces can meet and still get smoothed out by Auto Smooth.

Make VertCol (But)

A color can be specified per vertex. This is required for the VertexPaint option.

If the object DrawType is shaded, these colors are copied to the vertex colors. This allows you to achieve a radiosity-like effect (set MaterialButtons > VertCol on). If the mesh is double-sided, this is automatically turned off.

Make TexFace (But)

Assigns a texture per face. This will be set automatically when you use the UV-Editor to texture a real-time model. Unchecking this option clears all UV coordinates.

Decimator (NumSli)

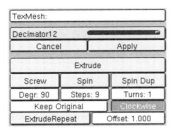

This slider will reduce your mesh faces to the number you indicate with the slider. Watch your mesh closely to see if the number of faces you demand is still enough to retain the desired shape.

NOTE *Mesh decimation will remove UV coordinates and vertex colors!*

Cancel (Button)

Resets the mesh to its original state before decimation.

Apply (Button)

Decimates according to the value indicated in the decimation slider. After using Apply there is no way back!

Extrude (But)

The most important of the mesh tools: Extrude Selected. In EditMode Extrude converts all selected edges to faces. If possible, the selected faces are also duplicated.

Grab mode starts immediately after this command is executed. If there are multiple 3DWindows, the mouse cursor changes to a question mark.

Click in the 3DWindow in which Extrude must be executed. Hotkey: EKEY.

Screw (But)

This tool starts a repetitive Spin with a screw-shaped revolution on the selected vertices. You can use this to create screws, springs, or shell-shaped structures.

Spin (But)

The Spin operation is a repetitively rotating Extrude. This can be used in every view of the 3DWindow; the rotation axis always goes through the 3D-Cursor, perpendicular to the screen. Set the buttons Degr and Steps to the desired value.

If there are multiple 3DWindows, the mouse cursor changes to a question mark. Click in the 3DWindow in which the Spin must occur.

Spin Dup (But)

Like Spin, but instead of an Extrude, there is duplication.

Degr (NumBut)

The number of degrees by which the Spin revolves.

Steps (NumBut)

The total number of Spin revolutions, or the number of steps of the Screw per revolution.

Turns (NumBut)

The number of revolutions the Screw turns.

Keep Original (TogBut)

This option saves the selected original for a Spin or Screw operation. This releases the new vertices and faces from the original piece.

Clockwise (TogBut)

The direction of the Screw or Spin can be clockwise or counterclockwise.

Extrude Repeat (But)

This creates a repetitive Extrude along a straight line. This takes place perpendicular to the view of the 3DWindow.

Offset (NumBut)

The distance between each step of the Extrude Repeat. Hotkey: WKEY.

Vertex Group Buttons

This group of buttons is meant for assigning vertices and weights to the bones of an armature. Besides the Weight button all options are only drawn when the active object is in EditMode.

Group Browse (MenuBut)

Browse the defined groups of vertices for this mesh. The text button shows the actual vertex group name. LMB-click to edit the name.

Weight (NumBut)

Sets the weight for groups and for use in WeightPaint.

New (But)

Creates a new vertex group.

Delete (But)

Deletes the actual vertex group.

Assign (But)

Assigns the selected vertices to the actual group.

Remove (But)

Removes selected vertices from the actual group.

Select (But)

Selects all vertices from the actual group.

Deselect (But)

Deselects all vertices from the actual group.

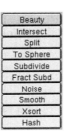

Intersect (But)

Select the faces (vertices) that need an intersection and press this button. Blender now intersects all selected faces with each other.

Split (But)

In EditMode, this command splits the selected part of a mesh without removing faces. The split sections are no longer connected by edges. Use this to control smoothing.

Because the split parts can have vertices in the same position, we recommend that you make selections with the LKEY. Hotkey: YKEY.

To Sphere (But)

All selected vertices are blown up into a spherical shape, with the 3D-Cursor as a midpoint. A requester asks you to specify the factor for this action. Hotkey: WKEY.

Beauty (TogBut)

This is an option for Subdivide. It splits the faces into halves lengthwise, converting elongated faces to squares. If the face is smaller than the value of Limit, it is no longer subdivided.

Subdivide (But)

Selected faces are divided into quarters; all edges are split in half. Hotkey: WKEY.

Fract Subd (But)

Fractal Subdivide. Like Subdivide, but now the new vertices are set with a random vector up or down. A requestor asks you to specify the amount. Use this to generate landscapes or mountains.

Noise (But)

Here textures can be used to move the selected vertices up a specific amount. The local vertex coordinate is used as the texture coordinate. Every texture type works with this option. For example, the Stucci produces a landscape effect. You can also use image textures to express them in relief.

Smooth (But)

This shortens all edges with both vertices selected and also flattens sharp angles. Hotkey: WKEY.

Xsort (But)

Sorts the vertices in the X direction. This creates interesting effects with (relative) vertex keys or build effects for halos.

Hash (But)

This makes the sequence of vertices completely random.

Rem Doubles (But)

Remove Doubles. All selected vertices that are closer to one another than the Limit are combined and redundant faces are removed.

Centre (But)

Each ObData has its own local 3-D space. The null point of this space is placed at the object center. This option calculates a new, centered null point in the ObData.

Centre New (But)

As above, but now the object is placed in such a way that the ObData appears to remain in the same place.

Centre Cursor (But)

The new null point of the object is the 3D-Cursor location.

Flip Normals (But)

Toggles the direction of the face normals. Hotkey: WKEY.

SlowerDraw, FasterDraw (But)

When leaving EditMode all edges are tested to determine whether they must be displayed as a wireframe. Edges that share two faces with the same normal are never displayed. This increases the "recognizability" of the mesh and considerably speeds up drawing. With SlowerDraw and FasterDraw, you can specify that additional or fewer edges must be drawn when you are not in EditMode.

Double Sided (TogBut)

Only for display in the 3DWindow, this can be used to control whether double-sided faces are drawn. You should turn this option off if the object has a negative size value (for example, an X-flip).

Hide (But)

All selected vertices are temporarily hidden. Hotkey: HKEY.

Reveal (But)

This undoes the Hide option. Hotkey: ALT-H.

Select Swap (But)

Toggles the selection status of all vertices.

NSize (NumBut)

The length of the face normals, if they have been drawn.

Draw Normals (NumBut)

Indicates that the face normals must be drawn in EditMode.

Draw Faces (NumBut)

Indicates that the face must be drawn (as wire) in EditMode. Now it also indicates whether faces are selected.

AllEdges (NumBut)

After leaving EditMode, all edges are drawn normally without optimization.

24.3.2. EditButtons, armatures

Rest Pos (But)

Disables all animation and puts the armature into its initial (resting) position.

Draw Axes (But)

Draw bone axes.

Draw Names (But)

Draw bone names.

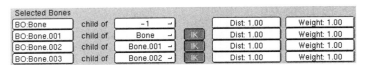

Buttons to name, organize, and build hierarchies of bones. See also Section 22.3.

24.3.3. EditButtons, camera

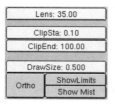

Lens (NumBut)

This number is derived from the lens values of a photo camera: 120 is telelens; 50 is normal; 28 is wide angle.

ClipSta, ClipEnd (NumBut)

Everything visible from the camera's point of view between these values is rendered. (Try to keep these values close to one another, so that the Z-buffer functions optimally.)

DrawSize (NumBut)

The size in which the camera is drawn in the 3DWindow.

Ortho (TogBut)

A camera can also render orthogonally. The distance from the camera then has no effect on the size of the rendered objects.

ShowLimits (TogBut)

A line that indicates the values of ClipSta and ClipEnd is drawn in the 3DWindow near the camera.

ShowMist (TogBut)

A line that indicates the area of the mist (see WorldButtons, Section 24.5) is drawn near the camera in the 3DWindow.

24.4. EditMode

When working in 3-D space, you can basically perform two types of operations: ones that affect the whole object and ones that affect only the geometry of the object itself but not its global properties (such as the location or rotation).

In Blender you switch between these two modes with the TAB key. A selected object outside EditMode is drawn in purple in the 3DWindows (in wireframe mode). To indicate the EditMode the object's vertices are drawn. Selected vertices are yellow; nonselected are purple.

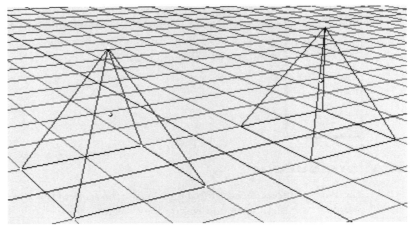

Vertices can be selected like objects with the RMB; holding SHIFT allows you to select more than one vertex. With some vertices selected you can use GKEY, RKEY, or SKEY for manipulating the vertices as you would for whole objects.

1. Add a cube to the default scene. Use the 3D-Cursor to place it away from the default plane or use GKEY to move it after leaving EditMode.

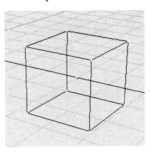

2. Switch the 3DWindow to a side view (PAD3), select the cube if it is deselected, and press TAB to enter the EditMode again.

3. Now press BKEY for the BorderSelect and draw a rectangle with the LMB around the top four vertices of the cube (you can only see two vertices, because the other two are hidden behind the first two!). The top vertices change to yellow to indicate that they are selected. You can rotate the view to make sure you really have selected four vertices.

4. Now press SKEY and move the mouse up and down. You will see how the four vertices are scaled. Depending on your movement you can make a pyramid or a chopped-off pyramid. You can now also try to grab and rotate some vertices of other objects to get a feeling for the EditMode.

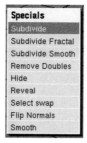

Specials
Subdivide
Subdivide Fractal
Subdivide Smooth
Remove Doubles
Hide
Reveal
Select swap
Flip Normals
Smooth

Using WKEY you can call up the Specials menu in EditMode. With that menu you can quickly access the functions often needed for polygon modeling. You can find the same functionality in the EditButtons (F9).

24.5. WorldButtons

The WorldButtons define global options for the scene. Only the options appropriate for the Blenders game engine are explained here.

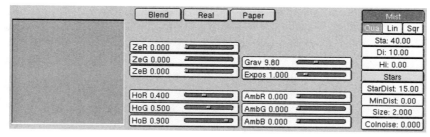

Figure 24-5: The WorldButtons

HoR, G, B (NumSli)

Here you define the color of the world, rendered where no other object is rendered.

Grav (NumSli)

Defines the gravity of the world. This influences the force you need to move an object up, for example, and how fast it will accelerate while falling.

Mist (TogBut)

Activates the rendering of mist. This blends objects at a certain distance into the horizon color.

Qua, Lin, Sqr (RowBut)

Determines the progression of the mist. Quadratic, linear, or inverse quadratic (square root), respectively. Sqr gives a thick, soupy mist, as if the scene is viewed under water.

Sta (NumBut)

The start distance of the mist, measured from the camera.

Di (NumBut)

The depth of the mist, with the distance measured from Sta.

24.6. SoundWindow

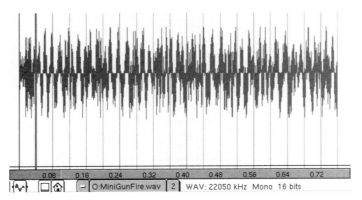

Figure 24-6: The SoundWindow

The SoundWindow is used to load and visualize sounds. You can grab and zoom the window and its contents like every other window in Blender.

The green bar indicates the position of the FrameSlider. This can be used to synchronize a sound with an Ipo animation. In the lower part of the window you also have an indicator of the sound length in seconds.

In the SoundWindow Header see the usual window buttons, user buttons, and some information about the sound.

25

REAL-TIME MATERIALS

Materials for Blender's game engine are applied with Vertex-Paint or UV-Textures. With Vertex Paint you can paint on meshes, giving them solid colors or patterns of color. Vertex Paint is also a very valuable tool for creating the suggestion of light on faces and even more important for varying textures. Without using the CPU-intense real-time lighting you can use it to create the impression of a colored lamp shining on objects, darken corners, or even paint shadows.

Textures have a big impact on the look and feel of your game or interactive environment. Textures allow you to create a very detailed look even with a low poly model. With alpha channel textures, you are also able to create things like windows or fences without actually modeling them.

25.1. Vertex Paint

To start Vertex Paint press VKEY or select the Vertex Paint icon 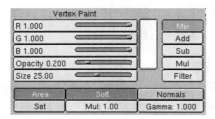 in the 3DWindow Header. The selected object will be drawn solid. You can draw on the vertices of the object while holding the LMB; the size of the brush is shown as a circle while drawing. Use the RMB to sample the color under the mouse pointer.

Figure 25-1: Vertex Paint–related Buttons in the Paint/FaceButtons

Enter the Paint/FaceButtons ![icon] to see the sampled color. Here you can also find more options to control Vertex Paint, as discussed below:

R, G, B (NumSli)

The active color used for painting.

Opacity (NumSli)

The extent to which the vertex color changes while you are painting.

Size (NumSli)

The size of the brush, which is drawn as a circle during painting.

Mix (RowBut)

The manner in which the new color replaces the old when painting: the colors are mixed together.

Add (RowBut)

The colors are added.

Sub (RowBut)

The paint color is subtracted from the vertex color.

Mul (RowBut)

The paint color is multiplied by the vertex color.

Filter (RowBut)

The colors of the vertices of the painted face are mixed together, with the opacity factor.

Area (TogBut)

In the back buffer, Blender creates an image of the painted mesh, assigning each face a color number. This allows the software to quickly see what faces are being painted. Then, the software calculates how much of the face the brush covers, for the degree to which paint is being applied. You can set this calculation with the option Area.

Soft (TogBut)

This specifies that the extent to which the vertices lie within the brush also determines the brush's effect.

Normals (TogBut)

This helps determine the extent of painting. The effect is one of painting with light.

Set (But)

The Mul and Gamma factors are applied to the vertex colors of the mesh.

Mul (NumBut)

The number by which the vertex colors are multiplied when Set is pressed.

Gamma (NumBut)

The number by which the clarity (Gamma value) of the vertex colors are changed when Set is pressed.

25.2. Texture Paint

To start Texture Paint select the Texture Paint icon ▨ in the 3DWindow Header.

NOTE   *Texture Paint needs a textured object to work (see Section 25.3). You also need to unpack a packed texture first (see Section 25.3.5).*

You can now paint on the texture of the object while holding the LMB. The RMB will sample the color located under the mouse pointer.

Enter the Paint/FaceButtons ▨ to see the sampled color. Here you can also find more options to control Texture Paint as follows:

R, G, B (NumSli)

The active color used for painting.

Opacity (NumSli)

The extent to which the color covers the underlying texture.

Size (NumSli)

The size of the brush.

25.3. The UV Editor

The UV editor is fully integrated into Blender and allows you to map textures onto the faces of your models. Each face can have individual texture coordinates and an individual image assigned. This can be combined with vertex colors to darken or lighten the texture or to tint it.

To start UV editing, enter FaceSelectMode with the FKEY or the FaceSelect icon in the 3DWindow Header. The mesh is now drawn Z-buffered. In textured mode
(ALT-Z) untextured faces are drawn in purple to indicate the lack of a texture. Selected faces are drawn with a dotted outline.

To select faces use the RMB. With the BKEY you can use BorderSelect, and the AKEY selects/deselects all faces. While in FaceSelectMode you can enter Edit-Mode (TAB) and select vertices. After leaving EditMode the faces defined by the selected vertices are selected in FaceSelectMode. The active face is the last face selected: this is the reference face for copy options.

RKEY allows you to rotate the UV coordinates or vertex colors.

25.3.1. Mapping UV textures

When in FaceSelectMode (FKEY) you can calculate UV textures for selected faces by pressing UKEY. The menu shown below gives you the following choices:

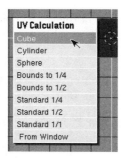

Cube

Cubic mapping, a requester asks for a scaling property.

Cylinder

Cylindrical mapping calculated from the center of the selected faces.

Sphere

Spherical mapping calculated from the center of the selected faces.

Bounds to

The UV coordinates are calculated using the projection of the 3DWindow and then scaled to a bound box of the desired size.

Standard

Each face gets the default set of square UV coordinates.

From Window

UV coordinates are calculated from the active 3DWindow.

25.3.2. The ImageWindow

To assign images to faces, open an ImageWindow with SHIFT-F10.

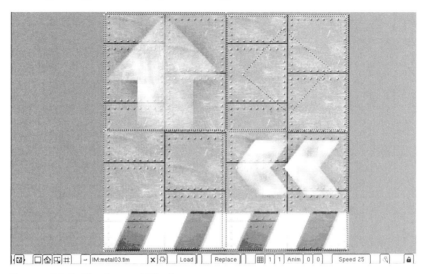

Figure 25-2: The ImageWindow

The first icon keeps UV polygons square while editing (this is a big help while texturing). Just drag one or two vertices around, and the others follow to keep the polygon square. The second one keeps the vertices inside the area of the image.

- With the UserBrowse (MenuButton) you can browse, assign, and delete loaded images on the selected faces.

- Load loads a new image and assigns it to the selected faces. Replace replaces (scene global) an image on all faces assigned to the old image. The small buttons to the right of the Load and Replace buttons open a FileWindow without the thumbnail images.

- The grid icon enables the use of more (rectangular) images in one map. This is used for texturing from textures containing more than one image in a grid and for animated textures. The following two number buttons define how many parts the texture has in the X and Y directions.

- Use SHIFT-LMB to select the desired part of the image in GridMode.

- The Anim button enables a simple texture animation. This works in conjunction with the grid settings, in a way that the parts of the texture are displayed in a row in game mode. With the number buttons to the right of the Anim button you define the start and end part to be played. Speed controls the playback speed in frames per second.

- With the lock icon activated, any changes on the UV polygons in the ImageWindow are shown in real time in the 3DWindows (in textured mode).

- Vertices in the ImageWindow are selected and edited (rotate, grab) like vertices in EditMode in the 3DWindows. Drag the view with the MMB; zoom with PAD+ and PAD-.

25.3.3. The Paint/FaceButtons

When in FaceSelectMode, you can access the Paint/FaceButtons with the icon in the ButtonsWindow Header. In the Paint/FaceButtons you'll find all functions to set the attributes for faces and access the Vertex Paint options.

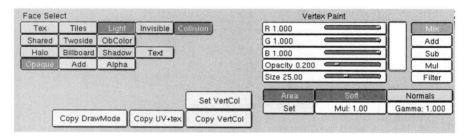

Figure 25-3: The Paint/FaceButtons

Face modes

The following modes always work on faces and display the setting of the active face. Two colored lines in the 3DWindow and the ImageWindow indicate the active face. The green line indicates the U coordinate, and the red line the V coordinate.

- To copy the mode from the active to the selected faces use the copy buttons (Copy DrawMode, Copy UV+tex, and Copy VertCol) in the Paint/FaceButtons.

- In FaceSelectMode the specials menu has some entries to quickly set and clear modes on all selected faces (see Figure 25-4).

Figure 25-4: The Specials menu for the FaceSelectMode

Tex

This enables the use of textures. To use objects without textures, disable Tex and paint the faces with Vertex Paint.

Tiles

This indicates and sets the use of the tile mode for the texture (see Section 25.3.2).

Light

Enables real-time lighting on faces. Lamps only affect faces of objects that are in the same layer as the lamp.

Lamps can also be placed on more than one layer, which makes it possible to create complex real-time lighting situations. (See also Section 26.7.)

Invisible

This makes faces invisible. However, because these faces are still calculated for collisions, this gives you an option to build invisible barriers, and so on.

Collision

The faces with this option are evaluated by the game engine. If this is not needed, switch off this option to save resources.

Shared

With this option vertex colors are blended across faces if they share vertices.

Twoside

Faces with this attribute are rendered two-sided in the game engine.

ObColor

Faces can have color that can be animated with the ColR, ColG, ColB, and ColA Ipos. Choosing this option replaces the vertex colors.

Halo

Faces with this attribute are rendered with the negative X-axis always pointing toward the active view or camera.

Billboard

Faces with this attribute are pointing toward the active view with the negative X-axis. This differs from Halo in that the faces are only rotated around the Z-axis.

Shadow

Faces with this attribute are projected onto the ground along the Z-axis of the object so that they can be used to suggest the shadow of the object.

Text

Faces with this attribute are used for displaying bitmap text in the game engine (see Section 25.4).

Opaque

Normal opaque rendered faces. The color of the texture is rendered as color.

Add

Faces are rendered transparent. The color of the face is added to what has already been drawn. Black areas in the texture are transparent, while white are fully bright.

Use this option to achieve light beam effects, glows or halos around lights. For real transparency use the next listed option, Alpha.

Alpha

The transparency depends on the alpha channel of the texture.

25.3.4. Available file formats

Blender uses OpenGL to draw its interface and the game engine. By using OpenGL we can provide great cross-platform compatibility.

In terms of using textures, we have to pay attention to several things before we're able to run the game on every Blender platform.

- The height and width of textures should be to the power of 64 pixels (e.g., 64 x 64, 64 x 128, 128 x 64, and so on) or Blender will have to scale them (in memory, not on disk!) to provide OpenGL compatibility

- The use of textures with a resolution above 256 by 256 pixels is not recommended if you plan to publish your game, because not all graphic cards support higher resolutions.

Blender can use the following file formats as (real-time) textures:

Targa

The Targa or TGA (.tga extension) file format is a lossless compression format, which can include an alpha channel.

Iris

Iris (.rgb) is the native IRIX image format. It is a lossless, compressed file format, which can include an alpha channel.

JPEG

This is a lossy compression (it uses a compression that leaves out the parts of the image the human eye can hardly see) file format (.jpg, .jpeg), designed for photos with very small file sizes. Because of its small footprint, JPEG is a very good format for distribution over the Net. However, it has no support for alpha channels, and because of the quality loss due to compression it is not a recommended format to work with during the design phase of a game.

25.3.5. Handling of resources

For publishing and to facilitate the handling of Blender's files, you can include all resources in the scene. Normally textures, samples, and fonts are not included in a file while saving, which keeps them on your disk and makes it possible to change and share them between scenes. But if you want to distribute a file you can pack these resources into the Blendfile, so you only need to distribute one file, thus eliminating the possibility of missing resources.

The functions for packing and unpacking are summarized in the Tools-Menu, shown in Figure 25-5. You tell that a file is packed if there is a little "parcel" icon to the right of the ToolsMenu, as shown in this example. Once you've packed a file, all newly added resources are automatically packed (AutoPack).

Figure 25-5: The ToolsMenu

When working with textures, sounds, or fonts you will notice a pack icon ⬚ near the file or datablock browse. This icon allows you to unpack the file independently.

The ToolsMenu entries

The options on the ToolsMenu do the following:

Pack Data

This packs all resources into the Blendfile. The next save will write the packed file to disk.

Unpack Data to current dir

This unpacks all resources to the current directory. It creates a textures directory for textures, a samples directory for sounds, and a fonts directory for fonts.

Advanced Unpack

This option calls the Advanced Unpack Menu, shown in Figure 25-6.

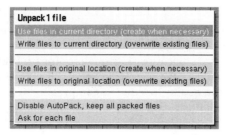

Figure 25-6: Advanced Unpack Menu

Advanced Unpack Menu entries

The Advanced Unpack Menu offers the following options:

Use files in current directory

This unpacks only files that are not present in the current directory. It creates files when necessary.

Write files to current directory

This unpacks the files to the current directory. It overwrites existing files!

Use files in original location

This uses files from their original location (path on disk). It creates files when necessary.

Write files to original location

This writes the files to their original location (path on disk). It overwrites existing files!

Disable AutoPack, keep all packed files

This disables AutoPack, so newly inserted resources are not packed into the Blendfile.

Ask for each file

This asks the user for the unpack options for each file.

25.4. Bitmap Text in the Game Engine

Blender has the ability to draw text in the game engine using special bitmap font textures. These bitmap fonts can be created from a TrueType or a PostScript outline font. (For an explanation of how to create a bitmap font see the tutorial "How to create your own bitmap fonts" at the Blender site.)

To get bitmap text or numbers displayed on a single face you need a special bitmap with the font rendered onto it. Then you must create a property named "Text" for your object and map the first character ("@") of the text bitmap on it. Check the Text face attribute for the face Paint/FaceButtons. The property can be any type, so a Boolean property will also be rendered as True or False.

26

BLENDER'S GAME ENGINE

Technically speaking the Blender game engine is a framework with a collection of modules for interactive purposes, like physics, graphics, logic, sound, and networking. Functionally the game engine processes virtual reality, consisting of content (the world, it's buildings) and behaviors (like physics, animation, and logic). Elements in this world — also called GameObjects — behave autonomously by having a set of tools called LogicBricks, and Properties. For purposes of comparison, the properties act as the memory, the sensors as the senses, and the controllers as the brain, and the actuators allow for actions in the outside world (like muscles).

At the moment, the controllers can be scripted using Python or simple expressions. The idea is that the creation of logical behavior can be edited in a more visual way in the future, so the set of controllers expands with AI state machines, and so on. Controllers could be split into control centers, like an audiovisual center, motion center, and such.

26.1. Options for the Game Engine

Figure 26-1 shows the GameMenu. Its options are discussed below.

Figure 26-1: The GameMenu

Start Game (PKEY)

Start the game engine, stop the engine with ESC; Blender will return to the Creator.

Enable All Frames

With this option checked the game engine runs without dropping frames. This is useful while recording to a Targa sequence or when you need to make sure that all collisions are calculated without loss on slower computers.

Show framerate and profile

With this menu option checked, the game engine will show some information on how fast the game runs and how the work is distributed.

Show debug properties

With this option checked, all properties marked for debug output (![D]) are printed on screen while the game engine is running.

Autostart

Enable autostart for the scene.

26.2. Options in the InfoWindow

In the InfoWindow ![i] (shown in Figure 26-2), you can set your personal defaults for certain aspects of Blender. These will be saved with the Blender default scene when you press CTRL-U.

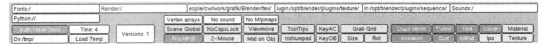

Figure 26-2: InfoWindow options

Some of the Blender game engine options in the InfoWindow are discussed below.

Vertex arrays

Disable the use of Vertex arrays. Vertex arrays normally speed up the calculation on complex scenes. If your OpenGL system does not support vertex arrays you can switch them off using this option.

No sound

Disable audio output.

No Mipmaps

Don't use texture mipmap; this can speed up the game but will result in rendered textures that are not so nice.

Python:

Here you can enter an additional path where Blender's Python interpreter should search for modules.

26.3. Command-Line Options for the Game Engine

When Blender is called with the option "-h" on a command-line (shell window or DOS window) it prints out the command-line parameters, as shown in Figure 26-3.

Figure 26-3: Blender command-line options

```
[cw@work cw]$ blender -h
Blender V 2.24
Usage: blender [options ...] [file]
Render options:
  -b <file> Render <file> in background
    -S <name>   Set scene <name>
    -f <frame>  Render frame <frame> and save it
    -s <frame>  Set start to frame <frame> (use with -a)
    -e <frame>  Set end to frame (use with -a)<frame>
    -a        Render animation
Animation options:
  -a <file(s)>  Playback <file(s)>
    -m       Read from disk (Don't buffer)
Window options:
  -w        Force opening with borders
  -p <sx> <sy> <w> <h>  Open with lower left corner at <sx>, <sy>
                        and width and height <w>, <h>
```

```
Game Engine specific options:
  -g fixedtime      Run on 50 hertz without dropping frames
  -g vertexarrays   Use Vertex Arrays for rendering (usually faster)
  -g noaudio        No audio in Game Engine
  -g nomipmap       No Texture Mipmapping
  -g linearmipmap   Linear Texture Mipmapping instead of Nearest (default)
Misc options:
  -d        Turn debugging on
  -noaudio  Disable audio on systems that support audio
  -h        Print this help text
  -y        Disable OnLoad scene scripts, use -Y to find out why its -y
[cw@work cw]$
```

Following is a discussion of the command-line options for the game engine:

-g fixedtime

With this option the game engine runs without dropping frames. This is useful while recording to a Targa sequence or when you need to make sure that all collisions are calculated without loss on slower computers.

-g vertexarrays

Disables the use of vertex arrays. Vertex arrays normally speed up the calculation on complex scenes. If your OpenGL system doesn't support vertex arrays you can switch them off using this option.

-g noaudio

Disables audio.

-g nomipmap

Don't use texture mipmap; this can speed up the game but will result in not-so-nicely rendered textures.

-g linearmipmap

Linear texture mipmapping instead of nearest (default).

26.4. The RealtimeButtons

The RealtimeButtons are meant for creating interactive 3-D worlds in Blender. Blender acts as a complete development tool for interactive worlds and includes a game engine to play the worlds. All this is done without compiling the game or interactive world; just press PKEY and it runs in real time.

The main view for working with the Blender game engine is the RealtimeButtons ( ) where you define your LogicBricks, which add the behavior to your objects (see Figure 26-4).

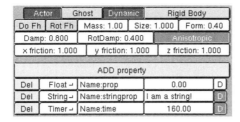

Figure 26-4: RealtimeButtons left part

TIP

The word games *is used here to mean all kinds of interactive 3-D content; Blender is not limited to making and playing games.*

The RealtimeButtons can logically be separated into two parts. The left part contains global settings for GameObjects. This includes settings for general physics, like the damping or mass. Here's where you also define whether an object should be calculated with the built-in physics, as an actor, or should be handled as an object forming the level (like props on a stage).

Settings for GameObjects

These are the settings for the GameObjects.

Actor

Activating Actor for an object causes the game engine to evaluate this object. The Actor button will produce more buttons as described below. Objects without the Actor button activated can form the level (like props on a stage) and are seen by other actors as well.

Ghost

Ghost objects that don't restitute to collisions, but still trigger a collision sensor.

Dynamic

With this option activated, the object follows the laws of physics. This option spawns new buttons that allow you to define the object's attributes in more detail.

Rigid Body

This button enables the use of advanced physics by the game engine. This, in turn, makes it possible to make spheres roll automatically when they make contact with other objects and the friction between the materials is non-zero. The rigid body dynamics are a range of future changes to the game engine. Use the Form factor to control the rolling speed.

Do Fh

This button activates the Fh mechanism (see Section 26.6). With this option you can create a floating or swimming behavior for actors.

Rot Fh

With this option set the object is rotated in such a way that the Z-axis points away from the ground when using the Fh mechanism.

Mass

The mass of a dynamic actor has an effect on how the actor reacts when forces are applied to it. You need a bigger force to move a heavier object. Use the Damp value to simulate air drag.

NOTE *Heavier objects don't fall faster! It is the air drag that causes a difference in the falling speed in our environment (without air, as on the moon, a feather and a hammer fall at the same speed).*

Size

The size of the bounding sphere, which determines the area in which collisions can occur. In future versions this will not be limited to spheres.

Form

A form factor, which gives you control over the behavior of Rigid body objects.

Damp

General (movement) damping for the object. Use this value for simulating the damping an object receives from air or water. In a space scene you might want to use very low or zero damping; air needs a higher damping. Use very high damping to simulate water.

RotDamp

Same as Damp but for rotations of the object.

Anisotropic

When an actor moves on a surface you can define a friction between the objects. Friction will slow down objects, because it is a force that works against any existing forces in the direction of the surface. It is controlled in the dynamic material settings (MaterialButtons (F5), see Section 26.6). This friction works equally in all directions of movement.

- With the Anisotropic option activated you can control the friction independently for the three axes. This is very helpful for racing games, where, for example, the car receives little friction in the driving direction (because of the rolling tires) and high friction sliding to the side.

- Below the object settings you define the properties of a GameObject. These properties can carry values, which describe attributes of the object like variables in a programming language. Use "ADD property" to add properties (see Section 26.5).

- The right part of the RealtimeButtons is the command center for adding logic to your objects and worlds. The logic consists of the sensors, controllers, and actuators.

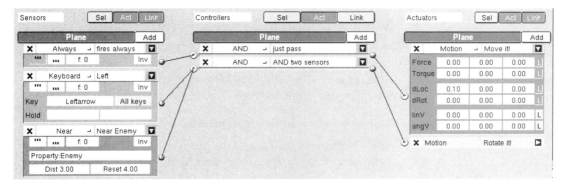

Figure 26-5: Example of some LogicBricks

- Sensors are like the senses of a life-form; they react to keypresses, collisions, contact with materials (touch), timer events, or values of properties.

- The controllers collect events from the sensors and are able to calculate them to produce a result. These are similar to the mind or brain of a life-form. Simple controllers just do an AND on the inputs. An example is to test if a key is pressed AND a certain amount of time has passed. There are also OR controllers, and you can also use Python scripting and expressions in the expression controller to create more complex behavior.

- The actuator actually performs actions on objects. A motion actuator, for example, is like a muscle. This muscle can apply forces to objects to move or rotate them. There are alsoactuators for playing predefined animations (via Ipos), which can be compared to a reflex.

The logic is connected (wired) with the mouse, sensors to controllers and controllers to actuators. After wiring you are immediately able to play the game! If you discover something in the game you don't like, just stop the game engine, edit your 3-D world, and restart. This way you can drastically cut down your development time!

26.5. Properties

Properties (Figure 26-6) carry information bound to the object, similar to a local variable in programming languages. No other object can normally access these properties, but it is possible to copy properties with the Property Copy Actuator (see Section 27.3.7) or send them to other objects using messages (see Section 27.3.11).

		ADD property			
Del	Bool ⌐	Name:BoolProp	True	False	D
Del	Int ⌐	Name:IntProp	0		D
Del	Float ⌐	Name:FloatProp	0.00		D
Del	String ⌐	Name:StringProp	I am		D
Del	Timer ⌐	Name:TimeProp	0		D
Del	String ⌐	Name:Result	Water.		D

Figure 26-6: Defining properties

- The big "ADD property" button adds a new property. By default a property of the float type is added. Delete a property with its Del button.

- The MenuButton defines the type of the property. Click and hold it with the LMB and choose from the pop-up menu.

- The Name text field can be edited by clicking it with the LMB. SHIFT-BACKSPACE clears the name.

IMPORTANT   *Property names are case sensitive. So "Erwin" is not equal to "erwin".*

The next field is different for each of the property types. For the Boolean type there are two radio buttons; choose between True and False. The string type accepts a string; enter a string by clicking in the field with the LMB. The other types use a NumberButton to define the default value. Use SHIFT-LMB for editing it with the keyboard; click and drag to change the value with the mouse.

Property types

The property types are as follows.

Boolean (Bool)

This property type stores a binary value, meaning it can be TRUE or FALSE. Be sure to write it all in capital letters when using these values in property sensors or expressions.

Integer (Int)

Stores a number like 1,2,3,4 . . . in the range from -2147483647 to 2147483647.

Float

Stores a floating-point number.

String

Stores a text string. You can also use expressions or the property sensor to compare strings.

Timer

This property type is updated with the actual game time in seconds, starting from zero. On newly created objects the timer starts when the object is "born."

26.6. Settings in the MaterialButtons

Some physical attributes can be defined with the material settings of Blender. The MaterialButtons can be accessed via the ⬤ icon in the header of the ButtonsWindow or by pressing F5. Create a new material or choose an existing one with the MenuButton in the header.

In the MaterialButtons you need then to activate the DYN button to see the dynamic settings (see Figure 26-7).

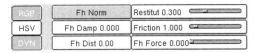

Figure 26-7: Material settings for dynamic objects

Restitute

This parameter controls the elasticity of collisions. A value of 1.0 will convert all the kinetic energy of the object to the opposite force. This object then has an ideal elasticity. This means that if the other object (e.g., the ground) also has a restitute of 1.0 the object will keep bouncing forever.

Friction

This value controls the friction of the object's material. If the friction is low, your object will slide like on ice; with high friction you get the effect of sticking in glue.

Fh Force

In conjunction with the Do Fh and/or Rot Fh (see Section 26.4) you make an object float above a surface. Fh Force controls the force that keeps the object above the floor.

Fh Dist

Fh Dist controls the size of the Fh area. When the object enters this area the Fh mechanism starts to work.

Fh Damp

This value controls the damping inside the Fh area. Values above 0.0 will damp the object movement inside the Fh area.

Fh Norm

With this button activated the object also gets a force in the direction of the face normal on slopes. This will cause an object to slide down a slope (see the example FhDemo.blend).

26.6.1. Specularity settings for the game engine

Figure 26-8 shows the specularity settings. A discussion follows.

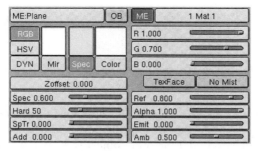

Figure 26-8: Specularity settings

26.6.2. Specularity settings in the MaterialButtons

These are the important specularity settings.

Spec

This slider controls the intensity of the specularity.

Hard

This slider controls the size of the specularity (hardness).

Spec color

Activating this button switches the RGB (or HSV) sliders to define the specularity color.

26.7. Lamps in the Game Engine

Lamps are created with the Toolbox (press the spacebar and then ADD Lamp). For a selected lamp you can switch to the LampButtons (F4) ☀ (see Figure 26-9) to change the properties of that lamp. These properties are the color, the energy, and so on. Because the game engine is fully integrated in Blender, some buttons are only useful for linear animation.

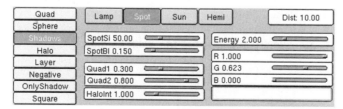

Figure 26-9: LampButtons, settings for Blender's game engine

Common settings for all lamp types are the energy and the color (adjustable with the RGB sliders).

To allow a face to receive real-time lighting in Blender's game engine, the face has to be set to Light in the Paint/FaceButtons ✎ (see Section 25.3). With the layer settings for lamps and objects (EditButtons, F9) you can control the lighting very precisely. Lamps only affect faces on the same layer(s) as the lamp. Per layer you can use eight lamps (OpenGL limitation) for real-time lighting.

Lamp types for the game engine

These are the lamp types for the game engine.

Lamp

Lamp is a point light source.

Spot

This lamp is restricted to a conical space. In the 3DWindow the form of the spotlight is shown with broken lines. Use the SpotSi slider to set the angle of the beam.

Sun

The Sun lamp type is a directional light. The distance has no effect on the intensity. Change the direction of the light (shown as a broken line) by rotating the lamp.

Hemi

The Hemi lamp type is currently not supported in the game engine.

The Lamp and Spot lights can be sensitive to distance. Use the Dist, Quad1, and Quad2 settings for this. The mathematics behind this are explained in the Official Blender 2.0 Guide (see Section A.5 in the Appendix).

26.8. The Blender Laws of Physics

All objects in Blender with the Dynamic option set (see Settings for GameObjects in Section 26.4) are evaluated using the physics laws as defined by the game engine and the user.

The key property for a dynamic object is its mass. Gravity, forces, and impulses (collision bounce) only work on objects with a mass. Also, only dynamic objects can experience drag or velocity damping (a crude way to mimic air/water resistance).

NOTE *Note that for dynamic objects using dLoc and dRot may not have the desired result. Because the velocity of a dynamic object is controlled by the forces and impulses, any explicit change of position or orientation of an object may not correspond with the velocity. For dynamic objects it's better to use the linV and angV for explicitly defining the motion.*

As soon we have defined a mass for our dynamic object, it will be affected by gravity, causing it to fall until it hits another object with its bounding sphere. The size of the bounding sphere can be changed with the Size parameter in the

RealtimeButtons. The gravity has a value of 9.81 by default: you can change this in the WorldButtons with the Grav slider. A gravity of zero is very useful for space games or simulations.

TIP *Use the Damp and RotDamp settings to suggest the drag of air or other environments. Don't use it to simulate friction. Friction can be simulated with the dynamic material settings.*

Dynamic objects can bounce for two reasons. Either you have Do Fh enabled and have too little damping or you are using a restitute value in the dynamic material properties that is too high.

NOTE *If you haven't defined a material, the default restitution is 1.0, which is the maximum value and will cause two objects without materials to bounce forever.*

In the first case, increasing the damping can decrease the amount of bounce. In the latter case define a material for at least one of the colliding objects, and set its restitute value to a smaller value.

The restitute value determines the elasticity of the material. A value of 0 denotes that the relative velocity between the colliding objects will be fully absorbed. A value of 1 denotes that the total momentum will be preserved after the collision.

26.8.1. Damping

Damping decreases the velocity in percent per second. Damping is useful to achieve a maximum speed. The greater the speed the greater the absolute decrease of speed due to drag. The maximum speed is attained when the acceleration due to forces equals the deceleration due to drag. Damping is also useful for damping out unwanted oscillations due to springs.

26.8.2. Friction

Friction is a force tangent to the contact surface. The friction force has a maximum that is linear to the normal—the force that presses the objects against each other (the weight of the object). The friction value denotes the Coulomb friction coefficient—the ratio of the maximum friction force and the normal force. A larger Friction value will allow for a larger maximum friction. For a sliding object the friction force will always be the maximum friction force. For a stationary object the friction force will cancel out any tangent force that is less than the maximum friction. If the tangent force is larger than the maximum friction then the object will start sliding.

For some objects you need to have different friction in different directions. For instance a skateboard will experience relatively little friction when moving it forward and backward, but a lot of friction when moving it side to side. This is called anisotropic friction. Selecting the Anisotropic button in the RealtimeButtons (F8) will enable anisotropic friction. After selecting this button, three sliders will appear, which enable you to set the relative coefficient for each of the local axes. A relative coefficient of zero denotes that along the corresponding axis no friction is experienced. A relative coefficient of one denotes that the full friction applies along the corresponding axis.

26.9. Expressions

Expressions can be used in the expression controller, the property sensor, and the property actuator, as listed in the following tables.

Table 26-1: Valid Expressions

Expression Type	Example
Integer numbers	15
Float number	12.23224
Booleans	TRUE, FALSE
Strings	"I am a string!"
Properties	propname
Sensornames	sensorname (as named in the LogicBrick)

Table 26-2: Arithmetic Expressions

Expression	Example
EXPR1 + EXPR2	Addition, 12+3, propname+21
EXPR1 - EXPR2	Subtraction, 12-3, propname-21
EXPR1 * EXPR2	Multiplication, 12*3, propname*21
EXPR1 / EXPR2	Division, 12/3, propname/21
EXPR1 > EXPR2	EXPR1 greater than EXPR2
EXPR1 >= EXPR2	EXPR1 greater than or equal to EXPR2
EXPR1 < EXPR2	EXPR1 less than EXPR2

Table 26-3: Boolean Operations

Operation	Example
NOT EXPR	Not EXPR
EXPR1 OR EXPR2	logical OR
EXPR1 AND EXPR2	logical AND
EXPR1 == EXPR2	EXPR1 equals EXPR2

Conditional statement: IF(Test, ValueTrue, ValueFalse)

Examples

Table 26-4: Expression Examples

Expression	Result	Explanation
12+12	24	Addition
property=="Carsten"	TRUE or FALSE	String comparison between a property and a string
"Erwin">"Carsten"	TRUE	A string comparison is done

26.10. SoundButtons

The SoundButtons ![icon] (Figure 26-10) are used for loading and managing sounds for the Blender game engine. See Section 24.6 for a method to visualize the waveform.

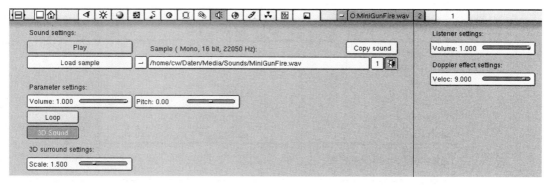

Figure 26-10: The SoundButtons

In the SoundButtons Header you can see the name of the SoundObject (here SO:MiniGunFire.wav). This name is set to the name of the sound sample by default.

Use the MenuButton to browse existing SoundObjects and create new SoundObjects. The blue color of the sound name indicates that more than one user uses the sound; the number button indicates the number of users.

26.10.1. Listener settings

The "Listener settings" on the right side of the SoundButtons define global settings for the listener. The listener is the current camera.

- The Volume slider sets the global volume of all sounds.
- The Veloc slider controls the overall strength of the Doppler effect.

26.10.2. Sound settings

In the SoundSettings section you can then assign or load samples for the SoundObject, so the SoundObject name doesn't have to be the name of the sample. For example, you can use a SoundObject, SO:explosion, and then load explosion_nuke.wav later.

You load samples using the Load Sample button in the SoundButtons. The sample name and the location on disk are shown in the text field to the right of the Load Sample button. Using the MenuButton to the left of the location, you can browse samples already loaded and assign one to the SoundObject.

Above the sample location Blender gives you some basic information about the loaded sample, like the sample frequency, 8-bit or 16-bit, and if the sample is stereo or mono.

- The NumberButton indicates how many SoundObjects share the sample. When the pack/unpack button (parcel) is pressed, the sample is packed into the .blend file, which is especially important when distributing files.
- The Play button plays the sound, you can stop a playing sound with ESC.
- The Copy Sound button copies the SoundObject with all parameters.

26.10.3. Parameter settings

The parameter settings are as follows:

- The Vol slider sets the volume of the sample.
- With the Pitch value you can change the frequency of the sound. Currently there's support for values between half the pitch (-12 semitones) and double the pitch (+12 semitones). Or in Hertz: If your sample has a frequency of 1,000 Hz, the bottom value is 500 and the top 2,000 Hz.
- The Loop button sets the looping for the sample on or off. Depending on the play-mode in the Sound Actuator this setting can be overridden.
- The 3D Sound button activates the calculation of 3-D sound for this SoundObject. This means the volume of the sound depends on the distance and position (stereo effect) between the sound source and the listener. The listener is the active camera.
- The Scale slider sets the sound attenuation. In a 3-D world you want to scale the relationship between gain and distance. For example, if a sound passes by the camera you want to set the scaling factor that determines how much the sound will gain if it comes toward you and how much it will diminish if it goes away from you. The scaling factor can be set between 0.0. All positions are multiplied by zero; no matter where the source is, it will always sound as if it is playing in front of you (no 3-D sound), 1.0 (a neutral state, all positions are multiplied by 1) and 5.0, which over-accentuates the gain/distance relationship.

26.11. Performance and Design Issues

Computers get faster every month, and nearly every new computer sold today has a hardware-accelerated graphics card. Still, there are some performance issues to think about. This is not only a good design and programming style, but also essential for the platform compatibility Blender provides. So to make a well-designed game for various platforms, keep these rules in mind:

1. Don't use properties in combination with AND/OR/Expr. controller as scripting language. Use the Python controller.
2. Use as few inter-object LogicBrick connections as possible.
3. Use ALT-D (instanced mesh for new object) when replicating meshes; this is better than SHIFT-D (copies the mesh).
4. Alpha mapped polygons are expensive, so use with care.
5. Switching off the collision flag for polygons is good for performance. The

use of Ghost is also cheaper than a regular physics object.

6. Keep the polygon count as low as possible. It's quite easy to add polygons to models, but very hard to remove them without screwing up the model. The detail should be made with textures.

7. Keep your texture resolution as low as possible. You can work with high-resolution versions and then later reduce them to publish the game (see Section 25.3).

8. Polygons set to Light are expensive. A hardware acceleration with a Transform and Lighting chip will help here.

9. Instead of real-time lighting use Vertex Paint to lighten, darken, or tint faces to suggest lighting situations.

27

GAME LOGICBRICKS

The game logic in Blender's game engine is assembled in the RealtimeButtons. Here you wire the different LogicBricks together. The following is a brief description of all LogicBricks currently available.

27.1. Sensors

Sensors act like real senses; they can detect collisions, feel (Touch), smell (Near), and view (Ray, Radar).

27.1.1. Always Sensor

The most basic sensor is the Always Sensor (Figure 27-1). It will serve as a good example of the buttons common to every sensor.

Figure 27-1: Common elements for sensors

The button labeled X deletes the sensor from the game logic. This happens without a confirmation dialog, so be careful.

The MenuButton to the right of the delete button (here labeled Always) allows you to choose the type of sensor. Click and hold it with the LMB to get the pop-up menu. Next to it is a TextButton, which holds the name of the sensor ("sensor2" in this case). Blender assigns the name automatically upon creation. Click the name with the LMB to change the name from the keyboard.

NOTE   *Name your LogicBricks and Blender objects to keep track of your scenes. A graphical logic scheme can become very complex.*

The small arrow button at the right hides the contents of the LogicBrick, so that it only shows the top bar. This is very handy in complex scenes.

The next row of buttons is used to determine how and with what frequency a sensor is "firing." This topic is a bit complex, so we will give examples in more than one part of this documentation.

General comments on pulses

Pulses coming from sensors trigger both controllers and actuators. A pulse can have two values, TRUE or FALSE. Each controller is always evaluated when it receives a pulse, whether the pulse is TRUE or FALSE.

The input "gate" of a controller remembers the last pulse value. This is necessary for controllers linked by multiple sensors because it can still perform a logical AND or OR operation on all inputs. Once a controller is triggered, and once all inputs have been evaluated, it can decide to either execute the internal script or send a pulse to the actuators.

Actuators react to a TRUE pulse by switching themselves on (making themselves active); they turn themselves off in response to a FALSE pulse.

The pulse buttons

The first button in the pulse mode buttons (Figure 27-2) activates the positive pulse mode. Every time the sensor fires a pulse it is a positive pulse. This can be used, for example, to start a movement with a motion actuator. The button next to it activates the negative pulse mode, which can be used to stop a movement.

Figure 27-2: Pulse mode buttons

NOTE   *If none of the pulse mode buttons are activated, the Always Sensor fires exactly one time. This is very useful for initializing stuff at the start of a game.*

- The button labeled "f:" (set to 41 here) determines the delay between two pulses fired by the Sensor. The value of "f:" is given as frames.

- The Inv button inverts the pulse, so a positive (TRUE) pulse will become negative (FALSE) and vice versa.

27.1.2. Keyboard Sensor

The Keyboard Sensor (shown below) is one of the most often used sensors because it provides the interface between Blender and the user.

- The pulse mode buttons are common to every sensor, and they have the same functionality as described for the Always Sensor.

- By activating the "All keys" button, the sensor will react to every key. In the Hold fields you can put in modifier keys, which need to be held while pressing the main key.

The Keyboard Sensor can be used for simple text input. To do so, enter the property that should hold the typed text (you can use BACKSPACE to delete characters) into the Target field. The input will be active as long the property in LogToggle is TRUE.

Python methods:

Import the GameKeys module (see Section 28.3.3) to have symbolic names for the keys.

`setKey( int key );`

> Sets the key on which the sensor reacts.

`int key getKey( );`

> Gets the key on which the sensor reacts.

`setHold1( int key );`

> Sets the first modifier key.

`int key getHold1( );`

> Gets the first modifier key.

setHold2(int key);

> Sets the second modifier key.

int key **getHold2**( );

> Gets the second modifier key.

list keys **getPressedKeys**( );

> Gets the keys (including modifier).

list keys **getCurrentlyPressedKeys**( );

> Gets the keys (including modifier) currently held.

27.1.3. Mouse Sensor

Currently, the Mouse Sensor can watch for mouse clicks, mouse movement, or mouseovers. To get the position of the mouse cursor as well you need to use a Python script. Use the MenuButton to choose between the Mouse Sensor types.

Left/middle/right button

This sensor (shown below) gives out a pulse when the correlating mouse button is pressed.

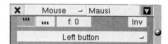

Python methods:

int xpos **getXPosition**( );

> Gets the mouse's X-position.

int ypos **getYPosition**( );

> Gets the mouse's Y-position.

Movement

This sensor (shown below) gives out a pulse when the mouse is moved.

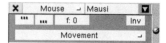

Python methods:

`int xpos` **getXPosition**`( );`

Gets the mouse x-position.

`int ypos` **getYPosition**`( );`

Gets the mouse y-position.

Mouse over

This sensor (shown below) gives a pulse when the mouse cursor is over the object.

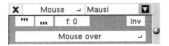

27.1.4. Touch Sensor

The Touch Sensor (shown below) fires a pulse when the object it is assigned to touches a material. If you enter a material name into the MA text field it reacts only to this material; otherwise it reacts to all touch.

Python methods:

The Touch sensor inherits from the Collision Sensor, so it provides the same methods, hence the method names.

---
setProperty`( (char* matname) );`

Sets the material the Touch Sensor should react to.

`char* matname` **getProperty**`( );`

Gets the material the Touch Sensor reacts to.

`gameObject obj` **getHitObject**`( );`

Returns the touched object.

`list objs` **getHitObjectList**`( );`

Returns a list of touched objects.

27.1.5. Collison Sensor

The Collision Sensor (shown below) is a general sensor used to detect contact between objects. Besides reacting to materials it is also capable of detecting an object's properties. Therefore you can switch the input field from material to property by clicking the M/P button.

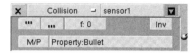

Python methods:

setProperty((char* name));

Sets the material or property the Collision Sensor should react to.

char* name **getProperty**( );

Gets the material or property the Collision Sensor reacts to.

gameObject obj **getHitObject**( );

Returns the colliding object.

list objs **getHitObjectList**( );

Returns a list of objects that have collided.

27.1.6. Near Sensor

The Near Sensor (shown below) reacts to actors near the object with the sensor.

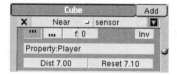

TIP *The Near Sensor senses only objects of the type Actor (a dynamic object is also an actor).*

If the Property field is empty, the Near Sensor reacts to all actors in its range. If filled with a property name, the sensor reacts only to actors carrying a property with that name.

You set the spherical range of the Near Sensor with the Dist NumberButton. The Reset value defines at what distance the Near Sensor is reset again.

Python methods:

setProperty((char* propname));

Sets the property the Near Sensor should react to.

```
char* propname getProperty( );
```

Gets the property the Near Sensor reacts to.

```
list gameObjects getHitObjectList( );
```

Returns a list of game objects detected by the Near Sensor.

```
gameObject obj getHitObject( );
```

Returns the object that triggered the sensor.

27.1.7. Radar Sensor

The Radar Sensor (shown below) acts like a real radar. It looks for an object along the axis indicated with the axis buttons X, Y, Z. If a property name is entered into the Prop field, it reacts only to objects with this property.

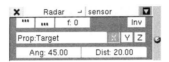

In the Ang field you can enter an opening angle for the radar that equals the angle of view for a camera. The Dist setting determines how far the Radar Sensor can see.

Objects can't block the line of sight for the Radar Sensor, though they can for the Ray Sensor (see Section 27.1.10). You can combine the two sensors to create a radar that is not able to look through walls.

Python methods:

```
setProperty( (char* name) );
```

Sets the property that the Radar Sensor should react on.

```
char* name getProperty( );
```

Gets the name of the property.

```
gameObject obj getHitObject( );
```

Returns the detected object that triggered the sensor.

```
list objs getHitObjectList( );
```

Returns a list of detected objects.

27.1.8. Property Sensor

The Property Sensor (shown below) logically checks a property attached to the same object.

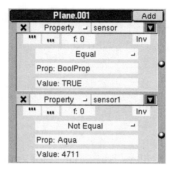

The Equal type Property Sensor checks for equality of the property given in the Prop field and the value in Value. If the condition is true, it fires pulses according to the pulse mode settings. The Not Equal Property Sensor checks for inequality and then fires its pulses.

- The Interval type property sensor fires its pulse if the value of property is within the interval defined by Min and Max. This sensor type is especially helpful for checking float values, which you can't depend on to reach a value precisely. This is most common with the Timer Property.

- The Changed Property Sensor gives out pulses every time a property is changed. This can, for example, happen through a property actuator, a Python script, or an expression.

Python methods:

---

setProperty((char* propname));

Sets the property to check.

---

char* propname **getProperty**( );

Gets the property to check.

```
setType( (int type) );
```

Sets the type of the Property Sensor.

1. Equal
2. Not Equal
3. Interval
4. Changed

```
char* propname getProperty( );
```

Gets the type of the Property Sensor.

```
setValue( (char* expression) );
```

Sets the value to check (as expression).

```
char* expression getValue( );
```

Gets the value to check (as expression).

27.1.9. Random Sensor

The Random Sensor fires a pulse randomly according to the pulse settings (50/50 pick).

TIP   *With a seed of zero the Random Sensor works like an Always Sensor, which means it fires a pulse every time.*

Python methods:

```
setSeed( (int seed) );
```

Set the seed for the random generation.

```
int seed getSeed( );
```

Gets the seed for the Random Sensor.

```
int seed getLastDraw( );
```

Gets the last draw from the Random Sensor.

27.1.10. Ray Sensor

The Ray Sensor (shown below) casts a ray for the distance set into the NumberButton Range. If the ray hits an object with the right property or the right material the sensor fires its pulse.

IMPORTANT *Other objects block the ray so that it can't see through walls.*

If no material or property name is filled in, the Ray Sensor reacts to all objects.

Python methods:

list [x,y,z] **getHitPosition( );**

Returns the position where the ray hits the object.

list [x,y,z] **getHitNormal( );**

Returns the normal vector how the ray hits the object.

list [x,y,z] **getRayDirection( );**

Returns the vector of the ray direction.

gameObject obj **getHitObject( );**

Returns the hit object.

27.1.11. Message Sensor

The Message Sensor (shown below) fires its pulse when a message arrives for the object carrying the sensor. The Subject field can be used to filter messages matching the subject.

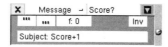

Python methods:

list bodies **getBodies( );**

Returns a list containing the message bodies arrived since the last call.

int messages **getFrameMessageCount( );**

Returns the number of messages received since the last frame.

setSubjectFilterText(string subject);

Sets the subject for the Message Sensor.

27.2. Controllers

Controllers act as the brain for your game logic. This reaches from very simple decisions like connecting two inputs and simple expressions to complex Python scripts that can carry artificial intelligence.

27.2.1. AND Controller

The AND Controller (shown below) combines one, two, or more inputs from sensors. That means that all inputs must be active to pass the AND Controller.

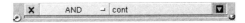

27.2.2. OR Controller

The OR Controller (shown below) combines one, two, or more inputs from sensors. OR means that either one or more inputs can be active to let the OR Controller pass the pulse through.

27.2.3. Expression Controller

With the Expression Controller (shown below) you can create slightly complex game logic with a single line of "code." You can access the output of sensors attached to the controller and access the properties of the object. (More on using expressions can be found in Section 26.9.)

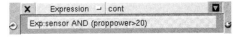

NOTE   *The expression mechanism prints out errors to the console or in the DOS window, so have a look there if anything fails.*

27.2.4. Python Controller

The Python Controller (shown below) is the most powerful controller in the game engine. You can attach a Python script to it, which allows you to control your GameObjects, ranging from simple movement up to complex gameplay and artificial intelligence.

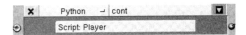

Enter the name of the script you want to attach to the Python Controller in the Script field. (The script must exist in the scene or Blender will ignore the name you type.)

NOTE   *Remember that Blender treats names as case sensitive! So the script "player" is not the same as "Player."*

Python for the game engine is covered in Section 28.2.

Python methods:

Actuator* **getActuator**(char* name ,);

Returns the actuator with "name".

list **getActuators**( );

Returns a python list of all connected actuators.

Sensor* **getSensor**(char* name ,);

Returns the sensor with "name".

list **getSensors**( );

Returns a Python list of all connected sensors.

27.3. Actuators

Actuators are the executing LogicBricks. They can be compared with muscles or glands in a life-form.

27.3.1. Action Actuator

The Action Actuator (shown below) offers the following action play modes.

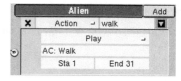

Play

Plays the action from Sta to End at every positive pulse the actuator gets. Other pulses while playing are discarded.

Flipper

Plays the action from Sta to End on activation. When the activation ends it plays backwards from the current position. When a new activation reaches the actuator the action will be played from the current position onward.

Loop Stop

Plays the action in a loop as long as the pulse is positive. It stops at the current position when the pulse turns negative.

Loop End

This plays the action repeatedly as long as there is a positive pulse. When the pulse stops it continues to play the action to the end and then stops.

Property

Plays the action for exactly the frame indicated in the property entered in the field Prop.

27.3.2. Motion Actuator

The Motion Actuator (shown below) may be the most important actuator. It moves, rotates, or applies a velocity to objects.

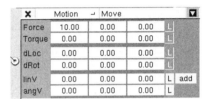

The simplest case of using a Motion Actuator is to move the object. This is done with the dLoc values in the third row. Every time the actuator is triggered by an impulse it moves the object by the amount given in the dLoc row. The three values here stand for X-, Y-, and Z-axis. So when you enter a 1.0 in the first field the object is moved one unit per time unit of the game. (The clock in the game engine ticks in frames, roughly 1/25 of a second; for exact timings use the Timer Property.)

The buttons labeled L behind each row in the Motion Actuator, determine whether the motion applied should be treated as global or local. If the button is pressed (dark green) the motion is applied based on the local axis of the object. If the button is not pressed the motion is applied based on the global (world) axis.

Force

Values in this row act as forces that apply to the object. This only works for dynamic objects.

Torque

Values in this row act as rotational forces (Torque) that apply to the object. This works only for dynamic objects. Positive values rotate counterclockwise.

dLoc

Offsets the object as indicated in the value fields.

dRot

Rotates the object for the given angle (36 is a full rotation). Positive values rotate clockwise.

linV

Sets (overrides current velocity) the velocity of the object to the given values. When "add" is activated the velocity is added to the current velocity.

angV

Sets the angular velocity to the given values. Positive values rotate counter-clockwise.

The Motion Actuator starts to move objects on a pulse (TRUE) and stops on a FALSE pulse. To get a movement over a certain distance, you need to send a FALSE pulse to the Motion Actuator after each positive pulse.

Python methods:

```
setForce( float x , float y , float z , bool local );
```

Sets the Force parameters for the Motion Actuator.

```
list [x,y,z,local] getForce( );
```

Gets the Force parameter from the Motion Actuator; local indicates whether the local button is set (1).

```
setTorque( list [x,y,z] );
```

Sets the Torque parameter for the Motion Actuator.

```
list [x,y,z] getTorque( );
```

Gets the Torque parameter for the Motion Actuator.

```
setdLoc( list [x,y,z] );
```

Sets the dLoc parameters from the Motion Actuator.

```
list [x,y,z] getdLoc( );
```

Gets the dLoc parameters from the Motion Actuator.

```
setdRot( list [x,y,z] );
```

Sets the dRot parameters for the Motion Actuator.

```
list [x,y,z] getdLoc( );
```

Gets the dRot parameters from the Motion Actuator.

setLinearVelocity(list [x,y,z]);

Sets the linV parameters for the Motion Actuator.

list [x,y,z] **getLinearVelocity**( );

Gets the linV parameters from the Motion Actuator.

setAngularVelocity(list [x,y,z]);

Sets the angV parameters for the Motion Actuator.

list [x,y,z] **getAngularVelocity**( );

Gets the angV parameters from the Motion Actuator.

27.3.3. Constraint Actuator

With the Constraint Actuator (shown below) you can limit an object's freedom to a certain degree.

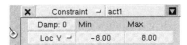

With the MenuButton you specify which channel's freedom should be constrained. With the NumberButtons Min and Max you define the minimum and maximum values for the constraint selected. To constrain an object to more than one channel simply use more than one Constraint Actuator.

Python methods:

setDamp(int damp);

Sets the Damp parameter.

int damp **getDamp**( );

Gets the Damp parameter.

setMin(int min);

Sets the Min parameter.

int min **getMin**( );

Gets the Min parameter.

setMax(int max);

Sets the Max parameter.

```
int max getMax( );
```

Gets the Max parameter.

```
setMin( int min );
```

Sets the Min parameter.

```
int min getMin( );
```

Gets the Min parameter.

```
setLimit( int limit );
```

Sets the limit for the constraint. None = 1, LocX = 2, LocY = 3, LocZ = 4.

```
int limit getLimit( );
```

Gets the constraint.

27.3.4. Ipo Actuator

The Ipo Actuator (shown below) can play the Ipo-curves for the object that owns the actuator. If the object has a child with an Ipo (in a parenting chain) and you activate Child in the actuator, the Ipo for the child is also played.

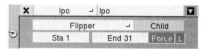

The Force button will convert the Loc Ipo-curves into forces for dynamic objects. When pressed, the L button appears, which takes care of applying the forces locally to the objects coordinate system.

Ipo play modes

The Ipo play modes are as follows.

Play

Plays the Ipo from Sta to End at every positive pulse the actuator gets. Other pulses received while playing are discarded.

Ping Pong

Plays the Ipo from Sta to End on the first positive pulse, then backward from End to Sta when the second positive pulse is received.

Flipper

Plays the Ipo for as long as the pulse is positive. When the pulse changes to negative the Ipo is played from the current frame to Sta.

Loop Stop

Plays the Ipo in a loop for as long as the pulse is positive. It stops at the current position when the pulse turns negative.

Loop End

This plays the Ipo repeatedly for as long as there is a positive pulse. When the pulse stops it continiues to play the Ipo to the end and then stops.

Property

Plays the Ipo for exactly the frame indicated by the property named in the field Prop.

Currently, the following Ipos are supported by the game engine:

Mesh objects

Loc, Rot, Size, Col

Lamps

Loc, Rot, RGB, Energy

Cameras

Loc, Rot, Lens, ClipSta, ClipEnd

Python methods:

`SetType( int type );`

Sets the type; 1 indicates the first play type from the MenuButton and so on.

`int type GetType( );`

Sets the type; 1 indicates the first play type from the MenuButton.

`SetStart( int frame );`

Sets the Sta frame.

`SetEnd( int frame );`

Sets the End frame.

`int frameGetStart( );`

Gets the Sta frame.

`int frameGetEnd( );`

Gets the End frame.

27.3.5. Camera Actuator

The Camera Actuator (shown below) tries to mimic a real cameraman. It keeps the actor in the field of view and tries to stay at a certain distance from the object. The motion is soft, and there is some delay in the reaction on the motion of the object.

Enter the object that should be followed by the camera (you can also use the Camera Actuator for non-camera objects) into the OB field. The field Height determines the height above the object at which the camera stays. Min and Max are the bounds of distance from the object to which the camera is allowed to move. The X and Y buttons specify which axis of the object the camera tries to stay behind.

27.3.6. Sound Actuator

The Sound Actuator (shown below) plays a SoundObject loaded using the SoundButtons (see Section 26.10). Use the MenuButton to browse and choose between the SoundObjects in the scene.

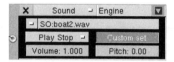

Sound play modes (MenuBut)

Play Stop

Plays the sound for as long as there is a positive pulse.

Play End

Plays the sound to the end when a positive pulse is given.

Loop Stop

Plays and repeats the sound when a positive pulse is given.

Loop End

Plays the sound repeatedly when a positive pulse is given. When the pulse stops the sound is played to its end.

Custom set (TogBut)

Checking the "Custom set" button will copy the SoundObject (sharing the sample data) and allows you to quickly change the volume and pitch of the sound with the NumberButtons that appear.

Python methods:

float gain **getGain**( );

Get the gain (volume) setting.

setGain(float gain);

Set the gain (volume) setting.

float pitch **getPitch**( );

Get the pitch setting.

setPitch(float pitch);

Set the pitch setting.

27.3.7. Property Actuator

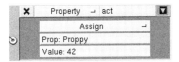

Property modes

Assign

Assigns a value or expression (given in the Value field) to a property. For example, with an expression like "Proppy + 1" the Assign works like an Add. To assign strings you need to add quotes to the string (" . . . ").

Add

Adds the value or result of an expression to a property. To subtract simply give a negative number in the Value field.

Copy

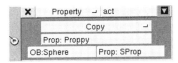

This copies a Property (here Prop: SProp) from the object with the name given in OB: Sphere into the property Prop: Proppy. This is an easy and safe way to pass information between objects. You cannot pass information between scenes with this actuator!

Python methods:

SetProperty(string name);

---

string name **GetProperty**( );

SetValue(string value);

---

string value **GetValue**( );

More on using expressions can be found in Section 26.9.

27.3.8. Edit Object Actuator

This actuator performs actions on objects itself, such as adding new objects, deleting objects, and so on.

Edit Object Actuator types

Add Object

The Add Object Actuator (shown below) adds an object to the scene. The new object is oriented along the X-axis of the creating object.

TIP *Keep the object you'd like to add on a separate and hidden layer. You will see an error message on the console or debug output when not following this rule.*

Enter the name of the object to add in the OB field. The Time field determines how long (in frames) the object should exist. The value 0 denotes it will exist forever. Be careful not to slow down the game engine by generating too many objects! If the time an object should exist is not predictable, you can also use other events (collisions, properties, and so on) to trigger an End Object for the added object using LogicBricks.

With the linV buttons it is possible to assign an initial velocity to the added object. This velocity is given in X, Y, and Z components. The L button stands for local. When it is pressed the velocity is interpreted as local to the added object.

Python methods:

setObject(string name);

Sets the object (name) to be added.

---

string name **getObject**( );

Gets the object name.

---

setTime(int time);

Time in frames the added object should exist. Zero means unlimited.

---

int time **getTime**( );

Gets the time the added object should exist.

---

setLinearVelocity(list [vx,vy,vz]);

Sets the linear velocity [Blender units per second] components for added objects.

---

list [vx,vy,vz] **getLinearVelocity**( );

Gets the linear velocity [Blender units per second] components from the actuator.

---

gameObject* **getLastCreatedObject**( );

Gets a pointer to the last created object. This way you can manipulate dynamically added objects.

End Object

The End Object type (shown below) simply ends the life of the object with the actuator when it gets a pulse. This is very useful for ending a bullet's life after a collision or something similar.

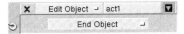

Replace Mesh

The Replace Mesh type (shown below) replaces the mesh of the object with a new one, given in the ME field. Remember that the mesh name is not implicitly equal to the object name.

Python methods:

---

setMesh(string name);

Sets the mesh for the Replace Mesh Actuator to "name".

---

string name **getMesh**( );

Gets the meshname from the Replace Mesh Actuator.

Track to

The Track to type (shown below) rotates the object in such a way that the Y-axis points to the target specified in the OB field. Normally this happens only in the X/Y plane of the object (indicated by the 3D button not being pressed). With 3D pressed the tracking is done in 3-D. The Time parameter sets how fast the tracking is done. Zero means immediately; values above zero produce a delay (are slower) in tracking.

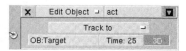

Python methods:

```
setObject( string name );
string name getObject( );
setTime( int time );
```

Sets the time needed to track.

```
int time getTime( );
```

Gets the time needed to track.

```
setUse3D( bool 3d );
```

Set if 3D should be used leading to full 3-D tracking.

27.3.9. Scene Actuator

The Scene Actuator is meant for switching scenes and cameras in the game engine or adding overlay or background scenes. Choose the desired action with the MenuButton and enter an existing camera or scene name into the text field. If the name does not exist, the button will be blanked!

Reset

Simply restarts and resets the scene. It has the same effect as stopping the game with ESC and restarting with PKEY.

Set Scene

Switches to the scene indicated into the text field. During the switch all properties are reset!

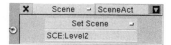

Python methods for all types of Scene Actuators

setScene(char* scene);

Sets the scene to switch to.

char* scene **getScene**( );

Gets the scene name from the actuator.

Set Camera

Switches to the camera indicated in the text field.

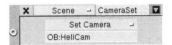

Python methods:

setCamera(char* camera);

Sets the camera to switch to.

char* camera **getCamera**( );

Gets the camera name from the actuator.

Add OverlayScene

Adds an overlay scene that is rendered on top of all other (existing) scenes.

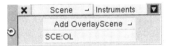

Add BackgroundScene

Adds a background scene which will be rendered behind all other scenes.

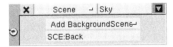

Remove Scene

Removes a scene.

Suspend Scene

Suspends a scene until Resume Scene is called.

Resume Scene

Resumes a suspended scene.

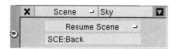

27.3.10. Random Actuator

An often needed function for games is a random value to get more variation in movements or enemy behavior. The Seed parameter is the value fed into the random generator as a start value for the random number generation. Because computer generated random numbers are only "pseudo" random (they will repeat after a long while) you can get the same random numbers again if you choose the same Seed.

Enter the name of the property you want to be filled with the random number into the Property field.

Random Actuator types

Following are the Random Actuator types.

Boolean Constant

This is not a random function at all. Use this type to test your game logic with a TRUE or FALSE value.

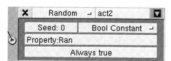

Boolean Uniform

This is the classic random 50-50 pick. It results in TRUE or FALSE with an equal chance. This is like an (ideal) flip of a coin.

Boolean Bernoulli

This random function (shown below) results in a Boolean value of TRUE or FALSE, but instead of having the same chance for both values you can control the chance of having a TRUE pick with the Chance parameter. A chance of 0.5 will be the same as Bool Uniform. A chance of 0.1 will result in 1 out of 10 cases in a TRUE (on average).

Integer Constant

For testing your logic with a value given in the Value field.

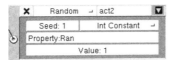

Integer Uniform

This random type randomly produces an integer value between (and including) Min and Max. The classical use for this is to simulate a dice pick with "Min: 1" and "Max: 6".

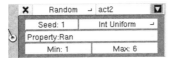

Integer Poisson

The random numbers are distributed in such a way that an average of Mean is reached with an infinite number of picks.

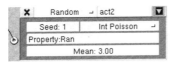

Float Constant

For debugging your game logic with a given value.

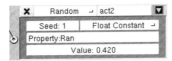

Float Uniform

This returns a random floating-point value between Min and Max.

Float Normal

Returns a weighted random number around Mean and with a standard deviation of SD.

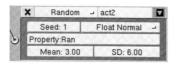

Float Negative Exponential

Returns a random number that is well suited to describe natural processes like radioactive decay or lifetimes of bacteria. The Half-life time sets the average value of this distribution.

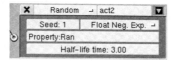

Python methods:

```
setSeed( int seed );
```

Sets the random seed (the init value of the random generation).

```
int seed getSeed( );
```

Gets the random seed (the init value of the random generation) from the actuator.

```
float para1 getPara1( );
```

Gets the first parameter for the selected random distribution.

```
float para2 getPara2( );
```

Gets the second parameter for the selected random distribution.

```
setProperty( string propname );
```

Sets the property to which the random value should go.

```
string propname getProperty( );
```

Gets the property name from the actuator.

```
setDistribution( int dist );
```

Sets the distribution; "dist = 1" means the fist choice from the type MenuButton.

```
int dist getDistribution( );
```

Gets the random distribution method from the actuator.

27.3.11. Message Actuator

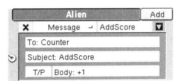

This LogicBrick sends a message out, which can be received and processed by the Message Sensor. The To field indicates that the message should be sent only to objects with the Property indicated by To. The subject of the message is indicated in the Subject field. With these two possibilities you can control the messaging very effectively.

The body (content) of the message can be either a text (Body) string or the content of a property when T/P is activated (Propname). (See Section 27.1.11 on how to get the body of a message.)

Python methods:

```
setToPropName( char* propname );
```

Sets the property name the message should be send to.

```
setSubject( char* subject );
```

Sets the subject of the message.

```
setBody( char* body );
```

Sets the body of the message.

```
setBodyType( int bodytype );
```

Sets whether the body should be text or a property name.

28

PYTHON

Python is an interpreted, interactive, object-oriented programming language. It combines remarkable power with very clear syntax. It has modules, classes, exceptions, very high-level dynamic data types, and dynamic typing. Python is also usable as an extension language for applications that need a programmable interface. And, Python implementation is portable to (at least) all platforms that Blender runs on. (Python is copyrighted but freely usable and distributable, even for commercial use.)

28.1. The TextWindow

The TextWindow (shown in Figure 28-1) is a simple but useful text editor, fully integrated into Blender. Its main purpose is for use in writing Python scripts, but it is also very useful for writing comments in the Blendfile or to explain the purpose of the scene to other users.

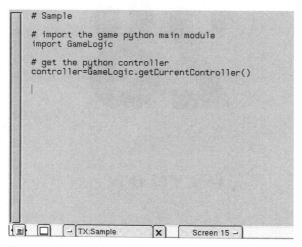

Figure 28-1: The TextWindow

The TextWindow can be displayed with SHIFT-F11 or by adjusting the IconMenu in the WindowHeader. As usual there is an IconBut to make the TextWindow full screen. The next MenuButton over can be used to switch between text files, open new ones, or add new text buffers. The X button deletes a text buffer after a confirmation. With the MenuButton on the right side you can change the font used to display the text.

By holding the LMB and then dragging the mouse you can mark ranges of text for the usual cut, copy, and paste functions. The key commands are:

28.1.1. Key commands for the TextWindow

ALT-C

Copies the marked text into a buffer.

ALT-X

Cuts out the marked text into a buffer.

ALT-V

Pastes the text from buffer to the cursor in the TextWindow.

ALT-O

Loads a text; a FileWindow appears.

CTRL-R

Reloads the current text—very useful for editing with an external editor.

SHIFT-ALT-F

Pops up the FileMenu for the TextWindow.

ALT-F

Find function.

ALT-J

Pops up a NumButton where you can specify a line number that the cursor will jump to.

ALT-U

Unlimited undo for the TextWindow.

ALT-R

Redo function; recovers the last undo.

ALT-A

Marks the whole text.

28.2. Python for Games

With Python integrated into the game engine you can influence LogicBricks, change their parameters, and react to events they trigger. You can also influence the GameObject that carries the Python controller directly by moving it, applying forces to it, or getting information from it.

In addition to the Python in the game engine, Blender includes Python for modeling and animation tasks.

28.2.1. Basic gamePython

The first step for using gamePython is to add at least a sensor and a Python controller to an object, then to add a new text file in the TextWindow. (Fill in the name of that text file in the Script field of the Python controller.) You should now have a game logic setup like the one shown in Figure 28-2.

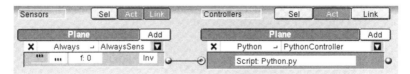

Figure 28-2: LogicBricks for a first gamePython script

Now enter the following script into the TextWindow (you don't need to type the lines starting with "#"; these are comments).

Figure 28-3: First script

```
 1 # first gamePython script
 2 # gets the position of the owning object
 3 # and prints it on the console
 4
 5 import GameLogic
 6
 7 controller = GameLogic.getCurrentController()
 8 owner = controller.getOwner()
 9
10 print owner.getPosition()
```

NOTE   *The print command and errors from the Python interpreter will appear on the console from which you started Blender (or in the DOS window, when running Blender under Windows). As such, it is helpful to size the Blender window in such a way that you can see the console window while programming Python.*

This basic script prints only the position of the object that owns the Python controller. Move your object and then restart the game engine with the PKEY to see the results changing.

Let's look at this script line by line. Line 5 may be the most important line here. Here is where we import the GameLogic module, which is the basis for all gamePython in Blender.

In line 7 we get the controller, which executes the script and assigns it to the variable `controller`. In line 8 we use the controller we got in line 7 to get the owner, the GameObject carrying the LogicBrick. (You can see that we use the method `getOwner()` to get the owner of our controller.) We now have the owner and we can use its methods for other things. Here in line 10 we use the `getPosition()` method to print the position of the GameObject as a matrix of the X, Y, and Z values.

You may wonder what other methods the Python objects have. Of course this is part of this documentation, but Python is self-documenting, so we have other ways to get that information. For example, add the following line to the end of the script from Figure 28-3:

```
1 print dir(owner)
```

Now start the game engine again, stop it, and look at the console window. You will see the following output:

```
[0.0, 0.0, 0.0]
['applyImpulse', 'disableRigidBody','enableRigidBody', 'getLinearVelocity', 'getMas
s',
'getOrientation', 'getPosition', 'getReactionForce','getVelocity', 'restoreDynamics
', 'setOrientation', 'setPosition', 'setVisible', 'suspendDynamics']
```

The first line above shows the position of the object; the next lines show the methods that the "owner" provides. For example, the getMass method will return the mass of a dynamic object.

With the knowledge of the dir() function you can ask Python objects for information, without consulting external documentation.

28.3. Game Python Documentation per Module

28.3.1. GameLogic module

```
SCA_PythonController getCurrentController( );
```

Returns the controller object that carries the script.

```
void addActiveActuator( actuator , bool active );
```

This method makes the Actuator "actuator" active ("active=TRUE") or inactive ("active=FALSE").

```
float getRandomFloat( );
```

This function returns a random float in the range of 0.0...1.0. The seed is taken from the system time, so you get a different sequence of random numbers at every game start.

```
setGravity( [gravityX,gravityY,gravityZ] );
```

Sets the world gravity.

28.3.2. Rasterizer module

```
int getWindowWidth( );
```

This function returns the width of the Blender window the game is running in.

```
int getWindowHeight( );
```

This function returns the height of the Blender window the game is running in.

```
void makeScreenshot( char* filename );
```

This function writes a screenshot of the game as a TGA file to disk.

```
enableVisibility( bool usevisibility );
```

This sets all objects to invisible when "usevisibility" is TRUE. The game can then set the visibility back to "on" for the necessary objects only.

```
showMouse( bool show );
```

Shows or hides the mouse cursor while the game engine runs, depending on the show parameter. The default behavior is to hide the mouse, but moving over the window border will reveal it again, so set the mouse cursor visibility explicitly with this function.

```
setBackgroundColor( list [float R,float G,float B] );
```

Sets the background color. Same as the horizon color in the WorldButtons.

```
setMistColor( list [float R,float G,float B] );
```

Sets the mist (fog) color. In the game engine you can set the mist color independently from the background color. To have a mist effect, activate "Mist" in the World-Buttons.

```
setMistStart( float start );
```

Sets the distance where the mist starts to have effect. See also the WorldButtons.

```
setMistEnd( float end );
```

Sets the distance from MistStart (0% mist) to 100% mist. See also the WorldButtons.

28.3.3. GameKeys Module

This is a module that simply defines all keyboard keynames (AKEY = 65 etc).
"AKEY". . . "ZKEY", "ZERO_KEY" . . . "NINEKEY", "CAPSLOCKKEY",
"LEFTCTRLKEY", "LEFTALTKEY", "RIGHTALTKEY", "RIGHTCTRLKEY",
"RIGHTSHIFTKEY", "LEFTSHIFTKEY", "ESCKEY", "TABKEY", "RETKEY",
"SPACEKEY", "LINEFEEDKEY", "BACKSPACEKEY", "DELKEY", "SEMICOLONKEY",
"PERIODKEY", "COMMAKEY", "QUOTEKEY", "ACCENTGRAVEKEY",
"MINUSKEY", "VIRGULEKEY", "SLASHKEY", "BACKSLASHKEY", "EQUALKEY",
"LEFTBRACKETKEY", "RIGHTBRACKETKEY", "LEFTARROWKEY",
"DOWNARROWKEY", "RIGHTARROWKEY", "UPARROWKEY", "PAD0", ..., "PAD9",
"PADPERIOD", "PADVIRGULEKEY", "PADASTERKEY", "PADMINUS",
"PADENTER", "PADPLUSKEY", "F1KEY" . . . "F12KEY", "PAUSEKEY", "INSERTKEY",
"HOMEKEY", "PAGEUPKEY", "PAGEDOWNKEY", and "ENDKEY".

28.4. Standard Methods for LogicBricks

All LogicBricks inherit the following methods:

```
gameObject*getOwner( );
```

This returns the owner of the GameObject the LogicBrick is assigned to.

28.4.1. Standard methods for sensors

All sensors inherit the following methods:

```
int isPositive( );
```

True if the sensor fires a positive pulse. Very useful, for example, to differentiate the press and release state from a Keyboard Sensor.

```
bool getUsePosPulseMode( );
```

Returns TRUE if positive pulse mode is active and FALSE if positive pulse mode is not active.

```
setUsePosPulseMode( bool flag );
```

Set "flag" to TRUE to switch on positive pulse mode and FALSE to switch off positive pulse mode.

```
int getPosFrequency( );
```

Returns the frequency of the updates in positive pulse mode.

```
setPosFrequency( int freq );
```

Sets the frequency of the updates in positive pulse mode. If the frequency is negative, it is set to 0.

```
bool getUseNegPulseMode( );
```

Returns TRUE if negative pulse mode is active and FALSE if negative pulse mode is not active.

```
setUseNegPulseMode( bool flag );
```

Set "flag" to TRUE to switch on negative pulse mode and FALSE to switch off negative pulse mode.

```
int getNegFrequency( );
```

Returns the frequency of the updates in negative pulse mode.

```
setNegFrequency( int freq );
```

Sets the frequency of the updates in negative pulse mode. If the frequency is negative, it is set to 0.

```
bool getInvert( );
```

Returns whether or not pulses from this sensor are inverted.

```
setInvert( bool flag );
```

Set "flag" to TRUE to invert the responses of this sensor; set to FALSE to keep the normal response.

28.4.2. Standard methods for controllers

Controllers have the following methods:

```
Actuator* getActuator( char* name , );
```

Returns the actuator with "name".

```
list getActuators( );
```

Returns a Python list of all connected actuators.

```
Sensor* getSensor( char* name , );
```

Returns the sensor with "name".

```
list getSensors( );
```

Returns a Python list of all connected sensors.

28.4.3. Standard methods for GameObjects

The GameObjects you got with getOwner() provide the following methods.

```
applyImpulse( list [x,y,z] , );
```

Apply impulse to the GameObject (N*s).

```
disableRigidBody( );
```

Disables the rigid body dynamics for the GameObject.

```
enableRigidBody( , );
```

Enables the rigid body dynamics for the GameObject.

```
setVisible( int visible );
```

Sets the GameObject to visible (int visible=1) or invisible (int visible=0). This state is true until the next frame-draw. Use enableVisibility(bool usevisibility); from the rasterizer module to make all objects invisible.

setPosition(*[x,y,z]* **);**

Sets the position of the GameObject according to the list of the X, Y, and Z coordinates.

pylist [x,y,z] **getPosition( );**

Gets the position of the GameObject as list of the X, Y, and Z coordinates.

pylist [x,y,z] **getLinearVelocity( );**

Returns a list with the X, Y, and Z components of the linear velocity. The speed is in Blender units per second.

pylist [x,y,z] **getVelocity( );**

Returns a list with the X, Y, and Z component of the velocity. The speed is in Blender units per second.

float mass **getMass( );**

Returns the mass of the GameObject.

pylist [x,y,z] **getReactionForce( );**

Returns a Python list of three elements.

suspendDynamics( );

Suspends the dynamic calculation in the game engine.

restoreDynamics( );

Suspends the dynamic calculation in the game engine.

29

INSTALLATION AND SUPPORT

29.1. Blender Installation

We want to ensure that installing Blender is as easy as possible. Usually the process consists of three easy steps:

1. Get Blender from the CD or by downloading it.
2. Uncompress the archive or use the installer.
3. Start Blender.

The Blender Windows version will work on 32-bit versions of Windows (Windows 9x, Windows Me, Windows NT, and Windows 2000). Get the installer archive from our website, or locate it on the CD.

1. Double-click the installer icon. The installer will load and present you with a splash screen and some important information about Blender. Read this information and click Next to proceed to the next screen.

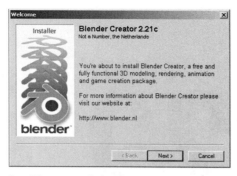

2.   Please read the license agreement carefully and agree by clicking Yes. The
     next screen displays some general information on Blender. Press Next to
     skip it.

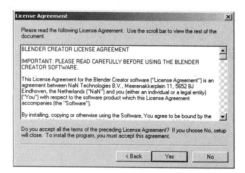

3.   In the Choose Setup Folder screen, enter a valid path where you want to
     install Blender. Optionally you can browse to a directory using the Browse
     button (indicated with the folder icon) next to the path. The path's default
     is C:\Program Files\Blender.

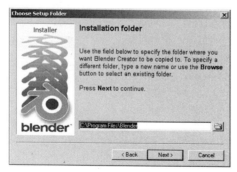

4.   After pressing Next in the Choose Setup Folder screen, Blender is installed
     on your hard disk.

     The installer offers you the option to start Blender after the installation by
activating the checkbox Start Blender. To start Blender later, you can use the
automatically created shortcut on your desktop or the entry in the Start menu.

29.2. Graphics Card Compatibility

by Daniel Dunbar

Blender requires a 3-D accelerated graphics card that supports OpenGL. We strongly recommend making sure you are using the latest version of the drivers for your graphics card before attempting to run Blender. (See "Upgrading your graphics drivers" below if you are unsure how to upgrade your graphics drivers.)

Additionally, here are some tips to try if you are having trouble running Blender, or if Blender is running poorly.

- Most consumer graphics cards are optimized for 16-bit color mode (High Color). Try changing the color mode you are using in the Display Properties.

- Some cards many not be able to accelerate 3-D at higher resolutions. Try lowering your display resolution in the Display Properties (Figure 29-1).

- Some cards may also have problems accelerating 3-D for multiple programs at a time. Make sure Blender is the only 3-D application running.

- If Blender runs but displays incorrectly, try lowering the hardware acceleration level in the Performance tab of the Advanced Display Properties (Figure 29-2).

29.2.1. Upgrading your graphics drivers

Graphics cards are generally marketed and sold by a different company than the one that makes the actual chipset that handles the graphics functionality. For example, a Diamond Viper V550 actually uses an NVidia TNT2 chipset, and a Hercules Prophet 4000XT uses a PowerVR Kyro chipset.

Often both the card manufacturer and the chipset maker will offer drivers for your card. We recommend always using the drivers from the chipset maker, which are often released more frequently and of a higher quality.

Table 29-1: Card Manufacturers

Company	Commonly Used Chipsets
3Dfx, http://www.3dfx.com	3Dfx
AOpen, http://www.aopen.com	NVidia, SiS
ASUS, http://www.asus.com	NVidia
ATI, http://www.ati.com	ATI
Creative, http://www.creative.com	NVidia
Diamond Multimedia, http://www.diamondmm.com	NVidia, S3
ELSA, http://www.elsa.com	NVidia
Gainward, http://www.gainward.com	NVidia, S3
Gigabyte, http://www.giga-byte.com	NVidia
Hercules, http://www.hercules.com	NVidia, PowerVR
Leadtek, http://www.leadtek.com	3DLabs, NVidia

Table 29-1: Card Manufacturers

Company	Commonly Used Chipsets
Matrox, http://www.matrox.com	Matrox
Videologic, http://www.videologic.com	PowerVR, S3

NOTE *If you are not sure which chipset is in your graphics card consult the section "Determining your graphics chipset" next.*

Once you know which chipset your graphics card uses, find the chipset maker in the table below, and follow the link to that company's driver page. From there you should be able to find the drivers for your particular chipset, as well as further instructions about how to install the driver.

29.2.2. Determining your graphics chipset

The easiest way to determine the graphics chipset used by your card is to consult the documentation (or the box) that came with your graphics card. Often the chipset is listed somewhere (for example, on the side of the box, in the specifications page of the manual, or even in the title like "Leadtek WinFast GeForce 256").

If you are unable to find out which chipset your card uses from the documentation, go to the Display Properties dialog (Figure 29-1), select the Settings tab, and look for the Display field, where you should see the names of your monitor and graphics card. Often the graphics card will also display its name or model and a small logo when you turn on the computer.

Once you know which graphics card you have, the next step is to determine which chipset the card uses. One way to find this out is to look up the manufacturer in the Card Manufacturers table (Table 29-1) and follow the link to the manufacturer's website. Once you are there, find the product page for your card model; the chipset that the card is based on should be listed somewhere on this page.

Table 29-2: Chipset Manufacturers

Company	Chipsets	Driver Page
3Dfx	Banshee Voodoo	http://www.3dfx.com/
3DLabs	Permedia	http://www.3dlabs.com/support/drivers/index.htm
ATI	Rage Radeon	http://www.ati.com/support/
Intel	i740 i810 i815	http://developer.intel.com/design/software/drivers/platform/
Matrox	G200 G400 G450	http://www.matrox.com/mga/support/drivers/home.cfm
NVidia	Vanta Riva 128 Riva TNT/GeForce	http://www.nvidia.com/view.asp?PAGE=drivers
PowerVR	KYRO KYRO II	http://www.powervr.com/Downloads.asp
Rendition	Verite	http://www.micron.com/content.jsp?path=Products/ITG

Table 29-2: Chipset Manufacturers

Company	Chipsets	Driver Page
S3 Graphics	Savage	http://www.s3graphics.com/DRVVIEW.HTM
SiS	300 305 315 6326	http://www.sis.com/support/driver/index.htm
Trident Microsystems	Blade CyberBlade	http://www.tridentmicro.com/videcomm/download/download.htm

Now that you know which chipset your card uses, you can continue with the instructions in the upgrading section (Section 29.2.1).

29.2.3. Display dialogs in Windows concerning the graphics card

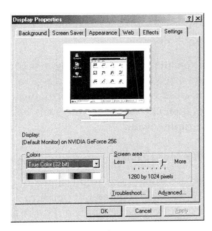

Figure 29-1: Display Properties

The Display Properties dialog has many useful settings for changing the function of your graphics card. To open the Display Properties dialog, go to Start > Settings > Control Panel and select the Display icon. Or, right-click your desktop and select Properties.

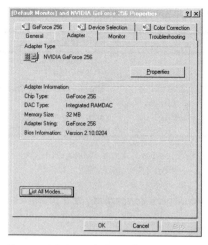

Figure 29-2: Advanced Display Properties

The Advanced Display Properties dialog has settings for controling the function of your graphics driver and often has additional settings for tweaking the 3-D acceleration. To open the Advanced Display Properties dialog, open the Display Properties as described above, then choose the Settings tab, and click the Advanced button in the lower right corner.

29.2.4. Graphics compatibility test results

In the table good (or bad) performance refers to the speed of general 3-D drawing and is an indication of how well a game will perform. Good (or bad) interactivity refers to how fast the interface responds on the graphics card and is an indication of how well the graphics card works for creating and editing 3-D scenes in Blender.

All tests are carried out with the latest drivers we could find. If the results on your system do not match ours, make sure you are using the latest drivers, as described in the upgrading section (Section A.2.1).

Table 29-3: Tested Chipsets

Chipset Manufacturer	Chipset Model	Windows 98	Windows 2000
3Dfx	Banshee	Works (very poor performance)	-untested-
	Voodoo 3000	Good performance, poor interactivity	Good performance, poor interactivity
	Voodoo 5500	Works (good performance)	-untested-
ATI	All-In-Wonder 128	Works (poor performance)	-untested-
	Rage II 3D	Works (poor performance)	-untested-
	Rage Pro 3D	Works (poor performance)	-untested-

Table 29-3: Tested Chipsets

Chipset Manufacturer	Chipset Model	Windows 98	Windows 2000
	Radeon DDR VIVO	Good performance, good interactivity	Good performance, good interactivity
Matrox	Millennium G200	OK performance, extremely poor interactivity, some drawing errors	OK performance, very poor interactivity, some drawing errors
	Millennium G400	Good performance, poor interactivity	Good performance, poor interactivity
	Millennium G450	Good performance, very poor interactivity	Good performance, very poor interactivity
NVidia	TNT	Good performance, good interactivity	Good performance, good interactivity
	Vanta	Good performance, good interactivity	Good performance, good interactivity
	TNT2	Good performance, good interactivity	Good performance, good interactivity
	GeForce DDR	Works (good performance)	-untested-
	GeForce 2	Works (good performance)	-untested-
PowerVR	Kyro	Good performance, good interactivity, some drawing errors	Good performance, good interactivity, some drawing errors
Rendition	Verite 2200	Works (poor performance), some drawing errors	-untested-
S3	Virge	OK performance, good interactivity	-untested-
	Trio 64	Works (poor performance)	-untested-
	Savage 4	-untested-	Works (poor performance)
SiS	6326	Works (poor performance)	-untested-

29.3. Where to Get the Latest Version of Blender

Blender is a constantly evolving 3-D creation suite, with new features being added on a regular basis. You can download the latest version of Blender Creator from the following URL: http://www.blender.nl/download.

The new features and bug fixes of each release can be found in the change logs in the News section, http://www.blender.nl/news.

29.4. Support and Website Community

Visit www.blender3D.com, where you will find a registered user base of over 250,000 Blender users worldwide, both professional and non-professional enthusiasts, alongside a string of award-winning graphic images, animations, and interactive content created by those users. You will also find a wealth of information to help you to continue to develop your game development skills.

24-hour support is available through the Blender Knowledge Base at http://www.blender3d.com/knowledgebase. Just type in your question for an instant answer.

For any support questions regarding your game kit, please email your questions to gamekit@blender3D.com. The support office is manned from 10 a.m. until 6 p.m. (Greenwich Mean Time plus two hours), Monday to Friday. If you send us an email, please try to describe your question with as much detail as you can. Sometimes, it is also a good idea to include your Blender file so that we can examine it for you.

Another useful resource is the Blender Discussion Server at http://www.blender.nl/discussion/index.php. There are 13 different discussion areas, with a dedicated area for the Blender Game Kit:

1. Blender Chat: For all your Blender-related chatting
2. "I made this!": Get feedback on your creations
3. Blender Publisher: For all your Publisher-related questions
4. Blender Game Kit: Discuss your experiences with other users around the world
5. Questions and Answers: The general help area for your questions to the community
6. Blender 3D Plug-ins: Discuss the plug-in program here
7. Blender Game Engine: Discussions about interactive 3-D content
8. Python: For Python-related questions
9. Website and Community L: Get involved
10. 3D Hardware: Discuss 3-D hardware problems, experiences
11. Blender Bugs: Check for known bugs
12. Render Daemon: Discuss the Render Daemon Open Source Project
13. Off Topic Chat: Here you can post anything you like

IRC: If you prefer to talk to someone in real time, you can always find helpful Blender users on the Blender chat box. Download an IRC client from the Internet (for example: http://www.mirc.com) and install it. Connect to an EFNet server and join the channel #blender3d. Not all IRC servers can find this channel. Here are a few good ones: irc.df.lth.se (port 6668), irc.phoenix.net, irc.ais.net, irc.telia.no, irc.nijenrode.nl, and irc.isdnet.fr.

29.5. Manuals and Further Reading

The following is a list of some printed and online resources, which may be of use to you as you continue to explore the potential of interactive 3-D design.

The Official Blender 2.0 Guide by Ton Roosendaal and Carsten Wartmann

This is the definitive guide to using Blender. See http://www.blender.nl/shop.

http://www.blender.nl/resource/index.php

These pages offer Blender users a variety of useful files, including Python scripts, plug-ins, models, textures, sounds, and more. Enthusiastic community members maintain these pages; if you have any comments or suggestions do not hesitate to contact them!

Game Design Theory & Practice by Richard Rouse

This book deals with the key game design topics including game balancing, story-telling, player motivations, artificial intelligence, level design, and play testing. See http://www.blender.nl/shop.

Game Architecture and Design

Learn the Best Practices for Game Design and Programming by Andrew Rollings and Dave Morris is a book that provides real-life case studies of what works and what doesn't. It takes the reader through all the necessary game-creation steps from seeing a game idea on paper to actually implementing that idea! See http://www.blender.nl/shop.

http://www.gamasutra.com

Dedicated to the art and science of game design.

http://www.digitalgamedeveloper.com

Contains news features, tools, and techniques for game developers.

GLOSSARY

Active Blender distinguishes between *selected* and *active*. Only one object or item can be active at any given time—for example, to allow visualization of data in buttons. *See also:* Selected.

Actuator A LogicBrick that acts like a muscle of a life-form. An actuator can move the object and also make a sound. See Section 27.3. *See also:* LogicBrick, Sensor, Controller.

Alpha The alpha value in an image denotes opacity; it is used for blending and anti-aliasing.

Anti-aliasing An algorithm designed to reduce the stair-stepping artifacts that result from drawing graphic primitives on a raster grid.

Back buffer Blender draws the interface in two buffers. This double-buffering system allows one buffer to be displayed, while drawing occurs on the back buffer. For some applications in Blender the back buffer is used to store color-coded selection information.

Bevel Beveling removes sharp edges from an extruded object by adding additional material around the surrounding faces. Bevels are particularly useful for flying logos, and animation in general, because they reflect additional light from the corners of an object as well as from the front and sides.

Bounding box A six-sided box drawn on the screen that represents the maximum extent of an object.

Channel Some DataBlocks can be linked to a series of other DataBlocks. For example, a material has eight channels to link textures to. Each IpoBlock has a fixed number of available channels. These have a name (LocX, SizeZ, enz.) indicating how they can be applied. When you add an IpoCurve to a channel, animation starts immediately.

Child Objects can be linked to each other in hierarchical groups. The parent object in such groups passes its transformations through to the child objects.

Clipping The removal, before drawing occurs, of vertices and faces that are outside the field of view.

Controller   A LogicBrick that acts like the brain of a life-form. It makes decisions to activate muscles (actuators), using either simple logic or complex Python scripts. See Section 27.2. *See also:* LogicBrick, Sensor, Python, Actuator.

DataBlock (or "block")   The general name for an element in Blender's object-oriented system.

Doppler effect   The Doppler effect is the change in pitch that occurs when a sound has a velocity relative to the listener. When a sound moves toward the listener the pitch will rise. When going away from the listener the pitch will drop. A well-known example is the sound of an ambulance passing by.

Double buffer   Blender uses two buffers (images) to draw the interface in. The content of one buffer is displayed, while drawing occurs on the other buffer. When drawing is complete, the buffers are switched.

EditMode   Mode to select and transform vertices of an object. This way you change the shape of the object itself. Hotkey: TAB. *See also:* Vertex (pl. vertices).

Extend select   Adds new selected items to the current selection (SHIFT-RMB).

Extrusion   The creation of a three-dimensional object by pushing out a two-dimensional outline and giving it height, like a cookie cutter. It is often used to create 3-D text.

Face   The triangle and square polygons that form the basis for meshes or for rendering.

FaceSelectMode   Mode to select faces on an object. Most important for texturing objects. Hotkey: FKEY.

Flag   A programming term for a variable that indicates a certain status.

Flat shading   A fast rendering algorithm that simply gives each facet of an object a single color. It yields a solid representation of objects without taking a long time to render. Pressing ZKEY switches to flat shading in Blender.

Fps   Frames per second. All animations, video, and movies are played at a certain rate. Above roughly 15 fps the human eye cannot see the single frames and is tricked into seeing a fluid motion. In games this is used as an indicator of how fast a game runs.

Frame   A single picture taken from an animation or video.

Gouraud shading   A rendering algorithm that provides more detail. It averages color information from adjacent faces to create colors. It is more realistic than flat shading, but less realistic than Phong shading or ray-tracing. The hotkey in Blender is CTRL-Z.

Graphical User Interface (GUI)   The whole part of an interactive application that requests input from the user (keyboard, mouse, and so on) and displays this information to the user. Blender's GUI is designed for efficient modeling in an animation company where time equals money. Blender's entire GUI is done in OpenGL. *See also:* OpenGL.

Hierarchy   Objects can be linked to each other in hierarchical groups. The parent object in such groups passes its transformations through to the child objects.

Ipo   The main animation curve system. Ipo blocks can be used by objects for movement and by materials for animated colors.

IpoCurve   The Ipo animation curve.

Item   The general name for a selectable element—e.g., objects, vertices, or curves.

Keyframe   A frame in a sequence that specifies all of the attributes of an object. The object can then be changed in any way and a second keyframe defined. Blender automatically creates a series of transition frames between the two keyframes, a process called *tweening*.

Layer   A visibility flag for objects, scenes, and 3DWindows. This is a very efficient method for testing object visibility.

Link   The reference from one DataBlock to another. A *pointer* in programming terms.

Local   Each object in Blender defines a local 3-D space, bound by its location, rotation and size. Objects themselves reside in the global 3-D space. A DataBlock is local, when it is read from the current Blender file. Nonlocal blocks (library blocks) are linked parts from other Blender files.

LogicBrick   A graphical representation of a functional unit in Blender's game logic. LogicBricks can be sensors, controllers, or actuators. *See also:* Sensor, Controller, Actuator.

Mapping   The relationship between a material and a texture is called the *mapping*. This relationship is two-sided. First, the information that is passed on to the texture must be specified. Then the effect of the texture on the material is specified.

Mipmap   A process to filter and speed up the display of textures.

ObData block   The first and most important DataBlock linked by an object. This block defines the object type—e.g., mesh or curve or lamp.

Object   The basic 3-D information block. It contains a position, rotation, size and transformation matrices. It can be linked to other objects for hierarchies or deformation. Objects can be empty (just an axis) or have a link to ObData, the actual 3-D information: mesh, curve, lattice, lamp, and so on.

OpenGL (OGL)   OpenGL is a programming interface mainly for 3-D applications. It renders 3-D objects to the screen, providing the same set of instructions on different computers and graphics adapters. Blender's whole interface and 3-D output in the real-time and interactive 3-D graphic is done by OpenGL.

Parent   An object that is linked to another object, the parent is linked to a child in a parent-child relationship. A parent object's coordinates become the center of the world for any of its child objects.

Perspective view   In a perspective view, the further an object is from the viewer, the smaller it appears.

Pivot   A point that normally lies at an object's geometric center. An object's position and rotation are calculated in relation to its pivot point. However, an object can be moved off its center point, allowing it to rotate around a point that lies outside the object.

Pixel   A single dot of light on the computer screen; the smallest unit of a computer graphic. Short for *picture element.*

Plug-in   A piece of (C-)code loadable during run time that makes it possible to extend the functionality of Blender without recompiling. The Blender plug-in for showing 3-D content in other applications is such a piece of code.

Python   The scripting language integrated into Blender. Python is an interpreted, interactive, object-oriented programming language.

Render   To create a two-dimensional representation of an object based on its shape and surface properties (like a picture for print or display on the monitor).

Rigid body   Option for dynamic objects in Blender that causes the game engine to take the shape of the body into account. This can be used to create rolling spheres, for example.

Selected   Blender distinguishes between *selected* and *active* objects. Any number of objects can be selected at once. Almost all key commands have an effect on selected objects. Selecting is done with the right mouse button. *See also:* Active, Selected, Extend select.

Sensor   A LogicBrick that acts like a sense of a life-form. It reacts to touch, vision, collision, and so on. See Section 27.1. *See also:* LogicBrick, Controller, Actuator.

Single user   Describes DataBlocks with only one user.

Smoothing   A rendering procedure that performs vertex-normal interpolation across a face before lighting calculations begin. The individual facets are then no longer visible.

Transform   Change a location, rotation, or size. Usually applied to objects or vertices.

Transparency   A surface property that determines how much light passes through an object without being altered. *See also:* Alpha.

User   When one DataBlock references another DataBlock, it has a user.

Vertex (pl. vertices)   The general name for a 3-D or 2-D point. Besides an X,Y,Z coordinate, a vertex can have color, a normal vector, and a selection flag. Also used as controlling points or handles on curves.

Vertex array   A special and fast way to display 3-D on the screen using the hardware graphics acceleration. However, some OpenGL drivers or hardware don't support this, so it can be switched off in the InfoWindow.

Wireframe   A representation of a three-dimensional object that shows only the lines of its contours, hence the name *wireframe*.

X-, Y-, Z-axes   The three axes of the world's three-dimensional coordinate system. In the FrontView, the X-axis is an imaginary horizontal line running from left to right; the Z-axis is a vertical line; and the Y-axis is a line that comes out of the screen toward you. In general, any movement parallel to one of these axes is said to be movement along that axis.

X, Y, and Z coordinates   The X coordinate of an object is measured by drawing a line that is perpendicular to the X-axis, through its centerpoint. The distance from where that line intersects the X-axis to the zero point of the X-axis is the object's X coordinate. The Y and Z coordinates are measured in a similar manner.

Z-buffer   For a Z-buffer image, each pixel is associated with a Z-value, derived from the distance in "eye space" from the camera. Before each pixel of a polygon is drawn, the existing Z-buffer value is compared to the Z-value of the polygon at that point. It is a common and fast visible-surface algorithm.

INDEX

F

G

K

key combinations, 38
key positions, 148
key presses, conventions, 38
Keyboard Sensor, 98, 101
    defined, 273
    Python methods, 273
keyframes, 82, 148, 172
    copying block of, 201
    deleting, 200
keys, 172
    inserting, 199
kinetic energy, 263
kinetic friction, 160

L

lamps, 30, 79, 251, 264
    adding, 79
    types, 264, 265
        Hemi, 265
        lamp, 265
        Spot, 265
        Sun, 265
LampButtons, 46, 264
layers, 8, 9, 156, 221
    transition, 9
    3DWindow, 220
left mouse button (LMB), 39
lens, 240
level creation and design, 139
lights. See lighting.
lighting, 27, 29
line, 18
linear
    animation, 13
    kinetic energy, 161
    velocity, 160, 291
linked copy, 51, 142
linking, 51
listener settings, 268
Load button, 7
Load Sample button, 268
Load Temp, 42
local
    coordinate system, 30
    origin, 30
LocalView, 49, 129, 222

location keyframe, 204. *See also* keyframes
logic, wiring, 261
LogicBricks, 71, 98, 255, 261, 271
    adding, 74
    animation curves and, 104
    chaining, 170
    collapsing, 74
    connecting, 72
    naming, 73, 99
    Standard methods, 304
low poly modeling, 109

M

mapping, 6
    UV textures, 248
Martin Strubel, 153
mass, 260, 265
material name (MA), 85
MaterialButtons (F5), 46, 86, 161, 262
materials, 23, 86, 245
    capitalization and, 86
    setting dynamic parameters, 162
MenuButton, 5, 41, 44
mesh, 22, 186
    attaching to armature, 192
    characters and, 186
Message Actuator, 107, 151, 297
    Python methods, 297
Message Sensor, 107, 151
    defined, 280
    Python methods, 280
MessageBody script, 151
messaging system, 107, 151
middle mouse button (MMB), 39
mipmap, 257, 258
    linear texture, 258
MMB, substitution, 39. *See also* middle mouse button
montage, 8, 9
motion, popping, 207
Motion Actuator, 74
    defined, 283
    force, 283
    Python methods, 284
    torque, 283
Motion Controller, 72
    force, 72

X

X coordinate, 17
X-axis, 16
XY axes, 16
XY coordinates, 17
XYZ coordinate, 25

Y

Y coordinate, 17
Y-axis, 16

Z

Z-axis, 18
zooming, 224

THE ART OF INTERACTIVE DESIGN
A Euphonious and Illuminating Guide to Building Successful Software

by CHRIS CRAWFORD

Renowned author Chris Crawford demonstrates what interactivity is, why it's important, and how to design interactive software, games, and websites that work. Crawford's mellifluous style makes for fascinating and idea-inspiring reading that encourages you to think about design in new ways.

2002, 352 PP., $29.95 ($44.95 CDN)
ISBN 1-886411-84-0

STEAL THIS COMPUTER BOOK 3
What They Won't Tell You About The Internet

by WALLACE WANG

This offbeat, non-technical book looks at what hackers do, how they do it, and how readers can protect themselves. The third edition of this bestseller adopts the same informative, irreverent, and entertaining style that made the first two editions a huge success. Thoroughly updated, this edition also covers rootkits, spyware, web bugs, identity theft, hacktivism, wireless hacking (wardriving), biometrics, and firewalls.

"If this book had a soundtrack, it'd be Lou Reed's Walk on the Wild Side.*"*
—*InfoWorld*

2003, 464 PP., $24.95 ($37.95 CDN)
ISBN 1-59327-000-3

PROGRAMMING LINUX GAMES

Discusses important multimedia toolkits (including a very thorough discussion of the Simple DirectMedia Layer) and teaches the basics of Linux game programming. Readers learn about the state of the Linux gaming world, and how to write and distribute Linux games to the Linux gaming community.

422 PP. , $39.95 ($59.95 CDN)
ISBN 1-886411-49-2

THE BLENDER BOOK
Free 3D Graphics Software for the Web and Video

by CARSTEN WARTMANN

Blender is a fast, powerful, and free 3D graphics and animation tool. *The Blender Book* shows you how to use Blender efficiently and creatively with clear step-by-step tutorials that teach all aspects of this often tricky program. You'll learn how to enhance your Web sites, graphic designs, and videos with the 3D graphics and animations you'll create in Blender.

316 PP. W/ CD-ROM, $39.95 ($59.95 CDN)
ISBN 1-886411-44-1

HOW NOT TO PROGRAM IN C++
111 Broken Programs and 3 Working Ones, or Why 2+2=5986

by STEVE OUALLINE

Find the bugs in these broken programs and become a better programmer. Based on real-world errors, the puzzles range from easy (one wrong character) to mind twisting (errors with multiple threads). Match your wits against the author's and polish your language skills as you try to fix broken programs. Clues help along the way, and answers are provided at the back of the book.

2002, 304 PP., $24.95 ($37.95 CDN)
ISBN 1-886411-95-6

PHONE:

1 (800) 420-7240 OR
(415) 863-9900
MONDAY THROUGH FRIDAY,
9 A.M. TO 5 P.M. (PST)

FAX:

(415) 863-9950
24 HOURS A DAY,
7 DAYS A WEEK

EMAIL:

SALES@NOSTARCH.COM

WEB:

HTTP://WWW.NOSTARCH.COM

MAIL:

NO STARCH PRESS
555 DE HARO STREET, SUITE 250
SAN FRANCISCO, CA 94107
USA

Distributed in the U.S. by Publishers Group West

UPDATES

Visit **http://www.nostarch.com/blendergamekit.htm** for updates, errata, and other information.